Sons,
Servants &
Statesmen

ALSO BY JOHN VAN DER KISTE

Published by Sutton Publishing unless stated otherwise

Frederick III, German Emperor 1888 (1981)
Queen Victoria's Family: A Select Bibliography (Clover, 1982)
*Dearest Affie: Alfred, Duke of Edinburgh, Queen Victoria's Second
Son* [with Bee Jordaan] (1984)
Queen Victoria's Children (1986)
*Windsor and Habsburg: The British and Austrian Reigning Houses
1848–1922* (1987)
Edward VII's Children (1989)
Princess Victoria Melita, Grand Duchess Cyril of Russia (1991)
George V's Children (1991)
George III's Children (1992)
*Crowns in a Changing World: The British and European
Monarchies 1901–36* (1993)
Kings of the Hellenes: The Greek Kings 1863–1974 (1994)
Childhood at Court 1819–1914 (1995)
Northern Crowns: The Kings of Modern Scandinavia (1996)
King George II and Queen Caroline (1997)
The Romanovs 1818–1959: Alexander II of Russia and his Family
(1998)
Kaiser Wilhelm II: Germany's Last Emperor (1999)
The Georgian Princesses (2000)
Gilbert & Sullivan's Christmas (2000)
*Dearest Vicky, Darling Fritz: Queen Victoria's Eldest Daughter and
the German Emperor* (2001)
Royal Visits in Devon and Cornwall (Halsgrove, 2002)
Once a Grand Duchess: Xenia, Sister of Nicholas II [with Coryne
Hall] (2002)
William and Mary (2003)
*Emperor Francis Joseph: Life, Death and the Fall of the Habsburg
Empire* (2005)

SONS, SERVANTS & STATESMEN

>⁃I◆▸◦◂I⁃◄

THE MEN IN QUEEN VICTORIA'S LIFE

JOHN VAN DER KISTE

SUTTON PUBLISHING

First published in the United Kingdom in 2006 by
Sutton Publishing Limited · Phoenix Mill
Thrupp · Stroud · Gloucestershire · GL5 2BU

British Library Cataloguing in Publication Data
A catalogue record for this book is available from the British Library.

ISBN 0-7509-3788-2

Typeset in 11/13pt Sabon.
Typesetting and origination by
Sutton Publishing Limited.
Printed and bound in England by
J.H. Haynes & Co. Ltd, Sparkford.

Contents

Illustrations

Acknowledgements

I wish to acknowledge the gracious permission of Her Majesty Queen Elizabeth II to reproduce material which is subject to copyright. All the other illustrations are from private collections.

Several people have assisted greatly in different ways during the writing of this book. Coryne and Colin Hall, Karen Roth, Katrina Warne, Sue and Mike Woolmans, Robin Piguet and Ian Shapiro have been their ever-supportive selves, always ready with information when needed. The staff at the National Archives and the Kensington Public Libraries have also assisted with access to primary sources and published information. As ever, my wife Kim and mother Kate have been a tower of strength, not least in reading the manuscript in draft form and making invaluable suggestions for improvement. Finally, my thanks go to my editors at Sutton Publishing, Jaqueline Mitchell and Anne Bennett, for helping to see the work through to publication.

Introduction

From her early days, Queen Victoria admitted to having 'very violent feelings of affection'. Her Hanoverian forebears had generally been an emotional family, not afraid to give vent to their feelings in front of others. They had nothing of the stiff-upper-lip quality so often associated with the typical Englishman. At the same time, she clearly had a fondness for masculine company, not in any immoral or amoral sense, but rather because she felt more at ease with the male of the species than with women. One modern biographer has remarked with considerable insight that she was a man's woman, and the men she liked best were 'strong and imperturbable men who made her laugh, maybe with a touch of the rascal about them'. Her husband was the exception to the rule, but most of the others she liked fit the description well.

Her dealings with men throughout her life therefore make for an interesting study. How did Her Majesty Queen Victoria of Great Britain, at the height of her nation's prestige and global pre-eminence deal and interact with her family, her most favoured servants and her prime ministers? How did a woman, the most renowned sovereign of her age yet at the same time a constitutional monarch who in practice wielded far less political power than her predecessors, reconcile the demands of matriarch and ruler?

Human beings are generally a mass of contradictions, and Queen Victoria was no exception. Sometimes she would complain that she could not defend her country as wholeheartedly as she could have done had she been a king. At the height of the Russo-Turkish war in 1877, she wrote that if only she was a man, she would 'give those horrid Russians . . . such a beating'. At others, she would admit the limitations imposed on her by her gender. 'We women are not *made* for governing,' she had admitted in 1852, 'and if we are good women, we must dislike these masculine occupations.' One day she almost railed at being a woman in a position which by its nature demanded certain masculine qualities, while on another she passively accepted the limitations of femininity, as there was naturally no alternative.

The attitudes she took to the most important men in her life on political and personal levels, her relationships with them and the psychological factors inherent in these are worthy of examination in their own right, and this is what I have endeavoured to do in this book. Her initial admiration for, then detestation of and finally grudging respect towards Lord Palmerston, and her liking of and later passionate hatred of Gladstone are in their way just as fascinating as her controversial and much-debated relationship with John Brown and her ever-changing feelings towards her eldest son and heir, the Prince of Wales.

PART ONE

Father Figures

ONE

'The daughter of a soldier'

King George III and Queen Charlotte had seven sons who survived to maturity. The fourth is one of the least remembered. Had it not been for marriage late in life, and for the daughter born to him and his wife eight months before he died, Prince Edward Augustus, Duke of Kent, might have been all but forgotten. Yet, though she would say little about her father during her long life, Queen Victoria occasionally referred to herself with pride as the daughter of a soldier. Discussing the armed forces with her ministers in November 1893, she remarked that she 'was brought up so to speak with the feeling for the Army – being a soldier's daughter – and not caring about being on the sea I have always had a special feeling for the Army.'[1]

Prince Edward Augustus was born at Buckingham House on 2 November 1767 and given his first name in memory of his uncle Edward, Duke of York, a dissolute young man who had died at the age of twenty-eight that same week. The circumstances of his birth, he would say self-pityingly, 'were ominous of the life of gloom and struggle which awaited me'.[2] In 1799 he was raised to the peerage, becoming Duke of Kent and Strathearn and Earl of Dublin.

Brought up with his brothers and sisters mostly at Kew Palace, Edward's early life was not so cheerless as he might have wished others to believe, notwithstanding the harsh regime and discipline at home to which he and his brothers were subjected as small boys. However, like his elder brothers he was quick to react against the frugality of his parents once he reached manhood, and soon found himself deep in debt, a state of affairs which would remain constant to the end of his days. According to one writer of a later generation, he considered that the Royal Mint existed solely for the benefit of royalty,[3] though he was not the only member of his family to do so. Wherever he was stationed on military service, be it North America, Gibraltar or Europe, he considered that as a king's son he had to live in comfort and maintain a certain sense of style. Any house in which

3

he lived, and the gardens which surrounded it, had to be refurbished to the highest standards, with no expense spared. The bills from builders, carpenters, glaziers and gardeners soon rapidly exceeded his parliamentary income and military pay.

In the Army he rose to the rank of field-marshal, but even by the standards of the day he was regarded as a merciless martinet. He thought nothing of sentencing a man to one hundred lashes for a basic offence like leaving a button undone. In 1802 he was appointed Governor of Gibraltar and considered he had been sent to restore order in what had become a rather undisciplined garrison. His conscientious efforts to do so, in particular to curb the drunkenness of the men, soon provoked mutiny, secretly encouraged if not instigated by the second-in-command, who was keen to get rid of him. Within a year he had been recalled to England.

Despite his reputation as a harsh disciplinarian, away from the parade ground some people found him one of the most likeable of the family. With the exception of the Prince Regent, he was probably the most intelligent of the brothers. The Duke of Wellington once said that he never knew any man with more natural eloquence in conversation than the Duke of Kent, 'always choosing the best topics for each particular person, and expressing them in the happiest language',[4] and the only one of the royal Dukes who could deliver a successful after-dinner speech. This favourable opinion was not shared by his siblings. The Prince of Wales, later Prince Regent and King George IV, so resented his air of righteous self-pity that he called him Simon Pure, and his sisters considered him so hypocritical that they named him Joseph Surface after a character in Sheridan's *The School for Scandal*.

Austere where creature comforts were concerned, he rose early in the morning, ate and drank little, and abhorred drunkenness and gambling. He was a close friend of the pioneer socialist Robert Owen, and it has been suggested that the Duke of Kent could claim to be the first patron of socialism,[5] at least in the annals of British royalty. He took a keen interest in Owen's workers' co-operatives, and in improving education for the working classes, in order that they might be able to better themselves. No slavish adherent to the Church of England, he sometimes attended dissenting services, much to the irritation of Manners Sutton, Archbishop of Canterbury. He actively supported over fifty charities, including a 'literary fund for distressed authors' and the Westminster Infirmary.

Despite enjoying a comfortable liaison for twenty-seven years with his mistress, Madame Julie de St Laurent, he was well aware of his royal obligations. Foremost among these was the promise of a generous parliamentary allowance on condition he contracted a suitable marriage in order to provide an heir to the throne. For the spendthrift sons of George III, such financial provision was an absolute necessity. The unexpected death in childbirth of Edward's niece, Charlotte, daughter of the Prince Regent and only legitimate grandchild of King George III, in November 1817, meant that he and his bachelor brothers – or brothers with mistresses, but without brides recognised by the Royal Marriages Act of 1772 – had to rectify the situation.

Naturally he made it known that he was willing to sacrifice his personal happiness for the sake of his country, subject to adequate remuneration. In May 1818 he married Victoire, Dowager Duchess of Leiningen, a widow of thirty-one with a son, Charles, aged fourteen, and a daughter, Feodora, aged eleven. The Duke and Duchess made their home at Kensington Palace where, on 24 May 1819, she gave birth to a daughter who was christened Alexandrina Victoria.

Because of his radical opinions, the Duke was disliked and feared by the Tories. A member of the Bathurst family, whose nephew Henry Ponsonby later became private secretary to Queen Victoria, dreaded the possibility of his eventually ascending the throne. Though he was no republican, he felt it did not matter 'much to us Englishmen what sort of men our Kings are, but I should be sorry if the Crown went to that odious and pompous Duke of Kent'.[6]

The Duke and Duchess planned to spend the winter of 1819–20 in Devon, ostensibly so the Duchess could benefit from the bracing sea air, but in fact to avoid the expense of living in London. He and his suite made arrangements to rent a modest house at Sidmouth on the Devon coast, where they arrived on Christmas Day 1819. It was an exceptionally severe winter, and after catching a heavy cold while out walking a few days later, Edward took to his bed with pneumonia. He had always been one of the healthiest members of the family, boasting that he would surely outlive his brothers, but he had spoken too soon.

Various friends came to Sidmouth to see him and condole with him on his illness, and the Duchess of Kent's younger brother, Prince Leopold of Saxe-Coburg, brought his doctor, Baron Stockmar. The latter examined the Duke but sadly admitted that he was beyond salvation. Early on the morning of 23 January 1820 he passed away, his wife kneeling beside him holding his hand. Within six days, his father, the blind and deranged King George III, had died as well, and in a nation which mourned its King, the death of the Duke of Kent went almost unnoticed.

As she was only eight months old at the time of his death, Princess Victoria could never remember her father. Brought up to obey the fifth commandment, she paid lip-service to the principle of honouring her parents and would occasionally speak of her 'beloved father'. Yet when people who had known him commented on how much she resembled him, she said pointedly that she had inherited far more from her mother. She and her father had certain characteristics in common, among them courage, truthfulness, strong powers of observation, and a love of order and punctuality.[7] However, as these virtues were shared by many other members of the family, it might be unwise to credit him unduly with passing them on to his daughter.

Some detected other distinct physical resemblances, such as the 'same frank eyes' and a 'proud curve of nostril'. In her later life, comparisons were drawn between their pride of race, sense of dignity, their uncompromising attitude when a certain course of action was decided on, their simple notion of right and wrong and their sharp definition of black and white, with no shading in between. In their private lives, it was considered that they had the same indifference to love and affection if the needs of state demanded any sacrifice. Above all, they were autocrats at heart, but with a genuine sympathy towards the poor.[8]

In at least three ways, Victoria was the exact opposite of her father. He was a spendthrift who ate but little, while she was as thrifty as her grandfather George III, and in later years she loved her food so much that whatever figure she had had as a young woman paid the price. Moreover, he was a six-foot giant of a man, while she was barely five feet tall.

Widowed a second time at only thirty-three years of age, the Duchess of Kent was very much a stranger in a strange land. It was less than two years since she had come to England, and she could barely speak English. The household was bilingual, and her infant daughter did not begin to speak English until she was three years old. The Duchess could hardly be blamed for contemplating a return to the safety and security of her old German home, Amorbach. But the Duke had left a wish that their daughter, whom he had told his friends to 'look at' well, as 'she will be Queen of England',[9] should be brought up in the country of her birth. Thanks to Prince Leopold, who came to her financial rescue, this was scrupulously observed.

Left fatherless at eight months, with no reassuring male presence in the household at Kensington Palace, the Princess destined to become Queen Victoria would spend much of her life looking for one father-figure after another.[10] Her 'wicked uncles', King George IV and his brothers, were considered unsuitable mentors. Most of them had once been notorious womanisers or adulterers, even bigamists, excessive spendthrifts, gluttons or drinkers, but now they had little energy for most of these vices. Even so, to the Duchess of Kent they were dissolute old men with whom she did not wish her daughter to be associated. Nevertheless, they took a friendly interest in her welfare, offering her rides in their carriages and sending her presents. However, the Duchess of Kent hated and feared them, convinced that they all regarded her small daughter as something of an interloper, or at best a reminder that her 'Drina' was the sovereign of the future whom her in-laws had conspicuously failed to provide. At the back of her mind was the fear that they would not hesitate to kidnap her or have her abducted, or at least attempt some subterfuge which would prevent her from coming to the throne.

* * *

The first genuine, or substitute, father-figure was her uncle, Prince Leopold of Saxe-Coburg Saalfeld. Born in December 1790, he was four years younger than his sister, the Duchess of Kent. A none-too-affluent German prince, he had distinguished himself during his military career in the Napoleonic wars, rising to the rank of lieutenant-general. In May 1816 he had married Charlotte, daughter of the Prince Regent, and experienced eighteen months of married bliss which were suddenly, tragically, ended when she died in childbirth in November 1817. Having been granted an annuity of £50,000 on his marriage, he could easily afford to be generous to others.

At first, the bereaved Leopold had been unable even to look at his baby niece, who inadvertently brought back bitter memories of his dead wife and the little son who had never lived. It took all his sister's powers of persuasion before he would set eyes on her, and after one reluctant look he shrank from doing so again for a time. Even to attend her christening required no mean effort on his part, and only when the baby's father died did he relent. From then on, he became in effect a second father to her. Having heard the sad news he hurried to Sidmouth, and three days after the Duke of Kent's death he accompanied the bereaved family on their return to Kensington.

Though denied the chance of being the husband of England's future Queen, Leopold realised that he was the uncle of a likely future one. After the ailing King George IV, the heirs to the throne were Frederick, Duke of York and William, Duke of Clarence. All three were in their fifties, the first two were childless and the Duchess of Clarence seemed sadly unable to bear any children who would live for more than a few months. Barring miracles, it was highly probable that within twenty years or so Victoria would succeed them to the throne.

Leopold became very attached to her, and for the next few years of his life he paid her weekly visits at Kensington. Disliked and distrusted by most of his in-laws in England as a crafty schemer, he had to behave with circumspection, lest he was seen to be playing too influential a part in the little girl's life. At one stage during this time, he imagined and hoped that he might become regent to her, in the event of her succeeding to the throne before she attained her majority.

The Duke of York died in January 1827, aged sixty-three. Few people expected either King George IV or his new heir, the Duke of Clarence, to outlive Victoria's eighteenth birthday, and Leopold thought it safe to assume that the government and ministers would prefer him as regent to any other of his niece's surviving Hanoverian uncles. In particular, the next in line of succession after Clarence and Victoria herself was Ernest, Duke of Cumberland, one of the most hated men in the kingdom. While the scandalous rumours about his private life, among them incest with a sister, murder of a valet and seduction of a friend's wife, were almost certainly nonsense, his reputation as a reactionary of the deepest dye was enough to put him beyond the pale as far as most members of the Houses of Parliament were concerned.

However, Leopold was aware that it would not do for him to make his case as prospective regent too assertively. Though George IV was Leopold's father-in-law, the King had never liked the conscientious, yet sanctimonious and avaricious young Coburg prince who had won the hand of his beloved late daughter. The

Duke of Clarence, who succeeded his brother George as King
William IV in June 1830, cared for Leopold and his Coburg kinsmen
even less. They were devoted to Princess Victoria, a feeling which
they did not extend to her mother.

It was fortunate for Leopold and his sense of ambition that a
greater destiny beckoned. In 1831 he was chosen as king of the
newly independent state of Belgium, but he continued to maintain a
regular correspondence with his niece. Far-sighted and astute, he
had a thorough understanding of the concept of constitutional
monarchy, and he was more than ready to impart his knowledge of
the subject to his young niece. Each year he wrote her a long
birthday letter imparting much affection as well as sound advice.

Her letters to him were very appreciative and similarly
affectionate. These were a sorely needed safety valve for her, as she
found it easier to be more frank and confiding with him than with
anybody at home whom she saw regularly. When King Leopold and
his second wife, Queen Louise, came to visit her in September 1835
and she met them at Ramsgate, her delight knew no bounds.

'He is *so* clever, *so* mild, and *so* prudent;' she wrote in her journal
after one of their conversations; '*he* alone can give me good advice
on *every* thing. His advice is perfect. He is indeed "il mio secondo
padre" or rather "solo padre"! for he is indeed like my real father,
as I have none, and he is so kind and so good to me, he has ever
been so to me.'[11]

Within three weeks of writing this entry, the bonds between uncle
and fatherless daughter had strengthened. 'He gave me very valuable
and important advice,' she recorded after another talk. 'I look up to
him as a Father, with complete confidence, love and affection. He is
the best and kindest adviser I have. He has always treated me as his
child and I love him most dearly for it.'[12]

Leopold's advice, though Victoria was too young to appreciate it,
was even more 'valuable and important' than she might have ever
thought possible. His liberal attitudes and the fact that he was king
of a state that had come into existence as part of a liberal nationalist
movement which was spreading through nineteenth-century Europe
were in themselves significant. Therefore his liberal outlook and her
own adolescent political inclinations, such as they were, helped to
make the future Queen Victoria more acceptable to a broader
section of public opinion in Britain than would have been the case
had she been schooled by her cousins and uncles.[13]

The moderately progressive views of the popular Augustus, Duke of Sussex and her late father were adequate proof that King George III's sons were not out-and-out reactionaries; and although he was often derided as a total buffoon, King William IV had his fair share of common sense when it came to overseeing the contentious passage of the Great Reform Bill in 1832. But though he was later to astonish his critics by proving a very successful and just King of Hanover, the much-hated and arch-conservative Ernest, Duke of Cumberland would never have done as a role model for his niece.

King Leopold was well aware of this. Three days before King William IV died in June 1837, the former wrote from Laeken to his niece to prepare her for what lay ahead. Not only would she entrust the Prime Minister, Lord Melbourne, and his ministers with retaining their offices, he told her, but she would 'do this in that honest and kind way which is quite your own, and say some kind things on the subject'. There was nobody else who could serve her so faithfully, and 'with the exception of the Duke of Sussex, there is no *one* in the family that offers them anything like what they can reasonably hope from you, and your immediate successor, with the mustaches [the Duke of Cumberland], is enough to frighten them into the most violent attachment for you'.[14] Until she married and produced an heir, next in line to the throne would be the dreaded Duke Ernest.

The other man *in loco parentis* for much of Victoria's childhood was Sir John Conroy, the Duchess of Kent's comptroller. Conroy served his employer faithfully, and she always had the utmost confidence in him. Wagging tongues suggested that they must be lovers. It was said that the Duchess was unsure of her second husband's fertility and, true to the Coburg sense of ambition, took a lover to ensure that she would have a child who would sit on the English throne,[15] and that Conroy might just have been the right man in the right place at the right time. Also current at the time was a story that Victoria had once entered her mother's bedroom and caught them in a compromising position.

All this was almost certainly exaggeration, but it was beyond doubt that the ever-scheming, manipulative Conroy worked hard to keep the princess from outside influences and make sure she was utterly subservient to her mother. Victoria's dislike of his arrogance soon turned into hatred, especially when he tried to force his will on her. Soon after King Leopold and Queen Louise returned to Belgium, she took to her bed with a fever, possibly a form of typhoid. Taking advantage of her illness, one day Conroy appeared in her bedroom with a document he had drafted, in which she consented to his appointment as her private secretary on her accession to the throne. He tried to force her to sign, but she stubbornly refused. Baroness Louise Lehzen, her devoted governess and the Duchess of Kent's lady-in-waiting, came stoutly to her defence, and he had to leave the room without her signature. He did so with bad grace, and from then on he was the Princess's sworn foe.

King Leopold had never trusted Conroy, and when he heard about the incident he was beside himself with anger. Conroy's influence over the Duchess of Kent, he told his niece some years later, was 'so strong that it would once have been called witchcraft'.[16] The comptroller's conduct 'was madness and must end in his own ruin, and that, although late, there was still time! – but no, he continued in the same way, as the events of 1837 did show'.[17] Conroy evidently considered that he was entitled to wield more power than he genuinely did, and his eagerness to take advantage of the Duchess of Kent's naïveté spurred him on to reckless ambition which, he must have realised, would eventually bring about his downfall.

By 1835 Victoria had been heir apparent for five years. After the deaths of the childless Duke of York in 1827 and King George IV three years later, she was heir to the throne. The kindly, genial King William IV and his warm-hearted consort, Queen Adelaide, were fond of their little niece, but the increasing hostility of the Duchess of Kent and Conroy prevented them from seeing her regularly. It was the ailing King's dearest wish that he would be spared long enough, until his heiress attained her eighteenth birthday, so that there would be no danger of the Duchess becoming regent – a regency in which 'King John' would hold sway.

* * *

From Victoria's earliest years, various members of the older generation were giving constant thought as to who would be her husband, and invitations to come to England were extended to a number of eligible potential candidates. In 1832 the Mensdorff-Pouilly princes, Hugo and Alfonso, sons of the Duchess of Kent's sister Sophie, had been invited to stay. During the following summer it was the turn of Alexander and Ernest Württemberg, sons of another maternal aunt, Antoinette. Princess Victoria found them handsome and amiable, but no matchmaking plans were ever pursued.

By 1836, as it was increasingly a question of when, and not if, she would be queen regnant, some urgency was applied to the matter. In the spring, two Coburg princes, Ferdinand and Augustus, sons of the Duchess of Kent's brother Ferdinand, came to stay for several weeks. Victoria liked them both, especially the nineteen-year-old Ferdinand, though he was ineligible, as he had just been married by proxy to Queen Maria Gloria of Portugal and was about to travel there to meet her for the first time. Victoria was very sad when the time came for them to depart, as she enjoyed the companionship of young men, as well as balls and other such entertainments.

In April 1836 King William IV invited the Prince of Orange and his sons William and Alexander to England. This was unwelcome news to King Leopold, especially as Belgium had recently broken away from Holland, and both countries were on distant terms. They arrived in May, and Victoria was invited to a ball at which they were present. Much to King Leopold's relief, his niece was unimpressed by them: 'they look heavy, dull and frightened and are not at all prepossessing.'[18]

That same month, on 18 May, she met her Coburg cousins, sons of Ernest, Duke of Saxe-Coburg, for the first time. On 23 May she wrote to tell King Leopold that she found both 'very amiable, very kind and good, and extremely merry, just as young people should be'. Albert, she continued, was 'extremely handsome, which Ernest certainly is not, but he has a most good-natured, honest, and intelligent countenance'.[19]

After they had gone, she confided in her uncle again, thanking him 'for the prospect of great happiness you have contributed to give me, in the person of dear Albert'. She was delighted with him, as he 'possesses every quality that could be desired to render me perfectly happy', and she hoped and trusted that 'all will go on prosperously and well on this subject of so much importance to me'.[20] He could not equal her zest for living, as he hated late nights and rich food, tended to fall asleep in company and found little pleasure in the dances, parties and entertainments on which she throve. For a high-spirited girl who enjoyed good living and could dance until dawn, this was something of a disappointment. Nevertheless, her Coburg cousin had made a lasting impression on her. She greatly admired him, even though she did not know him well enough to be in love with him.

* * *

Early in the morning of 20 June 1837, barely four weeks after Victoria's eighteenth birthday, King William IV passed away and his niece became queen. For the first two years of her reign, Queen Victoria was an isolated, even lonely, figure. Her ageing, worldly-wise Prime Minister, Lord Melbourne, provided her with the best company she could possibly want at the time, but as a young unmarried sovereign she was severely limited in her friendships. Perhaps she needed a father more than a consort. King Leopold was prudent enough to stay away from England during this period, as he foresaw that the English might think he was coming merely to 'enslave' her.[21] Yet it was a source of some concern to him that her letters had become increasingly imperious. When she wrote to him on political matters, they were not the outpourings of an eager young woman ready to learn, so much as the thoughts of the Queen of England.

Although she had never known him, maybe she felt more affection somehow for the father whom she never knew, or at least for his memory, than for the mother who had worked so hard, albeit sometimes misguidedly, on her behalf. For during the first two years or so of her reign, relations were extremely strained between Queen Victoria and the Duchess of Kent, and the influence of Lord Melbourne had obviously superseded that of the kingly sage of Laeken. Moreover, she seemed reluctant to marry, and King Leopold saw that if she was to loosen the connections with her Coburg heritage too much, the chance of bringing about the alliance he had worked for might be lost. It was time to expedite plans for the betrothal. One more meeting between her and her cousin Albert, he was sure, would be enough to make her reconsider. He planned to send the young man and his brother Ernest to visit her again in the autumn of 1839.

This put the Queen in a difficult position. Despite all the favourable reports about her cousin's character, she informed the King that it must be understood there was no engagement between them, and she was not in a position to make any final promise that year, 'for, at the *very earliest*, any such event could not take place till *two or three years hence*'. She might 'like him as a friend, and as a *cousin*, and as a *brother*, but not *more*; and should this be the case (which is not likely), I am *very* anxious that it should be understood that I am *not* guilty of any breach of promise, for *I never gave any*'.[22]

If King Leopold feared his niece's obstinacy, he was wise enough not to show it. A young virgin queen was bound to relish her independence at first, and then probably change her mind. He agreed that she was under no obligation to give any immediate answer, as long as she would allow the visit to take place. First, though, he relied on a little psychology. A few immediate calls from other Coburg relations first would put her in a more receptive frame of mind. Setting the stage for Albert 'and a renewal of warm Coburg family life'[23] would surely help to achieve the object. Her uncle Ferdinand and her cousins Augustus and Leopold, and their sister Victoire, arrived in September 1839, to be followed by another cousin, Alexander Mensdorff-Pouilly, son of Princess Sophie of Saxe-Coburg, soon afterwards. For almost the first time in her life, Queen Victoria could experience something of a happy family existence, with cousins whose jokes, nicknames and friendly teasing she could share as if they were all brothers and sisters. When the time came for their departure, she was as deeply affected as they were.

On 10 October Ernest and Albert reached Windsor Castle after a very rough sea crossing which had left Albert feeling particularly seasick. Nevertheless, the young suitor, who had vowed before leaving Coburg that he intended to win the hand of Queen Victoria or else return with a decision that all must be over between them, made the right impression at once. One sentence from her journal that day will suffice: 'It was with some emotion that I beheld Albert – who is *beautiful*.'[24]

In Albert, Queen Victoria was to find the next father-figure for whom she craved. King Leopold had been less accessible since becoming a sovereign in his own right, and with her new-found self-confidence she was inclined to resent his interference. In December she wrote to Albert of having just received what she thought was 'an ungracious letter' from their uncle in Belgium. 'He appears to me to be nettled because I no longer ask for his advice, but dear Uncle is given to believe that he must rule the roast [*sic*] everywhere. However, that is not a necessity.'[25]

The influence of her Prime Minister, Lord Melbourne, who had been such a valued mentor ever since her accession, was beginning to diminish. From their engagement later that week to her death some sixty years later, Albert was and would be the most important figure in her life and her most abiding influence.

From the beginning of their relationship, Albert was made well aware that his wife and monarch initially intended to be the senior partner in the marriage. Just before he left Coburg for the last time as a bachelor, he received a letter from his affianced, firmly rejecting his plan for a honeymoon at Windsor. 'You forget, my dearest Love, that I am the Sovereign and that business can stop and wait for nothing.'[26]

A few days later she demonstrated similar single-mindedness, in the face of a united front from Melbourne and the Duchess of Kent, about allowing the bridegroom to sleep under her roof before the wedding. English objections to such an idea, she retorted, were 'foolish nonsense'. On the night before the ceremony, they spent an hour reading over the Marriage Service and rehearsing with the ring.

The wedding itself took place on 10 February 1840 at the Chapel Royal, St James's. As she walked up the aisle, it was noticed that she was perfectly composed but unusually pale, her normally red countenance for once a similar colour to that of her satin dress. Moreover, the orange flowers in her wreath were shaking as much as if she was caught in a breeze. Even so, she made her responses firmly, and her promise to 'obey' her husband, which was retained at her personal request, rang throughout the chapel.

On the following day, 'the happiest, happiest Being that ever existed' poured out her feelings in a letter to King Leopold. Albert, she wrote, 'is an Angel, and his kindness and affection for me is really touching. To look in those dear eyes, and that dear sunny face, is enough to make me adore him. What I can do to make him happy will be my greatest delight.'[27]

Yet for some weeks he felt oddly sidelined in his married life. To his friend Prince William zu Löwenstein he complained that he was 'only the husband, and not the master in the house'.[28] He found she had a tendency to be wilful and thoughtless. Though at heart she was kind and good-natured, she still seemed inclined to be moody, sulky, peevish and temperamental at times. In some ways she was an old head on young shoulders, well aware of her responsibilities as Queen of England, yet because she had gone from a sheltered upbringing to becoming theoretically the most powerful woman in the land, she had little experience of dealing with other people. It saddened him that he was at first denied her confidence in anything to do with the running of their households, and that she was disinclined to let him take part in political business. He was not asked into the room when she was talking to the Prime Minister; she never discussed affairs of state with him, she changed the subject whenever he tried to talk to her about political matters and she would not allow him to see any state papers from government departments. When he tried to suggest it, she told him gently but firmly that the English were very jealous of foreigners interfering in the government of their country. She was exercising caution, as initially she had wanted to create him King Consort, only to be warned in no uncertain terms by Lord Melbourne that if the English were allowed into the way of making kings, they might well be got into the way of unmaking them.

Melbourne had considerable sympathy for Albert and the Queen's reluctance to share authority with anyone – even her husband. 'My impression', he wrote to George Anson, 'is that the chief obstacle in Her Majesty's mind is the fear of difference of opinion and she thinks that domestic harmony is more likely to follow from avoiding subjects likely to create difference.'[29]

Moreover, Albert had formidable allies in King Leopold and his confidential adviser, Baron Stockmar, both of whom were determined that he should be her right hand in her constitutional functions. On a visit to Windsor in August 1840, the King declared that the prince 'ought in business as in everything to be necessary to the Queen, he should be to her a walking dictionary for reference on any point which her own knowledge or education have not enabled her to answer'.[30]

Albert's patience, and a gradual recognition of his abilities by others, soon brought about a change for the better. Melbourne had initially been sceptical of this shy, unworldly young German prince. Though deeply devoted to the Queen himself, he was concerned for her future happiness, and never a trace of jealousy entered his soul. He readily knew that it would be to the benefit of all if she was able to find a husband worthy of her and act as her support in governing the kingdom. To the elderly Prime Minister, who knew his political career would soon be over, Albert's qualities of calm, intelligence and conscientiousness were evident. He began talking political matters with Albert and urged the Queen to do likewise, telling her that he understood everything so well and should be involved more in the regular business of the monarchy. When he left office for the last time in 1841, he advised her to put her trust in her husband.

The advice was well received. Soon Albert was reading despatches, being asked for his advice and making important decisions. He was given the keys to the boxes of confidential state documents. At ministerial meetings he was always by the Queen's side, ready to make his contribution when asked, and without exception all her prime ministers during his lifetime appreciated and valued his opinions, though at least one – the redoubtable Lord Palmerston – might not have been prepared to admit it, preferring instead to regard him as a royal busybody meddling in affairs beyond his station. When Albert encouraged Victoria to take a greater interest in European affairs and insist on the right to be consulted on them at all times, the ministers might disagree, wondering whether he was exceeding his brief as the consort of a constitutional monarch. But they soon realised that they were dealing with a man of intelligence whose grasp of affairs at home and abroad was always scrupulously well-informed and generally impartial. Before her marriage, she had been a somewhat partisan Whig, until Albert convinced her that it was the duty of the Crown to stand above party politics; she must give allegiance to neither Whigs nor Tories.

Like her Hanoverian predecessors, the Queen did not shrink at first from openly showing her support for 'our party'. Until then, it had been accepted as common practice that in Windsor the monarch could control the election of members of parliament. Under Stockmar's tutelage, and with Peel's ready endorsement, Albert decided that the Queen should no longer do so. There was no question of the Crown withdrawing completely from involvement in political questions; but it was important that the Queen was seen to respect the integrity of the elected government and its party, just as she demanded that they respect her power as sovereign.

Within two months of his wedding, Albert had already formed his own view of the two-party system and the fundamental differences between each. The Whigs, he had decided, sought change *'before change* is required', and 'their love of change is their great failing'. The Tories, on the other hand, *'resist change* long after the feeling and temper of the times has loudly demanded it and at last make a virtue of necessity by an ungracious concession'.[31]

Yet Queen Victoria never completely recognised the limits imposed on a constitutional monarch. At various times throughout her life, she submitted to a change of government with ill-concealed bad grace. Albert may have been better in masking his feelings, but it is doubtful whether he appreciated such limits himself. In this he was taking his lead from Baron Stockmar's ill-advised opinion that the prime minister of the day was merely the temporary head of the cabinet, with the monarch as 'permanent premier'.[32] Lord John Russell once called the monarch 'an informal but potent member of all Cabinets'.[33] On the fall of his Conservative administration in 1852, Lord Derby recommended that Her Majesty should send for Lord Lansdowne; Lord John Russell maintained that his own claim should be considered; but the Queen chose the more amenable, if ineffectual, Lord Aberdeen instead. In 1858 the Queen and the Prince Consort, on whom this title had been conferred by letters patent the previous year, wanted Lord Granville to head an administration in order to avoid calling Lord Palmerston a second time, but in vain. As will be examined later, their relations with the maverick Palmerston had been very variable, and they opposed his Italian policy at a crucial time for Anglo-European relations, but their reservations about making him head of government counted for little.

* * *

Albert initially saw it as his role to broaden his wife's education and undertake a certain amount of character-forming. She was painfully aware of her intellectual and cultural shortcomings, and she tended to avoid the company of clever people. He encouraged her to take a more intelligent interest in everything around her, introducing her to the wonders of art and science, and encouraging her to read more serious books. With his passion for music, and skill as a musician and composer himself, he extended her interest in and knowledge of music. She had been brought up to enjoy concerts and the ballet, but as in so many other artistic matters, she knew very little about them until he imparted his own grasp of and enthusiasm for the subject, particularly the work of Handel, which until then had never meant anything to her.

Gradually he became the dominant partner, the one who made the decisions. Where he had initially assumed the role of her unofficial secretary, in time the positions became reversed. In effect, she became his deputy in dealings with the ministers.[34] After their eldest daughter Victoria, Princess Royal, married Prince Frederick William of Prussia in January 1858, she wrote regularly to her mother about personal matters, but always discussed political business with her father. Such letters were not generally shown to the Queen.

It is unlikely that she would have been more than momentarily piqued if she had known. During the days of Melbourne's tutelage, her instruction in the matter of politics and government had been very enjoyable. In later years, thanks to Disraeli, the subjects would once again become interesting, in presentation if not in substance. However, while she was married, they were strictly for the male of the species, not for her. 'Albert grows daily fonder and fonder of politics and business,' she wrote to King Leopold in 1852, 'and is so wonderfully *fit* for both – such perspicacity and such *courage* – and I grow daily to dislike them both more and more. We women are not *made* for governing – and if we are good women, we must dislike these masculine occupations; but there are times which force one to take *interest* in them *mal gré bon gré*, and I do, of course, *intensely*.'[35] There spoke a reluctant political figure. How she would have viewed the election of women to parliament, let alone a woman prime minister, one can only speculate, but she would probably not have welcomed the concept.

In public and in private, the Queen became more serious and more dignified, less impulsive and impetuous. Before her wedding, she had been a high-spirited young woman, ready to tease and given to outbursts of almost uncontrollable laughter. With marriage to Albert, these high spirits were not extinguished altogether, but they were certainly dampened. In one sense, he taught her to be a queen, by assuming an appropriate sense of regal dignity. More than once, she admitted to him that it was he who 'entirely formed' her.

TWO

'My father, my protector, my guide and adviser'

It has sometimes been argued that Prince Albert was the true architect of Victorianism, rather than the Queen who gave the era its name. Had she lived and reigned as a virgin queen like Elizabeth I, Victoria might have remained true to her Hanoverian instincts – hard-working, but with her virtues of industry tempered somewhat by an easy-going nature, a tendency to self-indulgence and a total lack of prudery. Marriage to the straitlaced, methodical, ever-earnest Albert ensured that the opposite happened.

In this, he was doing no more than following the precepts laid down during his early years by the dour, high-principled Baron Stockmar. Albert's intense prudery can probably be ascribed correctly in part to the distress he suffered when his mother was banished from his life for adultery while he was still only a small boy, never to see him again, and by his concern with (bordering on disgust at) the infidelities of his father, a pattern which would be repeated by his brother Ernest. Stockmar's influence had some effect on the industrious if ever-philandering Ernest as well, particularly with regard to liberal and political leanings, but in the unimpeachably clean-living Albert he found a ready disciple in all aspects.

Even before marriage, Albert was making his moral standpoint clear to one and all. When the Queen was choosing her bridesmaids, he proposed that she should take into account the reputation of their parents, a view which amazed the easy-going Lord Melbourne. He argued that it was one thing to demand previous employers' references for stableboys and housemaids, but quite another 'for persons of quality'. Though Melbourne had his way on this occasion, Albert continued to make a stand wherever he could. In 1852, when Lord Derby (who was twenty years his senior) became Prime Minister, Albert treated him to a homily on prime-ministerial duties. These, he declared, included the responsibility of being

20

'Keeper of the King's (or Queen's) Conscience', and observing the Queen's insistence that the moral character of the Court must be beyond reproach.[1] One might say that Albert was even more Victorian than Victoria herself.

* * *

In his letters to the Queen, the Prince addressed her as his 'own darling', or his 'little wife', his *Fraüchen*. On the rare occasions when they were apart, such letters were full of endearments to her. She hated the moments of separation, and when he had to go to Coburg for his father's funeral in 1844 she missed him bitterly. It was the first time they had been apart for even just a night, and as she told King Leopold, 'the *thought* of *such* separation is quite dreadful'.[2]

The married life of Queen Victoria and Prince Albert may have been idyllic but, like any other marriage, it had its stormy moments. In January 1842 their eldest child, Vicky, then aged fourteen months, suddenly fell ill, though the problem was nothing much more than indigestion – certainly no life-threatening condition. When they returned home from a visit to Claremont, they found the infant very white and thin. Understandably anxious, Albert made some impatient remark which drew forth a sharp comment from the nurse, Mrs Roberts. 'That is really malicious,' he muttered under his breath to the Queen, who immediately lost her temper.

For some time he had been alarmed about the slapdash attitudes of some of the nursery staff. The main offender was the Queen's old governess and confidante, Baroness Lehzen, and his months of frustration with her and the over-mighty role she played in the royal household came to a head. The Queen accused him of wanting to drive Mrs Roberts away from the nursery while he as good as murdered their child. Horrified that his wife could ever say such a thing, he murmured to himself, 'I must have patience,' and went downstairs to cool off. When they met again there was a violent quarrel, the Queen retreating in floods of tears while her husband, seething with anger, wrote her a note claiming that their physician-in-ordinary, Dr James Clark, had 'mismanaged the child and poisoned her with calomel'. Calling her bluff, he declared that he would have nothing more to do with it; 'take the child away and do as you like and if she dies you will have it on your conscience.'[3]

Needless to say, Albert meant nothing of the kind. As the Queen would have been the first to know, he adored their daughter dearly and would never have done anything to jeopardise her health, or indeed that of any of their other children. Clark had been in royal service ever since being appointed the Duchess of Kent's physician while Victoria was still heir to the throne. Though a kindly man, his medical competence was questionable. In later years Lord Clarendon, Queen Victoria's plain-speaking Foreign Secretary, branded the royal doctors as unfit to attend a sick cat, Clark being the main butt of his verdict.

Albert wrote to Baron Stockmar that the Queen was 'naturally a fine character but warped in many respects by wrong upbringing'.[4] Lehzen, who has been acknowledged as 'the last irresponsible favourite' in British history,[5] was prevailed upon to retire from royal service and return to Germany, and with her departure a barrier between husband and wife was removed. Later the Queen would admit ruefully that Lehzen, like her arch-enemy Conroy, was one of those 'wicked people' who had estranged her from her mother.

Queen Victoria had a fiery temper, and with a quiet, less outgoing husband whose inclination was to reason with her on paper rather than argue face to face, there were inevitably difficult scenes throughout their married life. Albert was melancholic by nature and to those who did not know him well often gave an impression of utter world-weariness. This should not be taken as the sign of an unhappy marriage. There is no reason to doubt that they did not enjoy an extremely good marriage. Any European prince who was marrying the Queen of England would have been aware at the outset that such a matrimonial union would not always run smoothly, but Prince Albert of Saxe-Coburg Gotha was uniquely well-qualified in terms of temperament and intellect to make as successful a job of it as any of his contemporaries, had they been given the opportunity instead.

They knew that there would always be testing times. Another arose in 1853, when the Queen was suffering from postnatal depression and anxious about the condition of their newly born son, Leopold, who was puny and evidently not at all well. One evening, the Queen and Albert were compiling a register of prints, when Albert rebuked her for not paying attention to what they were doing. She lost her temper and was in hysterics, shouting and weeping, oblivious to his reasoning. When he tried to speak to her calmly about it, the result was another session of regal sulks, snapping and tantrums. Nonplussed, he sat down and wrote her a long letter, saying how astonished he was at the effect one or two hasty words from him could produce.

What the Queen needed was a man who would argue back, answer strong words with more of the same, shout her down, reduce her to tears, clear the air and then make it up with her. It was as if his reasonableness and his analytical turn of mind was counter-productive. Her tears unnerved him, probably undermined his self-confidence and made him fearful of losing his temper. The practice of writing notes to her was one he had learnt from Baron Stockmar as a means of cooling tempers. Regrettably, where Queen Victoria was concerned, it generally had the opposite effect and simply prolonged quarrels instead of having a short, sharp shouting-match which dealt with the matter at once. If such episodes emphasised Albert's father-figure role, the Queen could not have failed to find them unduly patronising, notwithstanding the fact that he acted with the best of intentions.

Stockmar's earnest analytical approach to such problems was responsible for Albert's sometimes misguided solutions to the quarrels. The old Baron, in whom Albert confided more freely about his marital problems than anybody else, always dreaded – perhaps excessively – the possibility of incipient madness in the Queen. As a result, he advised his young protégé that tempers must always be kept calm and face-to-face confrontations avoided at all costs. Had Albert been able to confide in other men (or women) sufficiently to seek their advice, he might have received a very different answer.

Nevertheless, such scenes between husband and wife were always quickly made up. These arguments were no more common than in most happy marriages, and they never did anything to undermine the closeness of their relationship.

* * *

Three years into their marriage, with a growing family, Queen Victoria and Prince Albert decided that they needed a home of their own. Buckingham Palace, their state residence in the capital, was hardly private, and Albert's regular requests for more funds from the public purse for rebuilding and improving it met with consternation from their ministers. Brighton Pavilion, so beloved by

Victoria's uncle, King George IV, was ugly, inconvenient and even less private. Windsor Castle was comfortable and imposing, but not homely enough.

In 1843 they visited the Isle of Wight and briefly considered buying Norris Castle, but they soon discovered it was beyond their means. Not long afterwards, Prime Minister Sir Robert Peel learnt that the adjoining Osborne House and its estate were soon due to be sold. Within two years they had rented it, and eventually they were able to buy it outright. Here they had a place of their own, within sufficiently easy reach of the mainland for visiting ministers and dignitaries, but in a suitably unspoilt setting. Here Albert could indulge his passion for farming and planting 'free from Departments, Crown, Woods & Forests etc', and they could bring the children up in pleasant rural surroundings close to the seaside.

'Here we are at the Whitsun holidays,' Albert wrote to Baron Stockmar, 'when the weary combatants in Parliament and the tired-out epicureans fly from town for a little fresh air. We do the same, exhausted partly by business, partly by the so-called social pleasures, and are off at noon to-day to the Isle of Wight . . . . Osborne is bought, and, with some adjoining farms, which we have also bought, makes a domain of 1,500 acres in a ring fence.'[6] Two days later, the Queen noted in her journal that 'It does my heart good to see how my beloved Albert enjoys it all, and is so full of admiration of the place, and of all the plans and improvements he means to carry out. He is hardly to be kept at home for a moment.'[7]

Albert was a man of diverse interests and talents. Whether he threw himself wholeheartedly into them because of dissatisfaction with his home life and a lack of friends at Court, even the difficulty faced by a naturally shy man of making friends in another country, can only be guessed at. Yet he worked hard at starting to bring the royal residences into the nineteenth century. He had the drains, sewerage and plumbing at Buckingham Palace and Windsor Castle modernised, and ensured that their new homes at Osborne and later Balmoral in the Scottish Highlands also benefited from such changes. He scrutinised the household accounts and was astonished to learn that hundreds of candles at the palace were snuffed out when only burned halfway down and then discarded, or else removed by the servants for their own use. This was one practice which he accordingly reformed, with the result that a substantial saving was made. He found a large collection of valuable paintings stacked and neglected in the cellars, and oversaw the restoration, cataloguing and in many instances rehanging of such works to full advantage.

* * *

Of Prince Albert's many achievements during his lifetime, perhaps none could ever compare with that of the Great Exhibition of 1851, the culmination of his interest in science and manufacture. He believed passionately in industrial Britain and thought that man might use his techniques to create a better world. While some saw it as just an enormous British shop-window, full of the products of the new industry, it was an attempt to fuse together utility and beauty, a celebration of the British Empire and advances in technology. In this he was inspired partly by the success of a recent French Industrial Exposition and partly by the enthusiasm of Henry Cole, an active member of the Royal Society of Arts, of which Albert was already President. He was also appointed President of a Royal Commission, and a total fund of £230,000 was raised. The Commissioners set up a competition for designing the building for the exhibition: 233 architects sent in designs, 38 from abroad, 51 from around England and 128 from London. The winning entry, from Joseph Paxton, proposed a glass house on a huge scale, the like of which had never been seen before.

The exhibition was held in the Crystal Palace, erected in Hyde Park, London. It opened on 1 May 1851, remaining open six days a week, and closed on 15 October. The original admission fee of 5s was reduced to 1s on four days each week, and on Fridays – and Saturdays from August onwards – it was 2s6d. The first major event of its kind in England, it had an enormous influence on the development of many aspects of society, including art and design, education, international trade and even the tourist industry, and also set a precedent for many more international exhibitions over the following hundred years.

Queen Victoria, Prince Albert and their family attended the opening of the exhibition. The day had been declared a public holiday, thousands lined the route the Queen would take, and inside the Palace were 25,000 invited guests and season ticket holders. Afterwards she wrote to King Leopold that it was 'the *happiest, proudest* day in my life, and I can think of nothing else. Albert's name is for ever immortalised with this *great* conception, his own, and my *own* dear country *showed* she was *worthy* of it.'[8] She came to visit almost daily from its opening until she left Buckingham Palace for Osborne at the end of July.

By the time it closed, over 6 million visitors had passed through its doors, though the precise total figure of 6,063,986 includes those who visited more than once. The profits exceeded £180,000, and on Albert's suggestion an acreage of land in Kensington Gore was purchased as a site for royal colleges and museums, notably the Victoria and Albert Museum and the Royal Albert Hall. The Crystal Palace itself was moved to Sydenham, where it was eventually destroyed by fire in 1936.

As a demonstration of industrial progress and a bringing together of all classes, the exhibition was an undoubted success. Writing to Prince Albert in rather patronising terms which would seem politically incorrect in the extreme to later generations, the Home Secretary, Sir George Grey, was particularly struck by the fact that it brought to London thousands of people who had never seen a train before, 'people speaking the strange tongues of Lancashire and Durham, and the official reports of their behaviour as they flocked through museums and gardens are full of unconcealed pride. Not a flower was picked, not a picture smashed.'[9]

Although the Great Exhibition made Prince Albert very popular in the country, he and the Queen were soon to find that this mood of euphoria did not last. When the Crimean crisis broke late in 1853 and Turkey declared war on Russia, Lord Palmerston, the Home Secretary, urged immediate support for the beleaguered Turks and joint action with France against the Russian Empire. When the Prime Minister, Lord Aberdeen, shrank from declaring war, Palmerston resigned. Public opinion, which was overwhelmingly on Palmerston's side, accused the Prince of having plotted to bring about his departure from the government and of carrying on pro-Russian intrigues through his relatives in Germany. It was rumoured that Palmerston had steamed open the Prince's letters and found evidence of treacherous correspondence with the Russians. Expecting him and the Queen to be sent to the Tower for treason, crowds gathered at Traitors' Gate in the hope of seeing their sovereign and 'the German lad' being taken through as prisoners.

War fever, the royal family and politicians were sure, had sent the whole country 'a little mad'. The press accused Albert of interference in the affairs of the War Office, where a senior officer had resigned his post after differences with the Commander-in-Chief, the Queen's notoriously reactionary cousin George, Duke of Cambridge.

So virulent were the attacks that Lord John Russell, as Leader of the House of Commons, strongly deprecated these calumnies, saying that the people of the country 'always just in the end, will, as a result of this experience, give a firmer and stronger foundation to the throne'.[10] The attacks on Albert were formally rejected in parliament by members of all parties, and the storm soon abated. Nevertheless, the Queen was bitter that politicians should have allowed passions in the country to have become so inflamed and that they had not come to the defence of her much-maligned husband sooner.

* * *

'I cannot ever think or admit that anyone can be as blessed as I am with such a husband and such a perfection as a husband; for Papa has been and is everything to me,' the Queen admitted candidly in 1858 to her eldest daughter, Victoria, Princess Royal, then newly married to Prince Frederick William of Prussia. 'I had led a very unhappy life as a child – had no scope for my very violent feelings of affection – had no brothers and sisters to live with – never had had a father. . . . Consequently I owe everything to dearest Papa. He was my father, my protector, my guide and adviser in all and everything, my mother (I might almost say) as well as my husband.'[11]

'Dearest Papa' was not quite perfection, however. 'That despising our poor degraded sex – (for what else is it as we poor creatures are born for man's pleasure and amusement, and destined to go through endless sufferings and trials?) is a little in all clever men's natures,' she told her daughter just over a year later. Albert himself was not free from such faults, though he would not have admitted it. He might laugh and sneer constantly at what his wife might have to live with, and at their 'unavoidable inconveniences', though he hated the want of affection, of due attention to and protection of them, and said that men who left all home affairs and the education of their children to their wives 'forget their first duties'.[12]

Such arguments would be returned to yet another year later, while the Princess was eight months pregnant with her second child. If only those selfish men, she lamented, who were the cause of such misery, 'knew what their poor slaves go through!'[13]

27

Much as Victoria loathed the *Schattenseite*, or shadow side, of child-bearing, the Hanoverian in her was certainly anything but frigid when it came to what might delicately be called her other role as a wife. When Dr James Clark told her, after the birth of her ninth baby, Beatrice, that she should not have any more children in case it seriously threatened her health, she is reputed to have asked with disappointment, 'Oh, James, can I have no more fun in bed?'[14] (Perhaps her instruction on the subject of birth control had been somewhat lacking.) Four years later, on one of the couple's last joint Highland excursions, she complained of the lack of facilities and substandard accommodation at an inn at Dalwhinnie: 'No pudding, and no fun.'[15] One cannot but smile gently at her allowing an admittedly cryptic reference in her diaries to 'fun', and even more, at the fact that she allowed this reference to be published in her *Leaves from Our Life in the Highlands* in 1868.

Fulfilling the roles of monarch, mother to a family of adolescents, wife and also expectant mother made demands on her patience which would have taxed any woman. Shortly before she became (in her preferred term) *enceinte* for the last time, she confided her fears to Sir James Clark, who told Albert that 'she felt sure if she had another child she would sink under it', and that Clark himself feared more for her mind than her health.[16] In March 1857, a month before the birth of Beatrice, she begged her husband to uphold her authority with the children, now aged between three and sixteen, and not scold her in front of them, as her physical condition caused her a deep sense of degradation. Her temper was further strained by feelings of jealousy where their eldest daughter was concerned. When the Princess Royal was betrothed to Prince Frederick William of Prussia, Albert began spending more and more time with her, coaching her in political and governmental matters and preparing her (a little too thoroughly, it must be said) for her future life in Germany. Victoria was angry with Albert for devoting too much attention to their unusually clever child and was also apparently angry with Prince Frederick William for preparing to devote his life to their child whom, Albert wrote to her bluntly, 'you are thankful to be rid of'.[17]

Albert was said to have been less physically passionate than his wife, a characteristic ascribed to prudery arising from psychological damage after his mother's expulsion from the family nest while he was still a boy. His lack of interest in other women amused, if not surprised, some of the more rakish gentlemen at Court. It was whispered that sometimes she had to coax him to bed, and it was even rumoured that, 'with her erotic Hanoverian inheritance', she debilitated him so much with her sexual demands that she hastened his early demise.[18]

For the sheltered young Queen of twenty, sharing a physical relationship was undoubtedly a revelation, something that the bowdlerised version of her journals that survives for posterity can only hint at but not completely disguise. Some commentators have called their love-life undoubtedly passionate, citing as evidence such details (recorded in Victoria's journal) as her unashamed pleasure in such actions as watching Albert shave in the mornings or his helping her to put on her stockings. Others think that he was sexually indifferent to her and regarded the whole business as procreational rather than recreational.[19]

Another measure of their interest in such matters can be discerned in a different way. For a couple who were generally considered by succeeding generations to be the last word in prudery, they had relatively uninhibited tastes in art. The Queen had their bedroom hung with paintings of male nudes. According to psychologist and author Dennis Friedman, this sprang from the hope that Albert would find them visually erotic.[20] For the sake of their marriage, one would like to think that he found his wife's present to him on his thirty-first birthday more to his liking. This was a vast painting by their favourite portraitist, Franz Xaver Winterhalter, *Florinda*, full of voluptuous women who had gone to a stream in order to bathe as nature intended. Elizabeth Longford suggests that they both developed sexually with each other, and that she loved him so much that the sudden lack of their love, including the sex, was what drove her into seclusion for so long after his death.[21]

Yet the Queen must have been aware that her Hanoverian vivacity far exceeded his Coburg fatalism. His indigestion and similar chronic symptoms, especially 'fainting fits', became more frequent over the years. All would be well in the end, Sir James Clark blandly assured her, but she was not convinced.

Neither was Baron Stockmar, who saw Albert in Coburg in September 1860 shortly after the latter had been involved in a horse-drawn carriage accident. The horses had bolted, Albert tried to rein in the beasts but failed, and his vehicle collided with a stationary wagon at a level crossing. He jumped clear, sustaining only cuts and bruises, and rushed to the aid of the wagon driver who was similarly shaken but not seriously hurt. After shock set in, Albert burst into tears, saying that he knew he would never see his beloved Coburg again. Stockmar came to see him while he was resting and said to himself afterwards that Albert was incapable of fighting a severe illness. If anything serious happened to him, he would surely die.

The Prince Consort later confirmed this gloomy outlook. 'I do not cling to life,' he told the Queen in conversation shortly before his last illness. If he had a severe illness, he said, he would give up at once and would not struggle for life.[22] Partly because of this it has been asserted, somewhat unconvincingly, that his marriage could not have been very happy, and that the withdrawn and introverted adolescent was drawn to Victoria, as she was to him, out of a shared need for emotional fulfilment, yet he was crushed by the affections of a woman on whom he depended but whom he could not have loved, 'because dependence and hostility go hand in hand', and from whom only death could release him.[23]

For present-day commentators to put such a construction on a relationship between two people, one of whom has been dead for over a century, is easy enough, yet perhaps a shade superficial. The marriage had its ups and downs, and Albert was one of those introspective souls who gave the impression of rarely, if ever, being totally happy and at ease with the world. Yet one should be careful of putting too negative an interpretation on the story of Victoria and Albert. It is difficult to avoid the conclusion that she was besotted with him, simply because she was less inhibited and more passionate about expressing her feelings, particularly in her journal (even the expurgated one which has survived her daughter Beatrice's censorious transcription), and also because she had a fiery temper. Though less demonstrative, Albert was surely in love with her, 'whatever love means', to use the words memorably spoken by one of their descendants at the time of his first betrothal over a century later.

What is beyond doubt is the fact that by 1861 he had aged well beyond his forty-two years. The year had begun sadly with the death, on 2 January, of the childless King Frederick William IV of Prussia, the Princess Royal's uncle by marriage, and the accession of his brother William, who had earlier given the misleading impression that he agreed – or at least did not take serious issue – with Albert's plans for bringing liberalism and democracy to the German kingdom, but now showed his true colours by angrily throwing Albert's letters into the fire. On 16 March the Queen's mother, the Duchess of Kent, became ill with the skin disease erysipelas and died. Thanks to Albert's peace-making skills, mother and daughter had been reconciled very soon after the wedding, and the Queen was so stricken with grief that rumours of her impending madness circulated throughout Europe. Later in the year, two of Albert's Coburg relations in Portugal, King Pedro V and his brother Prince Fernando, succumbed to typhoid fever.

This coincided with the news that the Prince of Wales, the incorrigible Bertie (the future Edward VII), had just had an affair with a lady of the night, Nellie Clifden, while at Army camp in Ireland. To add insult to injury, it seemed as if almost every court in Europe knew before the scandal reached his horrified parents at Windsor Castle. They both reacted with intense fury, Albert writing him an anguished letter on the subject and then travelling to Cambridge to see him in person. Though he forgave his son, the Queen took a long time to do so. The Prince Consort arrived back at Windsor dispirited and exhausted. Within a few days he had taken to his bed, suffering from the typhoid fever which would claim his life on 14 December.

'How am I alive after witnessing what I have done?' she wrote to Vicky in her grief, four days later. 'Oh! I who prayed daily that we might die together & I never survive him! I who felt in those blessed Arms clasped & held tight in the sacred Hours at night – when the world seemed only to be ourselves that nothing could part us!'[24]

To the few close friends who also knew the Prince Consort well, she would regularly lament her sad lot in life, particularly when precious anniversaries came around. Shortly after her forty-sixth birthday, in May 1865, she wrote to Queen Augusta of Prussia how she would 'rather sit and weep and live only with Him in spirit and take no interest in the things of this earth, for I believe that I am going further away from him and do not always see things so clearly as I used to! But I suppose that is God's will and one must acquiesce in that also. He commands that I shall live, and so He allows me for the present the power to continue, until I am with my Angel once more.'[25]

The feelings of insecurity which the Queen had known since childhood reappeared in widowhood. Now she had no husband to smooth her path or lighten her load, she held fast to old familiar ways. Sometimes family and friends thought she was living in the past. When Victoria was in her mid-seventies, a young lady-in-waiting, Marie Mallet, was struck by the 'curious charm to our beloved Sovereign in doing the same thing on the same day year after year'.[26] The ghost of the Prince Consort still held sway over a court which seemed to have been permanently set in stone since December 1861, over thirty years earlier. His widow resisted any efforts or suggestions to alter her time-honoured rituals or routines, and she remained fiercely resistant to change. There was no little comfort to be found in holding on to the past. Sometimes she would admit to feeling like a lost child.

The remarks of Benjamin Disraeli, who in time would become outwardly the most loyal of Queen Victoria's prime ministers, have been interpreted (or perhaps misinterpreted) as saying that the Prince Consort's untimely death was providential for the Crown. Shortly afterwards he remarked in conversation with Count Vitzthum, the Saxon ambassador, that the Prince had governed England for twenty-one years 'with a wisdom and energy such as none of our Kings have ever shown', and that had he lived longer, 'he would have given us, while retaining our constitutional guarantees, the blessings of absolute government'.[27] William A. Kuhn, biographer of Sir Henry and Lady Ponsonby, has construed this as saying that had Albert lived longer he would have become a dictator,[28] while David Duff would assert that, had his physical strength matched his determination, either parliament would have had to concede ground to 'King Albert' or the people would have called for the abolition of the monarchy[29] – something which, in view of the republican agitation of 1870–1, might not have been inconceivable. On the other hand, Elizabeth Longford asserted that Disraeli's gibe was a hollow one, and that there was nothing of substance in it.[30]

Queen Victoria remained in formal mourning for the rest of her life, thirty-nine years. Every letter she wrote was on paper with thick black borders. She always used the Prince Consort's copy of the Book of Common Prayer which the Duchess of Kent had given him as a wedding gift. At her insistence, all his rooms remained as they had been at the time of his death, with photographs taken to make sure that no alterations could be made – or, if any were inadvertently made, that they could be rearranged as they had been while 'he' lived. Visitors, particularly those outside the family, would be startled many years later to see steaming water carried into Albert's dressing-room in the morning as if he was about to shave.

Such details, such efforts to preserve the routines of his lifetime, were both a means of perpetuating mourning for the dear departed and a source of comfort.

No sovereign's consort ever made a deeper impact on his spouse's country, or their life and times, than Albert, Prince Consort. One need go no further than the verdict of Roger Fulford, admittedly a sympathetic rather than objective biographer but one whose assessment cannot be faulted, that his claim to greatness rested on his services to monarchy, and while he did not create the Coburg conception of monarchy – King Leopold of the Belgians, under Stockmar's guidance, deserved the credit for that – he 'seized the torch from them and sped it on its way with amazing verve and strength' – and 'can certainly claim to be the creator of the modern English monarchical tradition'.[31]

* * *

Only one of Queen Victoria's father-figures from the family now remained. King Leopold was ageing fast, though from his capital he was still ready to offer the occasional word of solace, encouragement and even warning to his bereaved niece. Within a few weeks of Albert's death, he was writing to warn her that it was time for grief to give way to duty, and that it was 'undoubtedly your interest for the sake of having no difficulties as well as that of the country that Pilgerstein [Palmerston] and his people should not be upset'.[32]

When she persisted in wallowing in her grief and withdrawing into herself, nobody counselled her more strongly against her seclusion than King Leopold. He knew that such a situation would only do her and the monarchy harm, and he found it necessary to remind her gently that the English were 'very personal': 'to continue to love people they must see them'. When the Prince of Wales married Princess Alexandra of Denmark in March 1863, they immediately adopted a high profile in the public eye and instantly gave the monarchy a presence in society life such as it had not seen for many years. Bertie and Alix, Leopold told her, were *'constantly before the public'*[33] and keeping a high profile for the monarchy which she would do well to emulate.

By this time, King Leopold was in poor health, though he paid one final visit to Queen Victoria in March and April 1865. Soon after returning home, he fell seriously ill with bronchitis, and he was never really well again. He died in his palace at Laeken on 10 December 1865, within less than a week of what would have been his seventy-fifth birthday. 'Dearly beloved Uncle Leopold is no more,' wrote the Queen in her journal, 'that dear loving Uncle, who has ever been to me as a Father, has gone to that everlasting Home, where all is peace and rest.'[34]

He had left a wish to be buried, not in Belgium beside his second wife, Queen Louise, but instead in St George's Chapel at Windsor, next to his first wife, the hapless Princess Charlotte. This desire was refused by the Belgian authorities, and he was laid to rest in the family vault at Laeken. Nevertheless, the preacher at Windsor paid tribute to him in the first Sunday service after his death, speaking to the congregation of 'the Nestor of [Europe's] sovereigns, not in age and experience only, but in wise and kindly counsel, in just and far-sighted prudence'.[35]

It was left to the Queen's second daughter, Alice, recently married to Prince Louis of Hesse and the Rhine, to tell her that now she was head of all the family.[36]

PART TWO

Prime Ministers

Queen Victoria's Prime Ministers

William Lamb, Viscount Melbourne (1779–1848) (*Whig*) – appointed
  April 1835
Sir Robert Peel (1788–1850) (*Tory*) – September 1841
Lord John Russell (1792–1878) (*Whig*) – July 1846
Edward George Stanley, Earl of Derby (1799–1869) (*Conservative*) –
  February 1852
George Hamilton-Gordon, Earl of Aberdeen (1784–1860)
  (*Conservative*) – December 1852
Henry John Temple, Viscount Palmerston (1784–1865) (*Liberal*) –
  February 1855
Edward George Stanley, Earl of Derby – February 1858
Henry John Temple, Viscount Palmerston – June 1859
Lord John Russell – October 1865
Edward George Stanley, Earl of Derby – June 1866
Benjamin Disraeli (1804–81) (*Conservative*) – February 1868
William Ewart Gladstone (*Liberal*) – December 1868
Benjamin Disraeli (from August 1876, Earl of Beaconsfield) – February
  1874
William Ewart Gladstone – April 1880
Robert Gascoyne-Cecil, Marquess of Salisbury (1830–1903)
  (*Conservative*) – June 1885
William Ewart Gladstone – February 1886
Robert Gascoyne-Cecil, Marquess of Salisbury – August 1886
William Ewart Gladstone – August 1892
Archibald Philip Primrose, Earl of Rosebery (1847–1929) (*Liberal*) –
  March 1894
Robert Gascoyne-Cecil, Marquess of Salisbury – June 1895

THREE

'I know how to value and appreciate real worth'

Queen Victoria's first official act of her reign was an appearance at her first Council, held at 11.30 a.m. on 20 June 1837 at Kensington Palace. Despite the short notice, there was a record attendance of privy councillors, eager to see their new sovereign who had ascended the throne only a few hours previously. The impression she made on everybody present remained with them for a long time, and some years later the 4th Earl of Rosebery described her appearance to his young grandson, the future Liberal prime minister. Her behaviour, he said, 'was perfectly composed & dignified' as she read out a written speech, appointed the Marquess of Lansdowne as president of her council and listened to Lansdowne reading out the places where she should be proclaimed. Several councillors, Rosebery observed, 'were affected to tears', none more so than the Prime Minister, Lord Melbourne.[1]

During the Queen's sixty-three years on the throne, ten different prime ministers held office. It was her supreme fortune that on her accession the first of them was ready and willing to be the perfect mentor, guiding her in the art of statecraft. William Lamb, 2nd Viscount Melbourne, had been a member of parliament since 1806, serving in Whig governments as Chief Secretary for Ireland and later as Home Secretary. In 1834 he was appointed prime minister by King William IV, though he only held office for a few months before being dismissed. As there was still a large Whig majority in the Commons, his Tory successor, Sir Robert Peel, found it impossible to govern effectively, and on his resignation in April 1835 Melbourne resumed office.

At the time of the Queen's accession he was fifty-eight years old. According to Elizabeth Longford, the three-year partnership between the inexperienced young sovereign and her political mentor was 'one of the romances of history'. King Leopold, she argued, was her second father and Melbourne her third, but as her association with the latter began after her childhood was over, it was more intense than anything which preceded it.[2] She was captivated by his worldly-wise store of knowledge and his irreverent wit. How could it have been otherwise of a statesman who could quote to her with a knowing smile that the Four Commandments repeated by a prominent politician's wife to her children were to fear God, honour the King, obey your parents and brush your teeth?

Within less than a month of her accession, she was writing to King Leopold of her delight and confidence in Melbourne. Here was somebody in England from the older generation whom she could trust: 'I have, alas! seen so much of bad hearts and dishonest and *double* minds, that I know how to value and appreciate *real worth*.'[3] Less than two years later, she was still just as partisan. 'God knows, *no* Minister, no friend EVER possessed the confidence of the Crown so entirely as this truly excellent Lord Melbourne possesses mine.'[4] Not only was he a valued political mentor, but his irreverent, cynical comments could always make her laugh. English physicians, he told her, 'kill you, the French let you die'. When the Duke of Richmond remarked that people often came out of prison worse than when they began their sentence, Melbourne added that the same applied to many other places: 'one often comes out worse of a ballroom than one went in.'[5]

If the Queen found the father-figure in him which she needed at such a vulnerable stage in her life, he was thrilled to have the regular company of a young woman who was in effect something of a daughter to him. His own family life had been unhappy. A tempestuous marriage had ended in separation, followed soon afterwards by the death of his wife from dropsy, and their only child, a son, was mentally defective and died as a young man. 'I have no doubt he is passionately fond of her as he might be of his own daughter if he had one,' the Hon. George Villiers told the diarist Charles Greville after a visit to Windsor, 'and the more because he is a man with a capacity for loving without having anything in the world to love. It is become his province to educate, instruct and form the most interesting mind and character in the world.'[6]

In many ways, Melbourne's influence on Queen Victoria was all to the good. He imparted to her much wisdom on the duties of a constitutional monarch and had the gift of making affairs of state seem less of a drudge and more interesting than they really were. Her only other prime minister who would ever manage to do this was Benjamin Disraeli – thus explaining why she responded so well to both men as a sovereign. No less important was the self-confidence Melbourne gave her through a judicious degree of praise and affection, and through a sense of sophistication in his table-talk. Several factors had combined to make her basically unsure of herself. She felt she was not properly educated and still had so much to learn, hence clever or learned people tended to make her feel inferior. She was also very small, barely standing five feet in height, and shared the lack of assurance often associated with women who were short in stature.

Less to Melbourne's credit was the impression he repeatedly gave her that the state of the country was better than it really was, and his failure to inculcate in her any pronounced sense of social conscience or genuine appreciation of the problems of the poor and starving. The lofty aristocrat in him deeply distrusted any thought of social change, and he made her think that unrest was more often than not due to a handful of agitators. His attitude to the discontented poor was equally insensitive. During the previous reign, when a particular group of agricultural workers had protested against their meagre wages in 1834, he endorsed the decision of the judge who tried them on a charge of 'unlawful assembly' and sentenced them to seven years' transportation to a penal colony in New South Wales, Australia, as an example to others, and only public pressure forced the government to remit the sentences of the men who would become known to posterity as the Tolpuddle martyrs.

Of the social realism portrayed by such writers as Charles Dickens, he was equally dismissive. One day in conversation he mentioned *Oliver Twist*. Commenting that it was all about (or among) workhouses, coffin makers and pickpockets, he remarked that he did not like 'that low debasing style; it's all slang; it's just like *The Beggar's Opera*; I shouldn't think it would tend to raise morals; I don't like that low debasing view of mankind.' When Victoria defended the book, he repeated that he did not like such things: 'I wish to avoid them; I don't like them in *reality*; and therefore I don't wish to see them represented.'[7] Quite how serious he actually was, or whether he was speaking with tongue in cheek, one will never know. When he told her that it was 'almost worthwhile for a woman to be beat, considering the exceeding pity she excites', he can hardly have meant his words to be taken seriously. He would surely never have said any such thing to his Queen unless he knew she had a sense of humour.

Nevertheless, if one assumes that his remarks about 'low debasing style' were genuinely representative of his views, then he certainly was a typical reactionary aristocrat, if no worse than any other such figure of the time. His opinions on the subject of workers' rights and ostrich-like attitude to the evils of society or the plight of the poor were in contrast to his liberal views on the upbringing of children. When the Queen told him that she thought solitary confinement and silence were suitable punishments for wilful youngsters, he begged to differ, saying he thought they must be 'very stupifying'. Nevertheless, his indulgence towards minors was severely limited in other directions. The work of such philanthropists as Lord Shaftesbury to improve the conditions of factory children who worked between twelve and fifteen hours a day in cotton mills or mines, he told her, was quite unnecessary, as reports of their conditions were greatly exaggerated; making the children work kept them out of mischief and prevented them from starving.[8]

The father-figure in him constantly made gentle suggestions to the Queen for the sake of her health. He warned her that over-eating was a Hanoverian family failing, and that she ought to eat only when she was hungry. In that case, she retorted, she would surely be eating all day, as she was always hungry. She should take more exercise and walk more if she did not want to get fat, he said, but she complained that walking made her feet swell. Anyway, she got stones in her shoes. Have them made tighter, he suggested. King Leopold added his support to Lord Melbourne's advice, telling her that poor Charlotte, his wife, had died through not walking enough.

Two of his favourite girls' names, Melbourne said, were Alice and Louise, and it was not surprising that Victoria would later name her second and fourth daughters thus. The Louise was to be partly in honour of her mother-in-law and also her aunt, Queen of the Belgians, but there had not been a royal Alice for some generations.

On her accession to the throne, the Queen pointedly ignored her mother, the Duchess of Kent, much of the time. She was one of the first to look askance at the close relationship between her daughter and the Prime Minister. 'Take care Victoria you know your Prerogative!' she warned. 'Take care that Lord Melbourne is not King.'[9] She need not have worried, for Melbourne scrupulously observed the limits of the royal prerogative.

* * *

Though nobody could ever hope to eclipse Melbourne as political mentor in the first two years of Victoria's reign, two other political personalities of the day had a decisive impact, albeit in different ways. The first was Arthur Wellesley, Duke of Wellington, the hero of the battle of Waterloo; the other was Melbourne's Foreign Secretary, Henry John Temple, 3rd Viscount Palmerston.

As the man who had defeated the arch-enemy Napoleon Bonaparte, no Englishman was more revered at the time than Wellington, and he was one of the most steadfast allies and defenders the Crown could ever have. Much as he might have disparaged, in an impatient moment, the sons of King George III as 'damned millstones' around the government's neck, nobody could be regarded as a more faithful supporter of the British monarchy than the Iron Duke. After attending the first privy council of Victoria's reign, he said that 'if she had been his own daughter he could not have desired to see her perform her part better'.[10]

A few weeks after her accession, Victoria was due to appear at a review of her troops, and despite the objections of her ministers she intended to appear on horseback. The Duke objected to her being forced into what he regarded as a piece of theatrical display on her part, especially as he had misgivings about her horsemanship. 'Much better come in her carriage,' he wrote to Lady Salisbury. 'I would not wish a better subject for a caricature than this young Queen, alone, without any woman to attend her, without the brilliant cortège of young men and ladies as ought to appear in a scene of that kind . . . . And if it rains and she gets wet, or if any other *contretemps* happens, what is to be done? All these things sound very little, but they must be considered in a display of that sort . . . . It is a childish fancy, because she has read of Queen Elizabeth at Tilbury Fort; but *then* there was the threat of foreign invasion, which was an occasion calling for display; what occasion is there now?'[11]

She had not ridden since her illness two years earlier, and there were doubts as to whether she would be able to hold her own properly on horseback. Melbourne likewise recommended that she should attend in a carriage, though for reasons of propriety, as she would be accompanied by a female attendant instead of riding on a horse between two men. Her verdict to them all was unequivocal: no horse, no review. She had her own way and went on horseback as she said she would.

Wellington felt exceptionally protective towards his young sovereign, and though he saw that she was 'quite satisfied' with Melbourne, looked with some dismay on her reliance on her Prime Minister, and feared her resistance to an eventual change in the government, which was inevitable. 'My opinion', he wrote to a friend after dining with Victoria at Buckingham Palace one night in February 1838, 'is that she does nothing without consulting him, even upon the time of quitting the table after dinner and retiring to bed at night.' Should the government be defeated and he or Sir Robert Peel, as the senior Tories, be asked to form an administration, 'I have always been and always shall be in front of the Battle. I cannot hold back.' He hoped the occasion would not arise, as in a minority administration they would find it difficult to govern 'when we cannot rely upon their support in any opinion of ours',[12] and he knew she would find it difficult to exercise her royal prerogative while still so young and inexperienced.

Two years later, the Queen's reputation plummeted with the 'Lady Flora Hastings affair' (see p. 47). During this sorry time it saddened Wellington that the Queen seemed to have so little affection or respect for her mother, though behind the scenes he urged both factions – the Hastings family and the Queen herself – to try to hush matters up as much as possible. At the time of the 'bedchamber crisis' (see pp. 45–6), she had briefly sent for Wellington as a possible prime minister in place of Peel, though he rejected the offer, partly on grounds of age – he was almost seventy years old – and as he thought it best if the prime minister was a member of the House of Commons.

By the end of 1839, Wellington's relations with the sovereign had become rather strained. When the matter of Prince Albert's annuity was discussed in parliament, it was fixed at £30,000, little more than half the sum granted to Prince (now King) Leopold on his marriage, a matter which still rankled with those at Westminster who were indignant at seeing such revenue go to a man who was now a European sovereign and in effect no longer a member of the British royal family. Despite Melbourne's greatest efforts to increase it, it was reduced to the lower figure.

The Queen was furious with the 'abominable infamous Tories', reserving her greatest venom for 'this wicked old foolish Duke [of Wellington]'. As her speech when she opened parliament in person on 16 January 1840 announcing her betrothal omitted the word 'Protestant', Wellington raised doubts about her future husband's religion and insisted on an amendment to the legislation authorising his income, ensuring that the word 'Protestant' appeared. He and Sir Robert Peel strongly opposed giving Albert precedence, and only when it was ascertained that the Queen could bestow whatever rank she wished on her husband by royal prerogative was the issue of precedence removed from the Naturalisation Bill.

When the list of guests for the royal wedding was drawn up, Melbourne had to persuade the Queen to invite Wellington, which she did with great reluctance. He was one of only five Tories out of 300 guests in the Chapel Royal, the others being Lord Liverpool, the two joint Lord Great Chamberlains (Lord Willoughby de Eresby and the Marquess of Cholmondeley) and Lord Ashley, who was married to a niece of Lord Melbourne's.

Within a few months, any differences were forgiven and forgotten. In August 1840 Wellington sat next to the Queen at dinner, and though he was a teetotaller who only drank iced water, he enjoyed the hospitality. 'She drank wine repeatedly with me;' he recalled, 'in short if I was not a milksop, I should become her Bottle Companion.' Six months later, he was invited to stand proxy for Albert's father, the Duke of Saxe-Coburg, at the christening of the Princess Royal. He was much flattered: 'I must be in favour to be thought of as a Beau Père!'[13]

* * *

Lord Palmerston's connections with Lord Melbourne extended beyond those of political colleagues. He was his brother-in-law, having married Melbourne's sister Emily, Lady Cowper, after the death of her first husband. Palmerston was entrusted by Melbourne with the duty of acquainting their sovereign with international affairs, and he spent much time with the Queen poring over maps and memoranda. He was won over by her charm, and he took much trouble to instruct her in the intricacies of foreign politics, providing her with specially drawn maps and an annotated *Almanach de Gotha*, teaching her to believe that these matters lay 'within the Sovereign's province', a move he would later come to regret. He taught her how to address her fellow sovereigns throughout Europe and how to end letters to them in her own hand, writing the appropriate endings for her in pencil, so she could copy over them herself before the pencillings were carefully erased.

He was also ever ready with advice as to what presents should be given to fellow sovereigns and their most distinguished subjects. Such instruction she found very helpful and enjoyable. Some three months before her accession, she wrote to King Leopold of having dined the previous Saturday with several guests, including Palmerston, 'with whom I had much pleasant and amusing conversation after dinner – you know how agreeable he is'.[14]

Palmerston was also slightly besotted with the Queen, though less so than Melbourne. In the first few months of her reign, both ministers attended on her as often as they could, even when there was no official need, and they rode regularly with her at Windsor. Tories and others regarded their constant hanging around with suspicion. Lord Aberdeen, another future prime minister, thought he saw parallels in the relationship between the Queen and her Prime Minister with that of the young King Edward VI and his Protector, Lord Somerset. Cartoons of the triumvirate were published, showing them riding together, or the Queen and Palmerston playing chess while Melbourne looked on. Soon the advice of King Leopold was being eclipsed by theirs.

However, these initial good impressions were to count for little against an episode which occurred at one point during Melbourne's administration. On a winter's night in 1839, Palmerston disgraced himself while staying at Windsor Castle by blundering into the bedroom of Mrs Brand, one of the Queen's ladies-in-waiting. As Charles Greville discreetly put it, the bold minister's 'tender temerity met with an invincible resistance'.[15] Once in the bedroom, Palmerston locked one door behind him and blocked the other with a piece of furniture. Finding him advancing on her in the middle of the night, Mrs Brand jumped out of bed and called for help, leaving him to retreat disappointed, if not chastened. Next day, Mrs Brand complained to Melbourne, who feared that the ensuing scandal would damage the Queen further and perhaps bring down the government. He ordered Palmerston to write an immediate letter of apology to Mrs Brand, which she accepted, but the Queen had already heard the news. It may have simply been a mistake on Palmerston's part, and that he was wandering around the long, ill-lit corridors in search of the bedroom of Lady Cowper, to whom he was still only engaged at the time. While the Queen was soon pacified by Melbourne's assurances that no harm had been intended, she neither forgot nor forgave her Foreign Secretary for such behaviour.

* * *

During the same year, 1839, the influence of Melbourne on Queen Victoria was beginning to fade. This was partly due to her growing maturity and her need for different counsel as well as company, but several events helped to weaken his authority.

The first was the 'bedchamber crisis'. Melbourne had repeatedly urged Victoria that if he should be defeated in parliament he would have to resign, and in that case, as it was her duty to work with all parties, she would have to accept that it might be necessary to ask one of the opposition leaders to lead the government. On 6 May the government's majority on a Bill to suspend the Jamaican Assembly was defeated by five votes. Next day he informed her that he would probably have to resign his position, and she should ask Peel or Wellington to form the next administration. She summoned the latter, who begged to be excused from forming an administration as he felt that, at seventy, he was too old. He recommended that she should send for Peel, who could be sure of securing support in the House.

With some reluctance she did so. On Peel's audience at the Palace with her, she told him that she would not agree to a dissolution of parliament; that she wanted the Duke of Wellington to be a member of the new government; and that whatever happened she intended to continue her friendship with her outgoing Prime Minister. Peel agreed to all this but told her respectfully of the difficulties of his parliamentary position. He asked her if she would be prepared to show confidence in her new ministers by changing he composition of her ladies of the bedchamber. As a result of Melbourne's partisanship, many female members of her household were wives or close relations of the Whig ministers, and he trusted that some of them would be replaced. As an incoming prime minister he had every right to do so, for the new government could hardly be expected to function properly if the monarch was still surrounded by his political opponents. Victoria refused to permit any changes at all, and when he told her regretfully that he could not, therefore, assume office, she triumphantly recalled Melbourne.

It was a short-term but hollow victory for the Queen, who was too inexperienced to realise that she had brought the Crown into disrepute by openly identifying it with one political party, and thus inadvertently brought into question her ability to perform a correct constitutional role of remaining above party. The Tories could argue with some justification that she was not their Queen, as the kingdom was still governed by a ministry which, as the Leader in the House of Lords emphasised, did not possess the confidence of the country. The prerogative powers of a monarch so closely identified with one party at the expense of another would surely be called into question.

One disgruntled newly elected Tory member of parliament, signing himself 'Laelius', wrote a letter to the Queen, to be published in *The Times*. 'You are a queen, but you are a human being and a woman,' he said. He warned her that she would find herself 'with the rapidity of enchantment the centre and puppet of a Camarilla, and Victoria, in the eyes of those Englishmen who once yielded to her in their devotion, will be reduced to the level of Madrid and Lisbon.' The consequences of her ill-thought reaction to the problem could be disastrous. 'Let not this crisis of your reign be recorded by the historian with a tear or a blush. The system which you are advised to establish is one degrading to the Minister, one which must be painful to the Monarch, one which may prove fatal to the monarchy.'[16] Ironically, 'Laelius' concealed the identity of the man who was to become her favourite Prime Minister and eternally devoted admirer, Benjamin Disraeli. For a while, the Tories would find it hard to forgive and forget their sovereign's behaviour.

Melbourne had clung to office, but he was embarrassed by the circumstances which had enabled him to do so, and out of loyalty he found himself somewhat reluctantly obliged to defend the Queen's conduct. 'I now frankly declare,' he said in a speech to the House of Lords, 'that I resume office because I will not abandon my Sovereign in a situation of difficulty and distress, when demands are made on her with which she ought not to comply.'[17]

One of Peel's earliest biographers, writing well within the Queen's lifetime, explained the crisis with admirable even-handedness. The Tory leader, he said, was 'little schooled in the ways of courts, and not particularly adroit in accommodating what he regarded as principle to their exigencies', while the Queen was inexperienced, too 'personally attached to the ministers who had surrounded her youthful throne', as well as mortified by any proposal to dismiss her ladies. Melbourne's judgement, he considered, was probably warped by his paternal regard for the sovereign over whose political education he had presided with rare devotion and discretion, and 'some of his colleagues might not be proof against the temptation of giving such advice to the Crown as would enable them to pose before the country as defending a royal lady against an insult alike unmanly and unconstitutional'.[18] It was an unusual situation in which everyone inadvertently was at fault, but a mistake which fortunately for all would not be repeated.

The damage done would have been limited had it not been for the tragic saga of Lady Flora Hastings, which was unfolding at the same time. Lady Flora was one of the Duchess of Kent's ladies, and a close friend of the detested Sir John Conroy. Early that year, she had returned to London from Scotland in a railway carriage with Conroy, and soon afterwards she complained of feeling unwell. Rumours began to circulate that she was pregnant, and worse still, with Conroy's child. The Queen and her old governess, Baroness Lehzen, were ready to believe the worst, and Melbourne foolishly did nothing to discourage them. In a desperate attempt to vindicate herself, Lady Flora underwent a medical examination which proved that, not only was she still a virgin, but also that the enlargement of her stomach was due to a cancerous tumour. Now painfully aware of the dreadful mistake she had made, the Queen did her best to make amends, but Lady Flora rapidly worsened and died in July. When the conscience-stricken sovereign sent a carriage to represent her at the funeral, it was stoned by angry crowds.

* * *

It was time for a new start for the Queen. Both her predecessors on the throne had experienced periods of intense unpopularity, and it would not do for her to forfeit any more the considerable fund of public goodwill which had greeted her on her accession. Her phase of hero-worshipping 'Lord M' was running its course.

Queen Victoria, it is said, was a man's woman, and 'the men whom she liked best were strong and imperturbable men who made her laugh, maybe with a touch of the rascal about them'.[19] The Hanoverian in her relished life and laughter, and without it she had a tendency to become morbid and introspective. Some of the men whose lives were to be bound up closely with hers recognised this. Melbourne had been quick to see it in her early days on the throne, while in later life the Ponsonby family and her youngest son-in-law, Prince Henry of Battenberg, would notice it equally.

Lord Melbourne remained in office for two more years. Not the least of his services to the Queen was his ready, if reluctant, acceptance of the inevitable. His period of influence on her and his days of power as head of government were coming to an end. Nevertheless, she was very touched when he took communion with her on Christmas Day 1839. 'It was a fine and solemn scene,' she wrote afterwards. 'I felt for one, my dearest Albert, – and wished he could be by my side, – also dear Lehzen, – but was *very* glad Lord Melbourne was there, the one whom I look up to as a father, and I was glad he took it [communion] with me.'[20]

While he was 'much affected' at her wedding to Prince Albert in February 1840, Melbourne was not so selfishly devoted to her as not to care deeply about her future happiness. Whatever initial reservations he may have had about the young man as his adored sovereign's husband and advisor were quickly dispelled, for he soon learnt to appreciate and respect Albert's conscientious approach and intelligence. The Prince, he foresaw, would soon acquire 'boundless influence'. He discussed political matters with Albert and urged the initially hesitant Queen to take her husband fully into her confidence. Albert had equal respect for Melbourne, aware that the outwardly imperturbable manner concealed the shrewdest of minds.

In May 1841 Melbourne's government was defeated by one vote, and parliament was dissolved at the end of June. The Queen was certain that the administration 'would gain by a dissolution', but when elections were held the Tories won with a clear majority. George Anson, Prince Albert's private secretary and treasurer, had dreaded the possibility of another bedchamber crisis, and on 12 June he expressed his fears to Melbourne. The latter was strangely unhelpful, advising him to 'let it alone until the time for action arrives'. Anson pointed out that the uncertainty kept the Queen's mind 'in perpetual agitation, when it ought to be perfectly calm, & that under existing circumstances this excitement might be attended by serious consequences'. The Tories were equally anxious, and Lord Ashley warned Anson that any repetition of the events of 1839 would 'destroy the position of the Queen, & it would be impossible to foresee the effect of it upon the country'. Peel, he said, had been deeply hurt by her conduct two years earlier and would probably be unable 'to place entire confidence in the disposition of the Queen before him . . . if it had been proposed to him to take office 6 months after that intrigue he was certain that nothing wd. have induced him.'[21]

Melbourne left office for what he knew was the last time. His last advice to the Queen was that she should put her trust in her husband. In another memorandum from Anson, the outgoing Prime Minister recommended that his successor, Sir Robert Peel, 'should write fully to Her Majesty, and *elementarily*, as Her Majesty always liked to have full knowledge upon everything which was going on. He would advise the Queen to be cautious in giving a verbal decision, that she should not allow herself to be *driven into a corner*, and forced to decide where she felt her mind was not made up and required reflection.'[22]

On Melbourne's departure from office, Victoria was particularly depressed. Throughout her life, at times of severe stress she was prone to 'sick headaches', worries about her appearance and supposed failing eyesight. On this occasion, any such symptoms were exacerbated by the fact that she was four months pregnant.

At first Melbourne continued to correspond with the Queen. Though it was a mainly harmless series of exchanges on social and personal matters, the very fact that she should be so closely in touch with her former Prime Minister was enough to provoke alarm. Baron Stockmar, who had been King Leopold's mentor from early days and also served Victoria and Albert during their formative years with advice, not least with helping on the Conroy problem, took it upon himself to bring this communication to an end. He wrote a lengthy memorandum for Anson to take to Melbourne and read aloud, stressing how unfair it was to Peel. 'This is a most decided opinion indeed, quite an apple-pie opinion!'[23] Melbourne retorted. Anson went on to say that Stockmar thought it a great pity, if he meant to continue writing to the Queen, that he should have made a recent speech in the House of Lords that appeared to attack government policy.

At this Melbourne was furious, leaping up from his sofa and pacing wildly up and down the room, exclaiming 'God eternally damn it! Flesh and blood cannot stand this.' He could not be expected to give up his position in the country, 'neither do I think that it is to the Queen's interest that I should'. When asked to consider the position in which he was placing the ministry, Melbourne thought deeply, muttering that he 'certainly cannot think it right'.[24]

Even so, he and the Queen continued to write to each other. A fortnight later, Stockmar found it necessary to make another personal intervention, and he warned Melbourne that he was encouraging the Queen in a course of action that could possibly get her into serious trouble. He advised that he should wait until after the Queen's second confinement, expected the following month, and then write and tell her that he thought it best all communications on politics between them should cease. Melbourne wrote to the Queen to say he thought it inadvisable for him to dine again at Buckingham Palace. Soon afterwards, Stockmar learnt that the correspondence had still not ceased, but another anguished letter from him was sufficient. Henceforth Melbourne's letters, while not coming entirely to an end, became more infrequent. Never again did he attempt to discuss politics with Victoria or even influence her at all. He knew Stockmar was right and was magnanimous enough not to bear him any grudge.

The Queen dreaded having to ask Peel to assume office. Charles Greville thought that she hated him 'from old recollections, and she never can forgive him, because she is conscious that she behaved ill to him'.[25] He lacked Melbourne's easygoing manner; diffident and gauche by nature, he was overawed at first by his sovereign, who in her turn found his apprehensive manner hard to deal with. However, his serious-minded nature was similar to that of Prince Albert. Both men were methodical, analytical characters who took their work very conscientiously. It was noticed by others that Peel was initially shy and awkward in her presence, and irritated her with a nervous twitch, in particular an inability to keep his legs still while speaking to her.

It was partly a sign of her deepening maturity, partly thanks to Albert's tactful handling of matters, that Queen Victoria quickly formed a better working relationship with Peel than with Melbourne. During Peel's premiership she became less malleable, more inquiring, more ready to accept ministerial decisions, much as she might initially disagree with them, once Peel and Albert had informed her of them and given her a chance to consider both sides of the issue. Shortly before Peel's appointment as prime minister, aware that the bedchamber crisis had left a lingering sense of awkwardness, Albert had made an effort to gain his trust and confidence.

Within a few months of his taking office, Queen Victoria's relations with Peel were excellent. One of her initial reservations about him had been that she found his manner pompous, a trait which could be ascribed to lack of ease. She soon readily admitted that he had a good voice, and she found his first speech from the throne most 'judicious'. By 1844 she could write to King Leopold that '*we cannot* have a better and a *safer* Minister'.[26]

One of Peel's first actions in office was to appoint Albert Chairman of the Royal Commission on Fine Arts, with particular responsibility for examining a scheme for the rebuilding of the Houses of Parliament, much of which had been destroyed by fire in 1834. That her new Prime Minister appreciated her husband so well and was ready to involve him in such important matters pleased and flattered the Queen, and it was not long before she began to revise her impressions of him more favourably. She called Peel Albert's 'second father'. Both men were in a sense liberal conservatives, who believed that the rising power of the middle classes demanded that the old order should make sensible, well-considered reforms, based not on intellectual text-book theory, but on the pragmatic needs of the British people and contemporary society.[27]

Thanks to another recommendation from Peel, from 1842 onwards Albert was invited to attend the ministers' audiences with the Queen. From that it was but a swift progression to his reading despatches to her, instead of the other way round. Whenever she expressed an opinion to her ministers, it would soon be a case of 'we' instead of 'I'.

It was to Peel that the Queen now readily turned for sympathy every time she considered what she regarded as her husband's humiliating constitutional position as the untitled, officially unrecognised husband of the Queen. Sometimes, particularly when he was given unduly lowly precedence on royal visits abroad, she wondered if 'it would have been fairer to him for me not to have married him'.[28] Something, the Prime Minister agreed, would need to be done. 'Oh! if only I could make him King,'[29] Victoria confided in her journal.

* * *

After his resignation, Melbourne's remaining seven years were marked by poor health. In 1842 he had a stroke and recovered slowly, spending more time at his country house, Brocket, than in London. He and his sovereign still met occasionally. At an evening at Chatsworth he was very excited at the thought of seeing her again, but she was distressed at the sad change in the appearance of the elderly man whom she had remembered as being so full of vitality. To his disappointment, she only chatted to him for a moment before dinner, and during the meal she soon turned her attention to the person who was sitting on her other side.

Sadly, he had to realise that her old friendship with him was little if anything more than 'the warm remembrance of a period that had been emotionally and politically dismissed'.[30] The widower who had lost not only his wife but also his child had served a Queen who had been his surrogate daughter and given him three years of great happiness, but left him lonely, even grieving, 'without further emotional resource'[31] once she married.

In the spring of 1848 he had a more severe stroke, and after lingering for some months he died on 24 November 1848, aged sixty-nine. The Queen was upset by the loss of one whose faults she had seen, but whom she still regarded as a true friend. 'One cannot forget how good and kind and amiable he was,' she wrote to King Leopold when told that Melbourne was seriously ill and not expected to recover, 'and it brings back so many recollections to my mind, though, God knows! I never wish that time back again.'[32] Some forty years after his death, she would remember her first Prime Minister kindly but not uncritically. 'The Queen does retain a most affectionate remembrance of Lord Melbourne,' she wrote to her private secretary, Sir Henry Ponsonby, 'though he was weak as a Minister.'[33]

* * *

After four years, Peel's position as prime minister was precarious. The Tories had become divided on the issue of the repeal of the Corn Laws. A protective duty had been introduced on imported corn in 1804, and some twenty years later a succeeding administration tried to relieve the distress caused by the high price of bread by introducing a sliding scale of duties according to price. A major trade depression in 1839, followed by poor harvests and potato famine in Ireland, worsened conditions and led to Peel's intention to repeal the Corn Laws altogether, despite the opposition within his party of a group of protectionists, one of whom was Disraeli. Thanks to support from the opposition, the measure was carried through in June 1846, but later that month the government was defeated in the Commons.

Much to the Queen's consternation, Peel and his Foreign Secretary, Lord Aberdeen, resigned, to be succeeded by a Whig administration led by Lord John Russell, with Palmerston resuming his old office as Foreign Secretary. The Queen regarded the departure of her outgoing ministers as 'irreparable losses' to them and to the nation. 'Never, during the five years that they were with me, did they ever recommend a person or a thing which was not for my or the Country's best.'[34]

Russell, who served as prime minister until 1852 (and again briefly from October 1865 to June 1866), was never destined to be a favourite of the Queen's. He 'had the true Whig's approach to the monarchy as a convenience rather than an institution for reverence'.[35] She found him dogmatic and opinionated, and once said he would be better company 'if he had a third subject; for he was interested in nothing except the Constitution of 1688 and himself'.[36]

Four years later, on 29 June 1850, Peel was thrown from his horse while out riding, broke his collar bone, and died three days later. The Queen was greatly upset: 'it does seem mysterious that in these troubled times when *he* could less be spared than any other human being, [he] should be taken from us.'[37] She and Albert had long since come to admire and respect the cotton-spinner's son whose lack of aristocratic lineage had proved no barrier to the assumption of high office, and whose readiness to put country and the common good before party had made it seem as if he was 'belonging to no party'. Later the following year, his son entered the Liberal government, and Victoria mused that it had been his father's misfortune 'to have been *kept down* to *old* Tory principles, for which his mind was far too enlightened'.[38]

* * *

With the Duke of Wellington, whose political career had long since come to an end, her early differences were soon forgotten. In the spring of 1850 he told her that, at eighty-one, he felt he should resign as Commander-in-Chief. He particularly wanted Prince Albert to succeed him. 'With the daily growth of the democratic power the executive got weaker and weaker,' he declared, 'and that it was of the utmost importance to the Throne and the Constitution that the command of the Army should remain in the hands of the Sovereign, and not fall into the hands of the House of Commons.'[39] Flattered as the Prince was, he declined on the grounds that it would encroach on the time he could spend with his wife and family. Wellington did the next best thing, by telling them he would send Prince Albert all the Commander-in-Chief's papers intended eventually for the Queen: 'let it be *done* first,' he suggested, '& *then* let the Queen *order* it.'[40] When the Queen's third son was born on 1 May 1850, she named him Arthur in the Duke's honour and invited him to be the boy's godfather.

There was still one last service Wellington could perform for the Crown. When Prince Albert was planning the Great Exhibition at Crystal Palace the following year, nobody else had any idea how to solve the problem of the sparrows which were making such a nuisance of themselves in the building. Only the victor of Waterloo had the answer. 'Try sparrow-hawks, Ma'am,' he suggested.

On 14 September 1852 the Duke died. Although he was aged eighty-three and had been in failing health for some time, life without such a towering figure was well-nigh impossible to imagine. 'One cannot think of this country without "the Duke," – our immortal hero!' she wrote in her journal. 'In him centered [*sic*] almost every earthly honour a subject could possess. His position was the highest a subject ever had, – above party, – looked up to by all, – revered by the whole nation, – the friend of the Sovereign; – and *how* simply he carried these honours!'[41]

She spared no expressions of praise as she wrote sorrowfully to King Leopold that Wellington was 'the pride and the bon génie, as it were, of this country! He was the GREATEST man this country ever produced, and the most *devoted* and *loyal* subject, and the staunchest supporter the Crown ever had. . . . We shall soon stand sadly alone; Aberdeen is almost the only personal friend of that kind we have left. Melbourne, Peel, Liverpool – and now the Duke – *all* gone!'[42] Her third son, Arthur, aged two, mourned the 'Duke of Wellikon', telling everyone that the great man was 'little Arta's godpapa'. The Duke would have rejoiced in the fact that, alone of Queen Victoria's sons, the lad who was resolved from infancy to be a soldier would honour his promise as an adult.

Thanks to the wishes of Prince Albert, on 18 November 1852 the Duke was given a magnificent, heraldic state funeral, with a centrepiece of a gigantic bronze funeral car, 21ft long, and an enormous coffin. The Queen watched the procession pass down the Mall, her eyes so full of tears that she could hardly make out the car. Even more moving was the sight of the Duke's charger, his master's boots reversed in the stirrups.

FOUR

'Such a good man'

During the first three decades of her reign, from her accession to his death twenty-eight years later, the Queen's relations with Lord Palmerston went from warm regard to intense irritation and finally to grudging admiration. While he was Foreign Secretary, she and Albert found 'Pilgerstein' (a nickname devised by Albert and King Leopold, a German pun on the words 'palmer' or 'pilgrim', and 'stone') extremely trying. Although it could not be denied that he was very knowledgeable and hardworking, they found him too impetuous, too ready to bluster and threaten other countries, and rude and undiplomatic. When he failed to keep the Queen informed of what was happening, he sent despatches before she had time to approve them, or delayed passing on boxes of papers for several days at a time, then sending her so many at once that she could not possibly go through them all in time. If taken to task, he would apologise, blaming his subordinates in the Foreign Office, and then carry on unrepentantly as before.

Palmerston's wife tried to impress on him that he must handle the Queen more carefully. She warned her husband that the sovereign did not have the intellectual capacity to respond to reason; he always thought he could convince people by arguments, and she did not have reflection or sense to feel the force of them. 'I should treat what she says more lightly & courteously, and not enter into argument with her, but lead her on gently, by letting her believe you have both the same opinions in fact & the same wishes, but take sometimes different ways of carrying them out.'[1]

That he strove to interfere in what the Queen and Albert regarded as their own province, that of foreign affairs, did not assist friendly relations. Throughout the first ten years or so of Victoria's reign, much of Europe was troubled with constitutional and national aspirations. Lands without constitutions were demanding them, while territories such as Hungary and the Italian dependencies of the

55

Austrian empire were seeking independence from what they saw as oppressive foreign rule.

As a Whig, Palmerston believed wholeheartedly in constitutional restraints on monarchs, rather than absolutism. He supported the attempts of Sardinia and France to drive the Austrians out of northern Italy. While he stopped short of believing in active armed interference in the internal affairs of other states, he tended to offer unsolicited advice, often expressed in trenchant language. As Prime Minister, Russell was often obliged to admit that in many ways his Foreign Secretary was not showing his sovereign sufficient courtesy and respect, which she had every right to expect. Yet Palmerston was popular with the public, seen as an unflinching upholder of British prestige abroad, and one who was never afraid to stand up to over-mighty foreign despots when necessary.

Several attempts were made to try to keep him out of mischief. It was suggested that he might be sent to Ireland as Lord Lieutenant, or offered the office of Home Secretary instead of Foreign Secretary, but to no avail. In August 1850 differences between monarch and minister came to a head, and after a heated conversation with Russell, the Queen demanded from him a promise in writing as to what she expected from her Foreign Secretary in future: that he would 'distinctly state what he proposes in a given case, in order that the Queen may know as distinctly to *what* she has given her Royal sanction' and that 'having once given her sanction to a measure, that it be not arbitrarily altered or modified by the Minister; such an act she must consider as failing in sincerity towards the Crown, and justly to be visited by the exercise of her Constitutional right of dismissing that Minister'. She expected to be kept informed of what passed between him and the Foreign Ministers before any important decisions were taken, to receive all foreign despatches in good time and to have drafts for her approval sent to her in sufficient time for her to make herself acquainted with their contents before they were finally sent.[2]

It was a reminder that the high-handed Palmerston would have to mend his ways in future. There would inevitably be a clash of wills between the sovereign and her husband, who saw foreign affairs as a kind of family trust, and a popular minister who had the support of the Commons and of the nation. Neither the Queen nor her husband were fully aware that power had almost imperceptibly slipped out of the hands of the Crown.

In September 1850 there was to be a further clash of opinions. The Austrian military commander, General Julius Haynau, known throughout Europe as 'General Hyaena', paid a visit to London as a private citizen. After his brutal repression in Hungary during the revolutionary fervour of 1848–9, his name was a byword for cruelty. He was easily recognised because of his long moustaches, and when he went to see the Barclays & Perkins Brewery at Southwark, a popular attraction among visitors to the city, the workmen physically attacked him, tore his clothes and pulled him by his moustaches through the gutter. He only escaped worse injury when he and his companions found refuge in a nearby tavern, eventually being rescued by the police. An Austrian exile, formerly editor of a liberal newspaper in Vienna and who had since taken a job as a clerk at the brewery, was probably behind the assault.

When she received a report of the incident, Queen Victoria told Palmerston that she thought 'it would be proper if a draft were written to the Austrian government expressive of the deep regret of this government at the brutal outrage on one of the Emperor's distinguished generals and subjects'.[3] Palmerston agreed and drafted a despatch, which he ended with a paragraph pointing out bluntly that somebody with Haynau's reputation should have known better than to expose himself to public opinion in this way. Haynau had been warned in Austria to expect something of the sort if he did set foot in London. When the Austrian government replied to the despatch (which was not seen by the Queen, as the royal family had just departed for Balmoral), they demanded that the draymen should be prosecuted. Palmerston assured Baron Koller, the Austrian ambassador in London, that such a move was pointless, as the draymen would be bound to cite Haynau's record of barbarities in Italy and Hungary as part of their case for the defence. When Palmerston replied to the government he firmly refused, adding that instead of striking him the draymen should have tossed him in a blanket, rolled him in the kennel and then sent him away in a cab.

When she read this despatch, the Queen was furious and demanded that it should be sent again with the 'objectionable' paragraph deleted. Palmerston told Russell, the Prime Minister, that such a despatch would need to be signed by a new Foreign Secretary. He then wrote a long explanatory memorandum to the Queen, praising the British people for their hospitable reception of foreigners and assuring her that feelings of indignation against

Haynau were not confined to Britain. Thinking better than to send it, he decided that the issue was too trivial to merit resignation and sent a new, modified despatch.

The truce was clearly not going to last, and Palmerston's over-confidence a year later proved his undoing. In December 1851 Louis Napoleon proclaimed himself President of the new Republic of France. The Queen and Russell agreed to adopt an attitude of neutrality at first but, to their annoyance, they soon found that Palmerston had already assured the French ambassador of British support. This was too much even for Russell to stomach, and he demanded his Foreign Secretary's resignation. The Queen's relief was short lived, for before long Palmerston had brought down Russell's government over the question of a need for a national militia, bringing Lord Derby to power for an administration which would last only ten months in 1852, at the end of which year Palmerston returned to government as Home Secretary.

Queen Victoria liked and respected Derby, her new head of government, but had her doubts about the calibre of his new cabinet. 'We have a most talented, capable, and courageous Prime Minister,' she wrote to King Leopold, 'but all his people have no experience.'[4] Derby's administration was seriously weakened after elections in July, and following a defeat in the House of Commons in December he resigned, with the amenable, 'safe' Lord Aberdeen replacing him as prime minister.

In September 1853 Aberdeen sent Palmerston, his Home Secretary, to Balmoral as minister in attendance. Lady Palmerston did not accompany her husband there, but warned him to conduct himself as tactfully as possible in the presence of his sovereign. 'Remember you have only one week to remain there, so you should manage to make yourself agreeable and to appear to enjoy the society.'[5] He evidently took her advice to heart, and when Queen Victoria and Prince Albert returned south later that year, they appeared to think more favourably of this maverick minister.

Unfortunately, the good impression he made was soon destroyed again when he provoked royal wrath by suggesting that the Queen's cousin, Princess Mary of Cambridge, should marry Emperor Napoleon III's cousin and heir, Prince Napoleon Jerome. The latter was thoroughly unsuitable, as he was not only a Bonaparte and therefore strictly a *parvenu*, but also a Roman Catholic. Lord Derby did not improve matters when he informed the Queen rather thoughtlessly that the French prince would probably make a far better husband than 'some petty Member of a petty German Princes House'.[6] Neither Mary nor Napoleon showed any enthusiasm for such a match, and the scheme was quietly dropped.

* * *

By this time, a new crisis was threatening to disturb the peace. England and France had long feared that Russia was proposing to dismember the Turkish Empire and take the Dardanelles under Russian control. In February 1854, when the outbreak of hostilities seemed all but certain, Queen Victoria admitted that her heart was 'not in this unsatisfactory war'. When she discussed it with Lord Aberdeen, he warned her that whatever happened, Palmerston was likely to succeed him as prime minister before long. She told him she would never feel safe with the latter, whereupon Aberdeen replied sadly that he feared Her Majesty 'would not be safe with me during war, for I have such a terrible repugnance for it, in all its forms'. Despite his pacifist caution, Victoria insisted that an immediate war would be the lesser of two evils, as it would prevent a worse one later; 'patching up was dangerous'.[7]

Aberdeen begged to differ, but in the end there was to be no patching-up. Three days later, on 28 February, Britain formally declared war against Russia in support of Turkey and in alliance with France. English and French warships were sent to the Black Sea to prevent Russian landings, and later that year troops were sent to the Crimea.

To those who knew him, it came as little surprise that Aberdeen proved an indecisive prime minister and reluctant head of government. In January 1855 the cabinet refused to accept a motion for a committee of inquiry into the management of the war, and a vote of no confidence was carried against the government. Aberdeen resigned and, as he had foreseen, only Palmerston was strong enough to form a ministry. He was accordingly appointed prime minister.

Despite the Queen's reservations about accepting him in office, Palmerston proved as determined as his sovereign to give utmost support to the Army and win the war. The Queen noted in her journal that to change her 'dear kind, excellent friend, Lord Aberdeen' had been a trial, as the incoming Prime Minister 'certainly does owe us many amends for all he has done, and he is without doubt of a very different character to my dear and worthy friend. Still, as matters now stand, it was decidedly the right and wise course to take, and I think that Lord Palmerston, surrounded as he will be, will be sure to do no mischief.'[8]

After the conflict ended in victory for England and France, the Queen paid her head of government his due. She and Albert agreed that of all the prime ministers they had yet had, 'Lord Palmerston is the one who gives the least trouble, & is most amenable to reason & most ready to adopt suggestions. The great danger was foreign affairs, but now that these are conducted by an able, sensible & impartial man [Lord Clarendon], & that he [Lord Palmerston] is responsible for the *whole*, everything is quite different.'[9] After a general election the following year, Palmerston increased his majority, and his grip on European politics seemed to Victoria indispensable. Yet this did not augur well for the future, as at seventy-three he seemed to be ageing fast. She was particularly anxious about his frail appearance, apprehensive as to what they would do if anything should suddenly happen to him.

Her concern for him was perhaps only increased when he went up in her estimation immeasurably by doing what each of his predecessors as prime minister had thought impossible. He persuaded a rather sceptical cabinet that they should assent to Prince Albert being made Prince Consort. On 25 June 1857 a Council was held at Buckingham Palace at which the delighted Queen conferred the title on her husband by Letters Patent.

In January 1858 there was an attempt in Paris on the lives of Emperor Napoleon III and Empress Eugenie. During their interrogation, the conspirators revealed that they were part of a group that had members in England and that their bombs had been made there. Palmerston was irritated by the political activities of some of the refugees who had settled in Britain and wanted to draft a Bill empowering the Home Secretary to expel anyone whom he suspected of plotting against a foreign head of state or government. The cabinet agreed it would be simpler to introduce a Conspiracy to Murder Bill instead, by which the crime of planning a murder was promoted from a misdemeanour to a felony and made punishable by a long term of imprisonment. The result, the Conspiracy to Murder Bill, resulted in a defeat for Palmerston on a vote on the second reading in February.

Professing herself 'much vexed and thunderstruck'[10] by the defeat, Queen Victoria sent again for Lord Derby to form a government.

In March 1859 his ministry introduced a Parliamentary Reform Bill which had a troubled passage through the House of Commons before leading to a motion of no confidence three months later, on which Derby resigned and Palmerston once again took office as prime minister. The Queen disliked having to change governments at a time of European crisis, in this case war between Austria and France, but she readily admitted that when she sent for Palmerston, he 'behaved very handsomely'.[11]

* * *

This premiership was to prove relatively untroubled. In fact, the Prime Minister showed a degree of concern towards his sovereign throughout which she found most touching. This was never more apparent than in November 1861, when he was the first person outside the family to express serious anxiety over the condition of the Prince Consort, who had never been robust and seemed seriously run down after a particularly stressful year. While the Queen's doctors blandly assured her there was nothing to be unduly concerned about, he recognised that the Prince was gravely ill and proposed calling a further physician, Dr Robert Ferguson. The Queen resented the suggestion, insisting that there was no need for further medical advice, and instructed Sir Charles Phipps, her Keeper of the Privy Purse, to thank the Prime Minister for his concern. The Prince, she said, was only suffering from 'a feverish cold'.

Palmerston was laid low at the time with gout, and although he genuinely mourned the death of the Prince Consort in December, he was privately a little relieved that in her grief the Queen did not wish to see anybody apart from members of her immediate family and household at first. He knew that she would be difficult to deal with, now that the prudent Albert was no longer there to guide or restrain her. He wrote to Russell after Christmas that he believed her determination 'to conform to what she from time to time may persuade herself would have been at the moment the opinion of the late Prince promises no end of difficulties for those who will have to advise her', and that they would need to deal with her gently.[12]

On 29 January 1862 Victoria received Palmerston at Osborne, for the first time since the Prince's death. He was deeply moved by the sight of her suffering, and in her words he could 'hardly speak for emotion'. On his first sight of her, sitting on the sofa in the drawing-room at Osborne, he too wept unashamedly for the man they had lost. His colleagues later saw tears in his eyes when he referred to the Prince Consort, and his sympathy for the bereaved Queen was beyond doubt. He assured her 'what a dreadful calamity it was' and agreed that the loss of his father was terrible for the Prince of Wales. The Queen was genuinely moved by her statesman's attitude 'and would hardly have given Lord Palmerston credit for entering so entirely into my anxieties'.[13]

During the crisis that arose over the disputed duchies of Schleswig and Holstein, ruled by Denmark, the Queen was on the side of counter-claimants Austria and Prussia, unlike her eldest son, the Prince of Wales, who had just married the daughter of the new King of Denmark, Christian IX. Most of her subjects strongly supported the Danish claims to the duchies, as did Palmerston. This led to a renewal of ill-feeling between him and the Queen, until he found it necessary to write to her that he could quite understand her reluctance 'to take any active part in measures in any conflict against Germany, but he is sure that Your Majesty will never forget that you are Sovereign of Great Britain'.[14] She wrote to King Leopold complaining about Palmerston and Russell, 'those two dreadful old men'. Britain stayed neutral during the ensuing war between Austria and Prussia on the one hand and Denmark on the other. Palmerston would have liked to go to the assistance of Denmark, but the majority of his cabinet colleagues opposed any declaration of hostilities on behalf of the Scandinavian kingdom.

Palmerston survived to the age of eighty, dying on 18 October 1865. Victoria mourned his death sincerely, admitting that he 'had often worried and distressed us, though as Prime Minister he had behaved *very well*. To think that he is removed from this world, and *I* alone, without dearest Albert to talk to or consult with!'[15]

* * *

In November 1865 Palmerston was succeeded by Lord Russell, who was keen to introduce further reform to the electoral system. He found his position weakened, as one wing of his supporters was strongly opposed to any such measure. Though she had no objection to such reform, the Queen lacked confidence and had no stomach for what could potentially be the worst ministerial crisis since the bedchamber affair. The general outlook was exacerbated by Prussia's recent declaration of war on Austria, and should the conflict escalate further in Europe, the last thing Victoria wanted was political instability at home. Lord Derby told her he could not support reform, and she begged him not to make it into a party question.

Russell insisted he would get his measure through Parliament, as his supporters would not allow it to be dropped, but he proved unsuccessful. In June 1866 he resigned after the defeat of his contentious Reform Bill, and Lord Derby formed an administration with Benjamin Disraeli as his Chancellor of the Exchequer. The Reform Bill passed its third reading the following year, and one million voters were newly enfranchised. Yet Derby's health was failing, and in February 1868 he resigned, to be succeeded by his Chancellor.

The Queen's attitude towards the colourful Disraeli had long been ambivalent. As a member of parliament he had attended her coronation and less than two years later, with other members of the House of Commons, was part of a deputation sent to Buckingham Palace to deliver a loyal address congratulating the Queen on her marriage. Naturally, she would not have remembered him from these occasions as one of many, yet she was aware of his career as a novelist, of his marriage to a widow twelve years older than himself and of his reputation as a politically ambitious social butterfly. It is, however, doubtful whether she was aware of his pseudonymous letter to *The Times* during the bedchamber crisis (see p. 46).

The fall of Russell's first ministry in February 1852 had brought a Tory administration under Lord Derby to power (as it would again in 1866), with Disraeli his Chancellor of the Exchequer and Leader of the House. Though Derby assured them of his ability, from what they had heard the Queen and Prince Albert initially found it hard to approve of a politician whom they considered pushy, irresponsible and unprincipled. In 1846 the Queen had called him 'that detestable Mr Disraeli' and denounced his opposition to repealing the Corn Laws as 'unprincipled and reckless', while Albert claimed that he 'had not one single element of the gentleman in his composition'.

Though his post as chancellor did not involve frequent audiences with the Queen, it involved writing letters regularly to her. As befitted a novelist and a man of his reputation, these were no ordinary letters. Almost at once she received interesting reports from him, presenting parliamentary debates in a vivid and entertaining style which greatly impressed her. Speeches might be 'elaborate, malignant, mischievous', or 'statesmanlike, argumentative, terse and playful', which constituted a pleasant change from the tedious factual accounts that had been sent her by others. As she had copied a number of Lord Melbourne's phrases into her journal, she now took to adding some of Disraeli's more picturesque observations likewise. His 'curious notes', she thought, were 'just like his novels, highly-coloured'.[16] For the first time since Melbourne's resignation, politics had become more interesting and less of a chore.

In April 1852 she invited the Disraelis to dinner at Buckingham Palace. She had already met Mrs Disraeli once before and found her 'very singular'. Now, for the first time she could see this fascinating couple close at hand. At almost sixty, Mary Anne Disraeli was dressed in her usual youthful fashion, her tinted hair crowned with an extravagant wreath of diamonds, velvet leaves and feathers, her dress an elaborate confection of white satin trimmed with looped-up flounces of gold lace and glittering with jewels. Such a startling appearance, and her frank conversation, did not impress the Queen, who thought her 'very vulgar'. Her husband she found 'most singular, – thoroughly Jewish looking, a livid complexion, dark eyes & eyebrows & black ringlets. The expression is disagreeable, but I do not find him so to talk to. He has a very bland manner, & his language is very flowery.'[17]

Within a year the government had fallen, and on leaving office Disraeli wrote letters to thank the Queen and Prince for their help and kindness. To Albert, he said that he would 'ever remember with interest and admiration the princely mind in the princely person'.[18] Ironically, not long before this Albert had had a conversation with Lord Derby about Disraeli, during which he remarked that he admired the latter's talents but suspected him of being a dangerous radical, if not a revolutionary, 'not in his heart favourable to the existing order of things'. Despite Derby's protestations that the man was greatly attached to the British constitutional system, Albert would not be deflected from his views. Disraeli, he was convinced, had 'democratic tendencies', and the potential to become 'one of the most dangerous men in Europe'.[19] He was not to know that the future Lord Beaconsfield would become such a doughty champion of the royal prerogative, while his chief political adversary during his premiership, Gladstone (a man whom Albert greatly admired), would turn out to be the standard bearer of 'dangerous radicalism' and a critic of the House of Lords, to a degree which would greatly perturb the Queen.

In April 1862 Disraeli was invited to spend the night as a guest at Windsor. Before leaving to attend parliament, he was granted an audience with the Queen, partly intended as a mark of favour for his appreciation of Albert and partly an opportunity for her to ask him not to try to displace Palmerston, to whom she had developed something of an attachment. She was anxious that there should be no governmental crisis 'brought about wantonly, for, in her forlorn condition, she hardly knew what she could do'.[20] He reassured her that her comfort and well-being were of prime importance. She was anxious about the Prime Minister, who was 'grown very old', and she feared she had seen 'a very great change' in him, though Disraeli was able to assure her that his voice in debate was as loud as ever.

That same afternoon, Disraeli was in the House of Commons to debate a suitable memorial to the Prince. He advocated a monument which should 'represent the character of the Prince himself in the harmony of its proportions, in the beauty of its ornament, and in its enduring nature. It should be something direct, significant, and choice, so that those who come after us may say: "This is the type and testimony of a sublime life and a transcendent career, and thus they were recognised by a grateful and admiring people."'[21] Anxious that the Queen should receive an accurate report of his speech, he wrote a copy out in his own hand and sent it to Windsor.

Naturally flattered and overwhelmed by his loyalty, she sent him a copy of the Prince Consort's speeches bound in white morocco, personally inscribed to Disraeli 'In recollection of the greatest and best of men from the beloved Prince's broken-hearted widow.' It was accompanied by a letter expressing 'her deep gratification at the tribute he paid to her adored, beloved, and great husband. The perusal of it made her shed many tears, but it was very soothing to her broken heart to see such true appreciation of that spotless and unequalled character.'[22]

One year later, Queen and politician saw each other from a distance. At the wedding of the Prince of Wales to Princess Alexandra in March 1863, seated in St George's Chapel, he caught sight of the Queen, partly hidden in the balcony above, overlooking the ceremony. He looked at her through his eyeglass, but she gave him such a penetrating look in return that 'I did not venture to use my glass again.'[23]

Evidently that occasion had been forgotten by February 1868. For the first time since Melbourne's final resignation, the Queen had a Prime Minister with whom she could establish the close personal relationship so important to her, and who made her feel appreciated as a woman as well as a queen. He had been fulsome in his praise of the Prince Consort, with whom his own acquaintance had been 'one of the most satisfactory incidents of his life'. Writing to her on acceptance of high office, he could 'only offer devotion', while venturing to trust that the Queen would 'deign not to withhold from him the benefit of your Majesty's guidance'.[24] The right tone was struck at once, and the contrast with Russell, Palmerston or Gladstone, who was destined to hold office as prime minister four times, could hardly have been greater.

Disraeli's first premiership was brief. He knew he would be unable to govern the country for long through a minority in the House of Commons, and he advised the Queen to dissolve parliament when the new electoral registers were ready. A general election in November resulted in a triumph for Gladstone, with a Liberal majority of 112 seats. The Queen showed her appreciation of Disraeli's services by creating his wife Mary Anne Viscountess Beaconsfield.

In earlier days, the Queen and Albert had been favourably impressed by William Ewart Gladstone. Had Albert lived longer, she might have kept to this view and been less dazzled by Disraeli. In March 1862 Gladstone, then Chancellor of the Exchequer during Palmerston's last administration, was summoned to an audience with the Queen at Windsor Castle. After a discussion on home and foreign affairs, she spoke to him of her great loss and how kind the nation had been in her time of sorrow. She intended to do her best, she assured him, 'but she had no confidence in herself'.

Too honest for his own good, he told her that he was not sorry to hear her use such language. To the unassuming, down-to-earth Gladstone, over-confidence was not a virtue. He failed to see that she was looking for reassurance and might have done better to disagree with her, no matter how gently. After the interview was over, he recognised his mistake and acknowledged that he could have 'gone a little further in the language of hope'. Nevertheless, the Queen found his presence comforting, as he had been 'very kind and feeling', and above all he had spoken with unbounded admiration of the Prince Consort, 'saying no-one would ever replace him'.[25]

His wife, Catherine, tried to steer him gently in the right direction. Before he went to see his sovereign again at Windsor that autumn, Mrs Gladstone advised her husband that 'contrary to your ways, do *pet* the Queen, and for once believe you can, you dear old thing'.[26]

One way in which he conspicuously failed to pet the Queen was in refusing her request, conveyed through her then private secretary,

General Grey, to support a motion in the House of Commons for the purchase of a small amount of gun metal for the Prince Consort's memorial in Kensington Gardens. In his reply to Grey, Gladstone pointed out that £50,000 had been voted in 1863 for the memorial. Not surprisingly, Victoria resented his attitude. It was left to Disraeli, as Chancellor of the Exchequer, to secure the assent of the House to the proposal. Also in 1863 Gladstone again incurred the Queen's displeasure during his period as Chancellor of the Exchequer and Minister at Attendance at Balmoral after she was involved in a carriage accident; he appeared to criticise her for risking life and limb by taking drives along darkened roads in the Highlands (see p. 116). She considered she had every right to continue to do so, and the only threats to her safety which ever resulted were due not to would-be assassins or kidnappers, but the shortcomings of 'confused' (in other words, drunk) coachmen. She was furious that Gladstone later told Palmerston about the accident.

Early in 1868 Gladstone succeeded Russell as leader of the opposition, and in September, after a dinner at Balmoral, the Queen found him 'very agreeable, so quiet & intellectual, with such a knowledge of all subjects, & [he] is such a good man'.[27] In November, shortly before he became Prime Minister, he was aware of rumours – as passed by Lord Clarendon to Lady Salisbury, among others – that he was 'utterly repugnant' to the Queen. It would be an exaggeration to say that she had conceived a strong antipathy to him at this stage, but it was common knowledge that she did not find him as easy to deal with as some of his predecessors.

Gerald Wellesley, Dean of Windsor, warned him that everything would depend on his manner of approaching her: 'Her nervous susceptibility has much increased since you had to do with her before, and you cannot show too much regard, gentleness, I might even say tenderness towards her.'[28] While she disapproved of his policy to disestablish the Irish Church and would undoubtedly tell him so, she fully realised that he was pledged to the principle before parliament and the country, and she would give him her customary loyal support in carrying on the government as long as he was able to do so. He had his first audience as prime minister with the Queen at Windsor on 3 December, a meeting which passed pleasantly enough.

But it was soon evident that Gladstone had none of Disraeli's sympathetic and intuitive knack of managing the Queen. Instead of giving her a clear summary of situations or problems, he bored and muddled her with long, over-earnest explanations which she found wearisome and unenlightening. His tendency to lecture, complicate and insist undermined the self-confidence which she had admitted early in her widowhood was in short supply but which she was now regaining. He wrote her lengthy letters of over-meticulous, minutely detailed arguments which would undoubtedly have appealed to Prince Albert and Baron Stockmar but which irritated her beyond measure. She said he treated her like a public meeting, though it never seemed to occur to her that this might have been avoided if she had invited him to sit in her presence instead of keeping him standing throughout. While she accepted the fact of his 'goodness', a quality which ought to have commended him to her, she could never bring herself to like him as a person or respect him much, and with his incomprehensible behaviour she often thought him either mad or a humbug. For his part, he was too down to earth and impatient of show to be able to stoop (as he might have seen it) to flatter her.

Another reason, advanced by Gladstone's first major biographer, John Morley, was the Queen's dread of 'enthusiasm', or what she saw as single-minded obsession. Gladstone, he considered, 'had a full measure of enthusiasm for causes',[29] such as his zeal for Home Rule. To the Queen, there was something of the fanatic about a man who was determined to pursue individual issues so doggedly. His interventionist manner might have pleased the Prince Consort, but she found the relaxed demeanour of Melbourne, Disraeli and later Salisbury a far more desirable quality.

Another early twentieth-century historian, Philip Guedalla, writing between the wars, suggested that there were three Victorias. Victoria I's reign was one of 'a romping sort of innocence' and 'a girlish Regency, appropriately based at Brighton, where she rode out with aged beaux, her ministers'. She was succeeded shortly after marriage by Victoria II, a sovereign who 'bore the unmistakable impress of her married life'.[30] Victoria III was the monarch of the 1870s onwards, when she had to some extent shaken off some of Albert's influences (though she would have been the last person to admit to such a thing) and was emerging from his shadow, the Victoria Regina Imperatrix guided, coaxed and flattered by the courtly Disraeli while being irritated and exasperated by the self-righteous Gladstone.

One of Gladstone's most recent biographers, Roy Jenkins, maintained that had the Queen possessed a vote, then in the first six general elections of her reign she would have cast hers for the incumbent government, be it Tory or Whig.[31] The break-point was 1868, after which she became more partisan than loyal and would have voted Conservative at all subsequent elections. While she moved to the right in political convictions, the man who had begun his parliamentary career as a Tory member of the House of Commons in 1832 and was to take the office of Liberal prime minister four times was moving firmly to the left.

Compared with his later ministries, Gladstone's first tenure of office, which lasted until 1874, was relatively serene. The Queen reluctantly accepted his Bill to disestablish the Irish Church, arguing that it would do little to solve the increasingly difficult Irish problem. However, she made her views clear by refusing to open parliament in person and thus give tacit approval to the measures, making the state of her health as an excuse. In February 1869 her physician, Sir William Jenner, told Gladstone that she declined to do so not entirely on account of health reasons but 'from an anxiety to avoid any personal interference in the great question pending with respect to the Irish Church'. She suggested to Gladstone that he could inform the press, if he liked, that she had been suffering 'more than normally from severe headache'.

This roused him to fury. Keen to get as close to the truth as possible, he discussed the matter with General Grey, who assured him that the Queen's daughter Louise was '*very* decided as to the ability of the Queen to meet any fatigue', and was indignant with Jenner for encouraging her 'fancies' about her ill-health.[32] Grey agreed that nothing except a peremptory tone on Gladstone's part would have any effect. He believed that 'the long, unchecked habit of self-indulgence that now makes it impossible for her, without some degree of nervous agitation to give up, even for ten minutes, the gratification of a single inclination, or even *whim*'[33] had made her increasingly disinclined to discharge her duties properly.

It was the problem between the Queen and her Prime Minister, his approach to what he called with a sigh 'the Royalty Question', or his efforts to bring the Queen out of her seclusion, which caused a gulf to open between them. He felt he had a duty to interfere in this issue, which was beginning to cause widespread and increasing discontent. 'To speak in rude and general terms,' he observed to Lord Granville, 'the Queen is invisible and the Prince of Wales is not respected.'[34] The raffish young man about town, whose infidelity to his beautiful young Danish wife made him look not unlike a reincarnation of some of his adulterous Hanoverian ancestors, made him popular among the smart set, but the more censorious of his mother's subjects were dismayed by the Prince's private life.

The Queen's pleas of ill-health were not unfounded. During a prolonged series of problems during the summer of 1871, Gladstone was sympathetic enough to earn her gratitude, even though he thought Sir William Jenner 'a feeble-minded doctor' when he begged the Prime Minister not to drive the Queen too hard lest her nerves give way. But Gladstone's constant pressure was strongly resented. In August he tried to persuade her to delay her departure for Balmoral, so she could prorogue in person the parliamentary session which had already been prolonged by a couple of debates, telling her it was her duty to do so. He should have known better. She would not be ordered about, and she angrily informed Lord Hatherley, the Lord Chancellor, that such interference was 'really abominable'. Overwork and worry had killed her beloved husband. She, the Queen, 'a woman no longer young, is supposed to be proof against all and to be driven and abused till her nerves and health give way with this worry and agitation and interference in her private life'. Unless the ministers supported her, she declared, she could 'not go on, but must give her heavy burden up to younger hands'.[35]

Gladstone found her reaction quite incomprehensible. To Sir Henry Ponsonby, her then private secretary, he raged that it was 'the most sickening experience' he had had in almost forty years of public life; 'smaller and meaner cause for the decay of thrones cannot be conceived.'[36] Two months later, in October, he wrote sadly to Lord Granville of 'the repellent power which she so well knows how to use has been put in action towards me on this occasion for the first time since the formation of the Government'.[37]

By now British disillusion with the royal family was rife. Republicanism, which had been gathering apace with discontent over the Queen's seclusion and the Prince of Wales's scandalous behaviour, was boosted by the overthrow of the Third Empire in France but received a major setback with the Prince's recovery from an almost fatal attack of typhoid fever in December 1871. Sir Charles Dilke, who had become renowned for his speeches calling for a republic, dismissed the news of the Prince's illness as 'a sham panic got up for the occasion to serve a political end'. Once the Prince was reported out of danger, many politicians could scarcely contain their glee. 'What a sell for Dilke this illness has been!' wrote Lord Henry Lennox to Disraeli.[38]

Gladstone claimed that nothing would reverse the monarchy's declining popularity sooner than by the Queen emerging from her seclusion; she had to shake herself out of the lethargy into which she had fallen since the Prince Consort's death, make more public appearances, spend less time away from the public gaze at Osborne and Balmoral, establish a residence in Ireland and, above all, let the Prince of Wales play a more active part in public affairs. His repeated insistence in letter after letter, increasingly pedantic and hectoring in tone, that she must play a more positive role, did his case no good. In his personal audiences with her, he bluntly reminded her of the need for her to be seen fulfilling more public engagements, but in vain.

Ironically, Gladstone could be regarded as one of the saviours of the Crown during the height of Victorian England's republican fervour. As the most radical of the Queen's prime ministers he could, believed Lady Ponsonby, have destroyed the monarchy if he had decided to 'show his teeth about Royalty'. Instead he risked incurring the opprobrium of his more left-leaning colleagues by defending the Queen so firmly. It was unfortunate that she would never realise how much she was indebted to him for doing so.

His plans to disestablish the Irish Church were not the end of it. He had two additional schemes involving Ireland, both of which would have linked the royal family more closely in the country. The first was the acquisition of a royal residence in Ireland, which he felt the Queen would do well to visit from time to time, thus going less to Balmoral. The second was the abolition of the post of Lord Lieutenant of Ireland, and the appointment of the Prince of Wales as a viceroy with a responsible secretary of state to assist him. Soon after becoming prime minister, Gladstone had been offered the use of a royal residence by John La Touche, a Dublin banker, and he asked the Queen to give the subject her earnest attention. Disraeli had had a similar plan but soon found that the Queen was so hostile to the idea that he decided to say no more about it.

Though she thought the offer was 'very liberal, and indeed noble',[39] Balmoral was necessary to her health, and nothing could take its place in her affections. She had had a grievance against Ireland since the royal visit in August 1861, when the Prince Consort had been the object of hostile demonstrations on account of an incautious comparison he had made between Irish and Polish discontent. To her, it was an insult never to be forgotten or forgiven.

The viceroy plan would have involved the Prince of Wales living in Ireland for several months each year. She thoroughly disliked the idea, saying it was a waste of time trying to connect the royal family with Ireland, as Scotland and England deserved it far more. The climate of Ireland was uncongenial to her, and it would also be bad for the Prince of Wales. Gladstone could not have disagreed more with this last opinion. He believed that the Prince of Wales was exercising a disastrous influence on society with his pleasure-loving way of life and told Ponsonby that he wanted to see the Court 'as pure as King Arthur's Round Table'. While Ponsonby was just as keen to see a solution to the problem on similar lines, he felt duty-bound to warn Gladstone that he had learnt from Tennyson's poem that the Round Table had also fallen short of perfection.

Lord Granville begged Gladstone to let the matter drop, but he would not accept such advice. While he had 'no wish to irritate', he thought that Queen and country had suffered in the past 'from want of plain speaking'. Returning to his argument, he wrote to the Queen pointing out that it was necessary to provide some means of 'remodelling' the life of the Prince of Wales 'by finding His Royal Highness that adequate employment from which, without any fault, he has hitherto been debarred'.[40] She retorted that he was putting forward this idea merely as an experiment, and 'she does not think Ireland is in a fit state at the present moment to be experimented upon'.[41]

Over-earnest and zealous, Gladstone was wise and far-seeing, but he lacked charm and the ability to persuade people. The more he tried to insist on the validity of his cause, the less the Queen was inclined to cooperate, or indeed listen to him. To Henry Ponsonby, she was ready to make comparisons between her Prime Minister and the relationship between the German Chancellor and his notoriously docile sovereign, Emperor William I, observing that '*she* has felt that Mr Gladstone would have liked to *govern* her as Bismarck governs the Emperor. Of course not to the same extent, or in the same manner; but she always felt in his manner an overbearing obstinacy and imperiousness (without being actually wanting in respect as to form) which she never experienced from *anyone* else, and which she found most disagreeable.'[42]

Anxious that credit should be given where it was due, Ponsonby insisted respectfully that Gladstone, unlike Bismarck, was 'honest and true', and she should believe that his loyalty and devotion to her as his sovereign was beyond question. To this she replied that he was indeed loyal, but he was, as Lord Palmerston had once said, 'a very dangerous man'.

FIVE

'The kindest of Mistresses'

In January 1874, after a series of by-election defeats, Gladstone declared that his government had been 'reduced to impotence', and dissolved parliament two and a half weeks later. A general election gave the Conservatives 350 seats to the Liberals' 245 and the Home Rulers' 57. Declaring that he intended to put 'an interval between Parliament and the grave', he announced his impending retirement. When he went to Windsor to resign, he found the Queen 'very kind', but he declined her offer of a peerage.

On 17 February she sent for Disraeli, and their meeting was little short of ecstatic. 'He repeatedly said whatever I wished shd. be done – whatever his difficulties might be!'[1] declared the Queen. When he fell to his knees before her to kiss her hand, he effusively assured her that he would plight his troth to 'the kindest of *Mistresses*'.[2]

In the following week she wrote to her eldest daughter, Alice, the Crown Princess of Prussia, that her outgoing Prime Minister was not merely 'a very dangerous man', as Palmerston had warned her. He was also 'very arrogant, tyrannical and obstinate, with no knowledge of the world or human nature'.[3] Alice was a more forward-thinking young woman, who had absorbed her father's political lessons well, had always admired Gladstone and believed that the Liberals were more in accordance with the prevailing tide of opinion. Mother and daughter were not united on the matter.

With Disraeli in power for the next six years, Queen Victoria would have a prime minister with whom she could work amicably, a minister who made her feel important and in whose company she could relax. It was almost like the early days of her reign with Melbourne, when ministerial visits became a pleasure, and business was leavened with gossip and pleasant conversations between the plump widow in her fifties and the septuagenarian eccentric who christened her 'the Faery'. Disraeli flattered her, regarding her with a certain wry amusement, but there was affection as well as unashamed adulation in his attitude. He knew exactly how to win her over with the phrases, gestures and compliments that would delight her. As he sometimes found it necessary to remind his colleagues, it had to be remembered that she was first and foremost a woman.

While she was shrewd enough to see through the theatricality in Disraeli's phrases, she relished it for its own sake. She was also well aware how much he enjoyed female company. When he received a box of primroses from Windsor he thanked her, saying that 'their lustre was enhanced by the condescending hand which showered upon him all the treasures of Spring'. Shortly before his death, he told the poet Matthew Arnold that everyone liked flattery, 'and when you come to royalty, you should lay it on with a trowel'.[4]

When compared with Gladstone, Disraeli's attitude to his sovereign during these years could not have differed more. While Gladstone could not resist hectoring the Queen to make a greater effort, Disraeli expressed public sympathy for her condition. He made supportive, not to say sycophantic, speeches about the onerousness of her burdens; and in his novel *Lothair*, published in 1870, he gave voice to one of the Queen's most firmly held convictions, namely that in forgetting its sense of duty, the aristocracy was degenerating into an indulgent and worthless caste.

Faced with an increasingly radical opposition party, Disraeli's Conservatives were becoming synonymous with policies with which the Queen was more naturally in sympathy. The young sovereign of 1837, a partisan Whig, had changed within thirty years and was now becoming into a true-blue Tory. In a series of public addresses at around this time, her Prime Minister was revealing the policy of the Conservatives as one which supported the monarchy, the House of Lords and the Church, believed in consolidating Britain's overseas possessions, recognised the importance of social reform and stood for a strong foreign policy, for the greatness of Britain as opposed to Gladstone's 'Little England' theory. While the Liberals were more internationalist, the Conservatives were the more truly national party. Disraeli saw the working classes as conservatives in the best sense, proud of belonging to a great country and keen to maintain its greatness. It was a philosophy which Queen Victoria could hardly disagree with or disapprove of.

How fortunate, he noted, that he was serving a female sovereign, as he owed everything to women. In the sunset of his life, he proclaimed that he still had a young heart, thanks to the influence of his Queen. It was as well that, unlike Lord Melbourne, he was not serving an inexperienced young sovereign, but a woman of middle age. As his contemporaries observed, the Prime Minister's many female friends were all grandmothers, and it must have been immensely rewarding for him to be dealing with the greatest grandmother of them all.

If Queen Victoria was the widow of Windsor, Disraeli was the widower of Hughenden, for Mary Anne had died at the age of eighty in December 1872. Yet the incorrigible old romantic still craved female company, and after his wife's death he had formed a deep, if rather one-sided, attachment with Selina, Countess of Bradford, a grandmother of fifty-four. Refusing to be broken-hearted when refused by Selina, the undaunted politician proposed to her sister of seventy-one, Lady Chesterfield, on the grounds that marriage to her would bring him closer to her sister. One must doubt how serious his intentions really were. Lady Chesterfield presumably did, for she turned him down, and he had to content himself with carrying on a passionate correspondence with both women.

Even so, Disraeli had no problem in keeping his promise to do by and large whatever the Queen wanted. Admittedly, after Gladstone, almost any prime minister would have come as a blessed relief; to have one whose political outlook was so well attuned to hers was indeed a bonus. The era of the Prince Albert-influenced liberalism was over, to be replaced by Disraeli's conservative persuasion – if indeed any persuasion was needed. During his six-year term of office, their ideas coincided more and more. She found herself accepting wholeheartedly his faith in the working together of the aristocracy and lower classes, his belief in a powerful foreign policy and his visions of imperial grandeur.

However, there were minor differences between monarch and statesman. The Queen's opinions regarding Church affairs were more strongly held than his, and in his policies of social reform to improve conditions for the working classes, his 'one nation' Tory democracy, the Queen was less interested. While she was kind-hearted, even sentimental to a degree, her social conscience was never pronounced, and she was still too ready to accept Lord Melbourne's glib assurances that dissatisfaction was generally caused by agitators; a *laissez-faire* attitude was her answer, on the grounds that social injustices would somehow rectify themselves if given time. When Queen Victoria spoke approvingly of the working classes, she had in mind the friendly Highland crofters and farm labourers whom she saw near Balmoral, not the underfed urban masses who lived in squalor in the poorer parts of London and the other industrial cities.

Even when Queen and Prime Minister were not in full accord on some political question, they could not argue for long. He had a way when they differed, she later told a future Prime Minister, Lord Rosebery, of saying 'Dear Madam' persuasively, 'and putting his head to one side'.[5] Gladstone's assertive, hectoring demeanour had got him nowhere, but Disraeli's intelligent approach could not fail. Sir Henry Ponsonby claimed that he had 'got the length of her foot exactly'.[6] Disraeli coaxed her, he deferred to her, he paid her extravagant compliments on her political judgement and expertise. On the publication in 1868 of extracts from her diaries, *Leaves from the Journal of Our Life in the Highlands*, he had congratulated her fulsomely as 'the head of the literary profession', and sometimes when discussing literature, he would slip in the phrase, 'We authors, Ma'am'.

Despite all the silver-tongued flattery, he never lost sight of the fact that the Queen was a woman of great ability. Now that he was encouraging her to think for herself, instead of always thinking how Albert might have reacted to particular problems had he still been alive, the Queen now followed her intuition, trusting her own judgement for perhaps the first time in her life. No longer was there a husband to insist that political impartiality on the part of the Crown was paramount, and her particular traits, her common sense, determination and, perhaps above all, her obstinacy, became more pronounced. Human nature being as it is, it was hardly surprising that with advancing years her views became less flexible. Even without Disraeli's encouragement, she would probably have become increasingly self-assured that she was always right. That he was her Prime Minister at the time may have done little more than to reinforce such characteristics.

In other ways, Disraeli helped to draw her out from the shadow of the Prince Consort. He showed her that she no longer needed to try constantly to improve herself, and that she did not owe it to herself and her country to be a paragon of culture, too intellectual or too serious-minded. He appreciated her for the woman she was and impressed on her the fact that she had no reason to feel inferior about any academic shortcomings. During her married life her intellectual self-confidence had been somewhat undermined by Albert's knowledgeable spirit and in the early years of her widowhood by Gladstone's cleverness. Though as well-informed as them, if less learned, Disraeli took care never to make her feel inferior. He even brought a sense of fun, or at least an air of gentle levity, into her life. At the same time, he introduced her to a new sense of vocation, and now she started to take a more lively interest in political affairs. Suddenly she no longer complained that she was overworked, and he took the right approach in urging her to make an effort as she began to busy herself with a renewed sense of purpose.

Other prime ministers, not least Gladstone, were used to her keeping their audiences with her short. With Disraeli they often lasted longer than an hour, and luncheon might be delayed as a result. Whereas she never thought twice about keeping Gladstone standing, she had a small gilt chair brought in for Disraeli. Once they were so engrossed in conversation that he forgot to keep an eye on the time. He had arranged to take a special train back from Windsor to London at five minutes past five. As the clock struck five he leapt to his feet, hurriedly explained why he had to go and rushed out of the room. Instead of being dismissed, he said later, he dismissed his sovereign.

Appropriately for a novelist, his letters were as full of sparkle as his conversation. While Gladstone's memoranda had been so ponderous that Victoria generally required a summary (if not a dictionary) before she could fully grasp them, Disraeli's were not only lively but succinct, very much to the point. Ponsonby noted with somewhat grudging admiration his 'wonderful talent for writing in an amusing tone while seizing the points of an argument'. Rather more expansively, Lady Augusta Stanley told Lord Clarendon that 'Dizzy writes daily letters to the Queen in his best novel style, telling her every scrap of political news dressed up to serve his own purpose, and every scrap of social gossip cooked to amuse her. She declares that she has never had such letters in her life, which is probably true, and that she never before knew *everything*!'[7]

On the occasion of the Queen's fifty-sixth birthday in May 1875, Disraeli wrote to her that she lived 'in the hearts and thoughts of many millions, though in none more deeply and more fervently than in the heart of him who, with humble duty, pens these spontaneous lines'.

How, it might be asked, did such a good judge of character as Queen Victoria accept or even tolerate his undisguised, almost excessive flattery, without wondering whether he might be making

fun of her or suspecting he was being 'false'? Yet she saw through
the outward show and relished Disraeli's extravagant style, seeing it
as simply an expression of a romantic temperament, and aware that
behind the façade he was scrupulously honest. There was no reason
this most eloquent of courtiers could not be an equally serious-
minded and trustworthy prime minister.

How much was she taken in by his extravagant compliments? Did
she ever feel that he was teasing her, or merely encouraging her to
come out of her shell? Though she lived a life of some seclusion in
widowhood, it is difficult to imagine that she can have been so
unworldly as not to take his elaborate, even exaggerated, courtliness
at face value. One must assume that she was amused by the
theatricality and good humour of his glowing phrases, though at the
same time she knew better than to be lured into some world of
make-believe more redolent of another age.

According to Algernon Cecil, Disraeli 'pursued a primrose path
of dalliance reminiscent of the Byronic age'. Though the showy
waistcoats of his younger days might have gone by the time he
assumed high office, 'his language remained flowery and his
flatteries were blatant'.[8] No matter how much he might pretend
otherwise, the concept of a 'Faery Queen' was not one to be taken
seriously. But no matter how blatant the flatteries were, Victoria
clearly enjoyed and was amused by being on the receiving end as
much as he relished bestowing such gilded compliments in the
first place.

During the six years of his premiership, their association
developed into something of an idyll, a partnership as much
romantic as political. In 1874 the Queen was fifty-four and Disraeli
sixty-nine. While others found the dumpy yet indomitably regal
Queen Victoria in her black, elaborately bustled dresses and white
widow's veil intimidating, to Disraeli she was invariably charming.
He appreciated her kindly eyes, her attractive voice, her silvery
laugh, her graceful movements and the warmly welcoming smile on
which so many others commented.

For her part, she found him attractive in her own way. This odd-
looking figure could by no stretch of the imagination be called
conventionally handsome, but to her he was undeniably poetic,
exotic and far more interesting than a good-looking but boring man
could ever be. His rouged cheeks, the single dyed curl on the
forehead and the rings he wore over white gloves might make give

him the appearance of a pantomime figure or a Lewis Carroll creation, but in the Queen's eyes, such quirks probably made him even more captivating.

She would never spend more than a night or two at Buckingham Palace, and as Disraeli baulked at the idea of going north to Balmoral, their meetings were generally held at Windsor Castle and Osborne House. He was a reluctant visitor to Windsor, which he called 'the Temple of the Winds', and he did not share her passion for fresh air. Neither did he enjoy the formalities of the Court, and would say that all was well as long as he was allowed to keep to his room, or a morning walk, but *toilette* and evening mannerisms would destroy him. Balmoral, with its freezing temperatures and generally wet weather, he liked even less. Above all, he was not immune to Her Majesty's occasionally exhausting company. 'What nerve! What muscle! What energy!' he groaned. 'Her Minister is very deficient in all three.'[9] Yet he was always unfailingly charming whenever he was with her; as he was too much the courtier to betray his feelings, the Queen never knew that he was not delighted with each visit. Whether in the audience chamber or at the dinner-table, she adored his company. If she saw any of her children, usually Princess Helena or Prince Leopold, laughing at his table talk, she would immediately want to know what he was saying.

Disraeli may have thought Windsor chilly, but Osborne in poor weather was even worse, not least because of the usually turbulent waters of the Solent to cross. Once she was installed at her island home, even if it was raining, the Queen would be seated in her large parasol-tent, erected on a lawn below the house, where she was surrounded by her dogs, footmen, Highland attendants and black-clad ladies-in-waiting as she ate her breakfast and dealt with her despatch boxes – before receiving her Prime Minister.

Disraeli's loss of his wife gave them something in common. After the death of Mary Anne, the Queen wrote to say that she knew exactly what he had lost and what he was suffering. To Lady Bradford he confessed that it was strange he always used to think that the Queen indulged in morbid sentiment, yet he was going through the same thing – and found it strangely irresistible. It is open to doubt whether either felt quite as much grief as they outwardly demonstrated, especially once the Queen had come through the first few years of widowhood, but there was comfort to be gleaned from the fact that their respective losses brought them even closer.

Unlike most of Victoria's other prime ministers, Disraeli was well aware that she would respond to a personal approach, that he needed to reach beyond the invisible barrier of the sovereign's status and the self-imposed dignity that she had acquired as necessary to her status. As such, he was one of the few men who dealt with her regularly and knew she had to be treated as a human being instead of as a deity on earth. More than most kings and queens, Victoria needed someone with whom she could be herself. Disraeli realised that her forbidding expression and stern demeanour hid a warm, even shy, personality, and that if handled with courtesy and tact, she would become a very different person. His efforts to woo her were as determined as his attempts to woo other women in the past, be they wives or widows and dowagers. While it was a discreet, respectful and innocent courtship, there was something of a whiff of courtship about it all the same.

Observers certainly suspected that Disraeli's personal relationship with the Queen included an element of courtship, albeit innocent and respectful. It was never anything if not decorous, for the old widower was an incurable romantic, and his wife's death probably allowed him a degree of licence to pursue his flirtation further than he might have done had she still been alive. His association with the Countess of Bradford was always more one of friendship and less an affair of the heart, and over the years he came to depend more on the Queen, who in a way epitomised the indulgent mother-figure he had long sought.

In his way, he must have believed that he was a little in love with the Queen, and he certainly never minded fostering the impression that the feeling was mutual. She was not in love with him, except in a strictly platonic sense, but the effect on her personality was very important. For the first time since the death of the Prince Consort, he made her feel desirable, ready for a little gentle flirtation, some joking and flattery, in a way which nobody else could, or would ever dare. It all proved invaluable in enhancing her personal self-esteem, as well as bringing into her life a sense of fantasy, a way to kindle her imagination. This make-believe world of the 'Faery Queen' which he created with gifts of primroses and snowdrops and violets added a sense of colour and gaiety to her existence. It was not exactly love, but something not unlike it.

Each February, sovereign and Prime Minister exchanged valentines. 'He wishes he could repose on a sunny bank, like young Valentine in the pretty picture that fell from a rosy cloud this morn,' he wrote on receiving one such card, 'but the reverie of the happy youth would be rather different from his. Valentine would dream of the future, and youthful loves, and all under the inspiration of a beautiful clime! Lord Beaconsfield, no longer in the sunset, but the twilight of his existence, must encounter a life of anxiety and toil; but this, too, has its romance, when he remembers that he labours for the most gracious of beings!'[10] Some years later she told Lord Rosebery how touched she had been when Disraeli sent her a small trinket box, a heart transfixed by an arrow on one side, and the single word *Fideliter* on the other.

* * *

Queen Victoria's platonic relationship with Disraeli never had any effect on her association with her Highland servant John Brown (see chapter 7). On the contrary, it was as if she had the best of both worlds. Her Prime Minister brought the poetical romance into her life, while the other made her feel secure at home. Between them they gave her all the moral support and attention she needed. One made her feel like a helpless widow, relying on him for protection, while the other made her feel like some desirable and almost mythical creature – an undoubted Queen.

Though they may not have realised it, Disraeli and Brown played complementary roles in drawing Queen Victoria out of her intense mourning for the Prince Consort. Although the passing of the years contributed, by the 1870s she was becoming less self-pitying and spent less time obsessively thinking about him, bewailing her loss. With these two very different men, her health, spirits and zest for life improved. Those who saw her exchanging banter with Disraeli during their regular audiences, or dancing with Brown at the ghillies' balls at Balmoral, were proof enough that 'the widow of Windsor' had recovered her natural vitality. The Hanoverian high spirits were triumphing once more over Coburg melancholy.

Disraeli was never remotely jealous of her relationship with John Brown; he knew that the Scotsman's presence did her good, and that she could divide her attentions, even her affections, between the two men. He understood how important the Highland servant was to her well-being, grateful that he had brought her out of her morbid frame of mind and her obsession with the memory of the Prince Consort. Maybe the Prime Minister had heightened her interest in life, but Brown had been the first to reawaken it. Unlike most other members of her circle, not least her family, Disraeli treated Brown with courtesy, and this only increased her admiration for this most understanding of prime ministers.

* * *

In foreign policy, the Queen and her Prime Minister were equally at one, not least on the question of the enhancement of British prestige. For too long, argued the Queen, people like Gladstone had allowed Britain to play a submissive, even negative, role, whereas Disraeli was ready to make a stand on behalf of British power in Europe.

Nevertheless, it was further eastwards that he achieved his most conspicuous feats. Monarch and Prime Minister were both well aware that if the Suez Canal was to come totally under French control, British commercial interests between the Mediterranean and the Red Sea would be at risk, as the waterway provided the shortest route between Britain and India, and over three-quarters of the ships using the canal were British. In November 1875 the Khedive of Egypt decided to sell his shares in the Canal, of which he owned nearly half, and he offered them to a French syndicate. Their acquisition would therefore have placed the Canal entirely in French hands.

Disraeli knew that the British government must buy the shares, and must do so quickly. Having rallied an unenthusiastic Cabinet behind him, he borrowed £4 million from the Rothschild banking house, and in November 1875 purchased the shares on behalf of the British government. 'It is just settled,' he wrote to the Queen in triumph; 'you have it, Madam. The French government has been out-generaled.'[11] Though it could hardly be considered as a gift from the Prime Minister to his sovereign, she was spellbound by this theatrical way and the myth that he had in effect presented his sovereign with this great waterway linking Britain to India, the Mother Country to its Empire, West to East. There could be no more striking proof of her country's greatness.

The next imperial gift to the Queen, in a manner of speaking, was an imperial crown. Disraeli's tactics in this sphere were aimed at satisfying two objectives: a satisfactory culmination of Victoria's intense interest in the Indian sub-continent of India, and also solving the age-old question of whether the title of Empress was superior to that of Queen.

None of Britain's overseas territories across the seas fascinated Queen Victoria more than India. The populations of Canada, Australia and New Zealand were basically Englishmen enjoying self-government, but the Indians were a subject people whom she saw as belonging in a sense to her personally. She felt a close affinity with India and regarded herself as being directly responsible for the country and its people's welfare.

Disraeli, who had once been considered as a possible Viceroy of India, agreed with her wholeheartedly. He too saw the land as his sovereign's personal domain and thought it would benefit everyone if British rule could be represented more directly by the monarch. The Prince of Wales had also long wanted to visit India, and knowing that his mother had a habit of thwarting him in any public role he was keen to assume, he took care to enlist Disraeli's approval for the idea.

An Indian royal tour accorded precisely with Disraeli's grand design. As expected, the Queen was less enthusiastic, and it took all his diplomatic skills to obtain her consent. She questioned the cost, wondered whether Princess Alexandra should accompany her husband or not (though to Alix's lasting dismay, Bertie would not let her join him), wondered also about the personal characters of the Prince's intended travelling company, and not least about the likelihood of the notoriously unfaithful socialite Prince getting into trouble. Nevertheless, the tour fulfilled everyone's expectations, the heir carrying out a demanding schedule of appearances and functions with his usual enthusiasm. To the Indians he was not a representative of the British government but a living symbol of the monarchy, and there could have been no better proof of the fact that the Queen was as much the sovereign of India as she was of Great Britain.

Inevitably, this reinforced her aspirations to assuming the title of Empress of India, a title which sounded infinitely superior to Queen. Every major European monarchy, such as Russia, Germany and Austria, was an empire, as was France until the fall of Napoleon III in 1870. 'Empress Victoria' would therefore consign to history the European concept that its archdukes, grand dukes and crown princes were superior to mere princes.

Disraeli's plans complemented the Queen's wishes, and, as Prime Minister, it was up to him to see that the scheme was put into action. There were sound political reasons for the introduction of the Royal Titles Bill, beyond the matter of personal, or even national, vanity. Such a title would confer an aura of stability and permanence on British rule in India. A British Empress of India might make Tsar Alexander II of Russia less inclined to advance further into Asia, as Queen Victoria could now face him as an undisputed equal across the North-West Frontier. If the Prince of Wales's tour had struck the first blow for British prestige in India, the Queen's assumption of the title of Empress would strike the second.

On 1 May 1876 the Royal Titles Bill was passed, and a delighted Queen Victoria was declared Queen–Empress. Though she was imperial only as far as India was concerned, she enthusiastically signed herself 'VR & I' (Victoria Regina et Imperatrix) whenever possible. In recognition of his work, Disraeli was given a huge portrait of his sovereign, itself a copy of a painting by Heinrich von Angeli.

Well aware of Disraeli's advancing years, the Queen was increasingly anxious about his health. She would chide him if he visited her when he had a cold and once, when they both had colds, he claimed that 'the kingdom was never governed with such an amount of catarrh and sneezing'. It amused her when he wrote to Ponsonby, claiming to have recovered his youth by doing what the doctor had warned him against – drinking very good wine.

In the summer of 1876 he was seventy-one and feared his health might be unequal to much more exertion in the House of Commons. He told the Queen that he must either resign – something she would not countenance – or continue his premiership from the House of Lords. This gave her the chance to present him with a title, as he had only recently conferred one on her himself, and that summer she elevated him to the peerage as the Earl of Beaconsfield. On 11 August 1876 he delivered his last speech in the House of Commons, and thereafter he remained Prime Minister from the House of Lords. It was thus as Earl of Beaconsfield that he gave his blessing to the Queen's official assumption of her title on 1 January 1877. At noon that day in Delhi, Queen Victoria was proclaimed Empress of India by the Viceroy, Lord Lytton. The occasion was celebrated that evening at Windsor with a sumptuous banquet at which, proudly sporting her

Indian jewellery, the Queen heard the Earl make such a lively address that it might have been taken straight from one of his novels.

* * *

During Disraeli's first premiership, in 1868, the Queen had sent him bouquets of flowers. Accompanying one such gift from Windsor was a letter from Princess Helena to Mary Anne Disraeli. Her mother, the Princess wrote, 'heard him say one day that he was so fond of May and all those lovely spring flowers that she has ventured to send him these, as they will make his rooms look so bright'.[12]

In his second term of office he reciprocated this practice, choosing though to send her not exotic blooms like lilies or orchids, but spring plants such as snowdrops and primroses. Each time she sent him another offering, she was rewarded with one of his lyrical letters. In time, his ardent imagination had converted the dowdy and dumpy sovereign into something altogether more poetic. Like Edmund Spenser's Elizabeth I, he told her, she was a 'Faery Queen', her flowers an offering from the fauns and dryads of the woods of Osborne; and camellias, blooming in the natural air, became 'your Majesty's Faery Isle'. Primroses meant that 'your Majesty's sceptre has touched the enchanted isle'.

When she sent him snowdrops, he fastened them to his breast to prove to his generally bemedalled fellow guests at an official banquet that he had also been decorated by a gracious sovereign. 'Then, in the middle of the night,' he told her, it occurred to him that it might all be enchantment, 'and that perhaps it was a Faery gift and came from another monarch: Queen Titania, gathering flowers, with her Court, in a soft and sea-girt isle, and sending magic blossoms, which, they say, turn the heads of those who receive them.'[13] Some might have viewed the Victoria–Disraeli association merely in terms of a wily and accomplished old seducer toadying to a plain and susceptible widow. But in both appearance and manner, Disraeli was a combination of all those men to whom she was always attracted. He had become her mentor, her counsellor, her best friend, maybe even lover in a strictly platonic sense, embodying the nonchalant cynicism of Lord Melbourne, the solicitude of Prince Albert and the 'take me as I am' spirit of John Brown. Yet there were limits to his powers of persuasion, and even he had no more success than her Liberal prime ministers when it came to asking her to open parliament.

Sometimes she could betray her irritation with him, especially if she felt he and her dinner guests were raising the conversation above her intellectual norm – something which had brought out a latent sense of inferiority in her relations with Albert. In 1876 he was dining at Windsor with the Queen and the German Empress Augusta, who had been renowned since her youth for being something of a bluestocking. The Empress, he noted afterwards, was becoming 'involved in some metaphysical speculation' with another guest, and later he was himself spellbound by her, 'who threw out all her resources, philosophical, poetic, political – till the Faery was a little jealous, for she had originally told Lady Ely that some one "was not to make his pretty speeches to Augóosta, who only wanted to draw him to her!!!!"'[14]

* * *

In 1878 Disraeli was partly responsible for another British triumph, namely the Congress of Berlin. During the previous year, Russia had declared war on Turkey, having a vested interest in seeing the Turkish Empire dismantled, while to Britain it was a safeguard against Russian designs on India. To surrender any Turkish territory to the Russians could threaten land and sea routes to India.

Some thought that Disraeli instigated, if not actively encouraged, her detestation of Gladstone. He had every reason to stimulate her antipathy towards his great rival, as the more she hated Gladstone, the more she would support Disraeli's anti-Russian policies. She was outraged at Russia's declaration of war against Turkey, and even more so at successive Russian victories. If she were a man, she proclaimed, she would like to go and give those horrid Russians 'such a beating'.[15]

Disraeli refused to pay too much attention to reports of mistreatment of Christian subjects by their Turkish masters. Reports reaching London of Bulgarian peasants being murdered by Turkish troops he dismissed as 'coffee-house babble'. Gladstone, then leader of the opposition, fulminated against the Turks in his pamphlet *The Bulgarian Horrors and the Question of the East*, a document which Disraeli denounced as 'contemptible' and 'the product of an unprincipled maniac'. Pragmatically he refrained from declaring war, somewhat to the dismay of his sovereign, who wanted him to act more assertively, urging him to tell Russia that

Britain was resolved to declare war if she reached, and refused to quit, Constantinople.

While he was almost as Russophobe himself, Disraeli preferred to be in a position to threaten Russia with war if she showed any signs of occupying Constantinople. Having worked the Queen up into a belligerent frame of mind, he played on this to bring his divided cabinet round to a more warlike attitude, while relying upon their ambivalent attitude to help restrain her from calling on them to carry out her desire to give the Russians 'a beating'.

Victoria was not the only bellicose member of her family. At a dinner party Disraeli found himself seated next to the Duchess of Teck, who asked him why he had not declared war. 'What are you waiting for, Mr Disraeli? The Queen is for you: the Army's for you – what *are* you waiting for?' Unabashed, he answered, 'The potatoes, Ma'am.'[16] Had some of his Cabinet colleagues had their own way, nobody would have waited. In particular, Disraeli's Foreign Secretary, Lord Salisbury, represented those who had the utmost sympathy with the Christian subjects of the Turkish Empire in Europe and who regarded Russia as their protector. Salisbury, Disraeli complained to the Queen, apparently thought 'that the progress of Russia is the progress of religion & civilisation'.[17]

Britain remained neutral throughout the nine-month conflict. An armistice between Russia and Turkey was signed in January 1878, but rumours that Russia had ignored the terms of the armistice and was marching on Constantinople finally enabled Disraeli to stir his irresolute Cabinet into action. War credits were passed, arrangements were made to move troops from India to the Mediterranean and reserve forces were called up. This was what he had always foreseen and hoped for, and for him it would suffice. While he had no intention of being stampeded into war, it would surely convince Russia of Britain's determination to stand firm. He had judged correctly, for the arrival of the British fleet off Constantinople halted the Russians. Hastily imposing the Treaty of San Stefano on the retreating Turks, Russia concluded the war.

The Queen and her government were not satisfied with some of the treaty's provisions, and Russia was persuaded to agree to a conference of the Great Powers, to be staged in Berlin under the presidency of Bismarck. It opened in June 1878, and Disraeli, it was said (by himself as well as others), returned from it having achieved 'peace with honour'. A more sober assessment later prevailed. He was ill-equipped to represent Britain on his own at such an event. His knowledge of geography was extremely vague, and he admitted that it held little interest for him; his meagre command of foreign languages extended only to rather poor French, or 'grocer's French', as it was described; and his memory was beginning to fail him. Before leaving England, he told the Queen that he would attend the Congress, 'exhibit his full powers' and then leave the better-qualified Lord Salisbury to complete the details. Nevertheless, what he lacked in basic administrative qualities he made up for in his sense of history, the lessons of the past and their implications for the future for Europe, and above all in his diplomatic instincts, which sprang from a remarkable understanding of human nature.

The Treaty of Berlin was signed on 13 July. Some of Disraeli's Cabinet and supporters were disappointed that Russia had not been humiliated, and thought Turkey had been shabbily treated, while the annexation of Cyprus smacked of the imperialism so derided by the Liberals. But the delighted Queen sent him a huge bouquet of 'Windsor Flowers' on his return to Downing Street, as well as offering him the Garter, a dukedom and a peerage for his brother or his nephew. Rather than 'Peace with Honour', quipped one cynic, it was 'Peace with Honours'.

In fact, of all the honours he could have had, Disraeli was content to accept only the Garter. 'He will not trust himself now in endeavouring to express what he feels to your Majesty's kindness,' he wrote. 'He thinks he is ennobled through your Majesty's goodness quite enough, though with infinite deference to your Majesty's gracious pleasure, he would presume to receive the Garter; but, as he always feels, your Majesty's kind thoughts are dearer to him than any personal distinction, however rich and rare. The belief that your Majesty trusts, and approves of him is more precious than rubies!'[18]

On returning home from Berlin, he was treated like a conquering hero. The Queen's feelings on the situation were aptly summarised by *The Times*, as it declared that the Prime Minister was now 'at the pinnacle of Ministerial Renown', as well as 'the favourite of his Sovereign and the idol of Society'.[19]

* * *

Disraeli never lost sight of the fact that he was serving the Queen of England. Though cynical by nature, he always retained a deep reverence for the monarchy and the throne. Perhaps it was as well that his sovereign was a woman and not a king, for she fired his imagination. Maybe he saw himself as a knight in shining armour, another Sir Francis Drake or Sir Walter Raleigh to a latter-day Queen Elizabeth. He gave her new confidence in herself, instead of indulging her unduly in her complaints that, as a widow, she had too many demands placed upon her by her country and her ministers.

In some ways, Disraeli's influence was questionable. During his second period of office, Victoria was inclined to think of him as the servant of the Crown, rather than of the people who had elected his government to power. Perhaps she saw the government of the country as a partnership between the sovereign and her prime minister, to which they each brought their accumulated knowledge and experience. Disraeli kept the Queen well informed as to what was going on, and he was constantly asking her opinion and advice. Now, to an extent which she had perhaps never known before, she was completely and willingly absorbed in the day-to-day business of government, and probably for the first time she could see herself as all-important.

Such intimacy between sovereign and prime minister might have passed without comment, had there not been a sense of something unconstitutional in the air. Sometimes the two of them spent hours in close discussion, frequently writing directly to each other without using the customary third person and without the prior knowledge of the Queen's private secretary, who felt theirs was unnaturally close for a working relationship.

He was not alone in thinking that the influence they had on each other was excessive, particularly if Disraeli was inadvertently encouraging the Queen to be something more than a constitutional monarch. His utterances about her being the 'Directress' and 'Arbitress' of Europe were probably not meant to be taken seriously, but such theatrical expressions were bound to be interpreted by others as indiscreet, not to say tactless. It was as if he never hesitated to encourage her authoritarian spirit, or to use her name to further his policies. To her, Disraeli's policy became 'our' policy; and 'our' policy thus became the 'imperial policy of England'. To criticise his measures or policies seemed to her like criticism of the Crown. It was an ill-advised stance for a constitutional monarch.

As it was, Queen Victoria's concept of the role of a constitutional monarch was changing. It was hard to avoid the belief that Disraeli was giving the Queen too self-important an opinion of her role as head of state. By the time of his second premiership, or at any rate during it, she was adamant she would not become a mere cipher, with a role restricted to signing Bills and opening parliaments. Almost imperceptibly, she was developing a somewhat exaggerated idea of her royal prerogative and strongly objected to any signs that her ministers might be encroaching on it.

Lady Ponsonby believed that 'Dizzy' had 'worked the idea of personal government to its logical conclusion, and the seed was sown' by Baron Stockmar and the Prince Consort. While they lived, they had kept matters in proportion, but despite themselves they had inadvertently been responsible for establishing 'the superstition in the Queen's mind about her own prerogative'. Now they had gone, there was always the danger that the situation could be used by an unscrupulous minister to his own advantage and the country's ruin. 'If there comes a real collision between the Queen and the House of Commons (say, for instance, that the country insists on Gladstone for the next Liberal Prime Minister) it is quite possible she would turn restive, *dorlotède* [pampered] as she has been by Dizzy's high-sounding platitudes, and then her reign will end in a fiasco *or* she prepares one for the Prince of Wales.'[20]

* * *

Disraeli had shrewdly walked the tightrope which enabled him to keep the country out of war with Russia, and it was to be a short yet inglorious war during the last year of his premiership which led to a rare argument with his sovereign. In January 1879 fighting broke out in southern Africa between the Zulus and the British, a conflict provoked by Sir Bartle Frere, who was determined to break Zulu power, seeing in it a threat to British expansion and commercial interests in the area. Lord Chelmsford, the British commander, had greatly underestimated the Zulus' fighting spirit, and under his leadership the Army was severely defeated.

Louis Napoleon, ex-Prince Imperial of France and only child of the former Emperor Napoleon III and Empress Eugenie, was living in exile in England with his widowed mother. He had attended the Royal Military Academy, Woolwich, and begged to serve with the British Army in South Africa. The Queen and the Empress readily assented, much to Disraeli's dismay. He tried to stop the Prince from going, he told his colleagues. 'But what can you do when you have to deal with two obstinate women?'[21] While serving with the Army in June he was killed by the Zulus in an ambush. His mother and the Queen grieved over his loss, and Disraeli wrote to Victoria that it was a tragedy, 'equalled only by the death of Emperor Maximilian of Mexico' (see p. 124).[22]

To make amends, the Queen decided that Louis Napoleon should be given as splendid a funeral as possible. Disraeli feared the effect such a display of loyalty to the Bonapartes would have on Anglo-French relations, and he and his ministers saw no reason they should make such a public gesture of penitence. He had to persuade the Queen against placing the Order of the Bath on the Prince's coffin with her own hands, and she was so angry when she learnt that none of the Cabinet were going to attend the funeral that, to placate her, it was agreed that the War Minister and the Colonial Minister should both be there. After the ceremony on 12 July, she telegraphed to Disraeli that everything had gone very well. To Lady Chesterfield he wrote that he hoped the French government would be as joyful; in his opinion, 'nothing could be more injudicious than the whole affair'.[23]

Despite this tragedy, the Queen gave unstinting support to those of her servants engaged in the thankless task of maintaining law and order in the imperial outposts, and firmly resisted any suggestions to supersede Frere and Chelmsford. Although Disraeli upheld the concept of the British Empire, to him it was a noble cause for peace and goodwill. The concept of colonial wars was more or less anathema, and he resented those who were responsible for the conflict and subsequent bloodshed.

In July, after Chelmsford had finally managed to defeat the Zulu forces at Ulundi, he returned home as a conquering hero, readily forgiven his earlier errors. The Queen shared in the general enthusiasm, but her Prime Minister considered it very ill-judged. When she pressed him to receive Chelmsford at Hughenden, he demurred, saying that 'it would be hardly becoming . . . for Lord Beaconsfield to receive him, except in an official interview'. He justified his stance by explaining that Chelmsford was indelibly associated 'with the policy of the unhappily precipitated Zulu War, the evil consequences of which to this country have been incalculable', and was responsible for 'having invaded Zululand "avec un coeur léger", with no adequate knowledge of the country he was attacking, and with no precaution or preparation. A dreadful disaster occurred in consequence,' after which he was panic-stricken and appealed to the government for reinforcements 'in order to reduce a country not larger than Yorkshire'. He added how painful it was for him to differ from Her Majesty where public affairs were involved, not only because he was bound to her 'by every tie of duty and respectful affection', but also as he had 'a distinct and real confidence in Your Majesty's judgment, matured, as it is, by an unrivalled political experience, and an extensive knowledge of mankind'.[24]

The Queen was 'grieved and astonished' to receive his letter. She said that she wanted him to receive Chelmsford, in order to hear everything from him and those who had actually gone through the experiences, 'and not to decide on condemning people in most difficult and trying positions from the Cabinet, pressed by an unscrupulous Opposition (at least a portion of it) and still more unscrupulous press – without allowing them to state their own case and defend themselves!' Chelmsford, she admitted, had made mistakes, but she could not bear injustice or a want of generosity towards those who had had to deal with such difficulties, 'and who ought to be supported from home and not condemned unheard'.[25]

Disraeli was likewise 'grieved' at having incurred the Queen's displeasure, but stuck to his position, pointing out that Chelmsford's letters had become 'confused, he might say incoherent, vacillating and apparently without resource'.[26] He added that the military authorities supported his view that a new commander should be appointed. These differences were all the more painful to him, he wrote the same day to Lady Ely, as it was a source of grief that anything he should say or do should be displeasing to Her Majesty: 'I love the Queen – perhaps the only person in the world left to me that I do love; and therefore you can understand how much it worries and disquiets me, when there is a cloud between us.'[27]

Despite her requests for Disraeli to retract his views, he would not be swayed. In September the Queen received Chelmsford warmly at Balmoral, conferring on him a knighthood and the Grand Cross of the Order of the Bath. She urged Disraeli to be more generous and receive him at Hughenden, as well as his two subordinate officers. Disraeli made his views on the issue known by receiving the officers at home, while grudgingly granting Chelmsford a few minutes' formal talk at Downing Street.

* * *

This momentary stand of defiance was soon forgotten by the Queen. In the spring of 1880 Disraeli called a general election, but a vigorous campaign by Gladstone, leader of the opposition, resulted in Conservative defeat and a new Liberal administration. The Queen was stunned to learn the results of the voting, declaring she would 'sooner abdicate than send for or have any communication with that *half-mad fire brand* who would soon ruin everything, and be a Dictator'.[28]

On 25 April Disraeli left Downing Street for the last time. Two days later he travelled sadly to Windsor to take formal leave of his sovereign, a poignant occasion for both. Like Napoleon, he said, he had been beaten by the elements – six bad harvests in succession. She presented him with bronze statuettes of herself, John Brown, the royal pony and her dog Sharp; he tactfully expressed himself 'much delighted' with them, and he promised to visit her again. They continued to correspond, but as in the case of Melbourne's letters to her after he had left office in 1841, it was necessary to keep it quiet. As the Queen's private secretary, Sir Henry Ponsonby disapproved, fearing it might compromise the impartiality of the Crown. Yet Disraeli was wise enough to avoid political topics most of the time, and when the Queen asked him for advice, he took care to keep it as neutral as possible.

Gladstone's audience on taking office was brief. He thought his sovereign had been 'natural under effort'. She considered that he looked ill and haggard, and was surprised when he told her that he intended to be his own Chancellor of the Exchequer as well as Prime Minister. In view of his state of health, she probably persuaded herself – mistakenly – that this 'half-mad firebrand' of seventy would be unable to shoulder the burdens of high office for long.

On 28 February 1881 the Queen and Disraeli dined together at Windsor Castle. With a chest infection that was developing into bronchitis, he was far from well, and perhaps he had a presentiment that it would be their final meeting. Her gift of flowers a few days later elicited an effusive letter of thanks. 'No Sovereign could decorate a subject with a new order', he wrote, 'which could have conferred greater pleasure, than the box, which contained yesterday the harbingers of spring, and which now adorn my writing table.'[29]

A few days later she received her last letter from him, a short note of thanks scrawled in pencil after she had enquired as to his health, to which he answered there was 'little prospect of my being visible before Easter. I am ashamed to address Your Majesty not only from my room, but even my bed.'[30] He sensed that he would probably never leave his bed again.

'We are so anxious about dear Lord Beaconsfield who has been very ill for the last fortnight,' she wrote to the Princess of Wales on 11 April. 'It is a great sorrow to me and a cause of grief and anxiety to the nation at large.'[31] Towards the end, she offered to come and visit him, but he declined, allegedly with the comment that she had better not: 'she would only ask me to take a message to Albert.'[32]

On 19 April he died, aged seventy-six. The Queen was overwhelmed with grief. Tradition prevented a sovereign from attending the funeral of a subject, but three of her sons, the Prince of Wales, the Duke of Connaught and the Duke of Albany, attended the obsequies as he was laid to rest beside Mary Anne in the churchyard at Hughenden. She sent two wreaths of primroses and on the accompanying card wrote, 'His favourite flowers from Osborne, a tribute of affection from Queen Victoria.' Above his seat in the chancel at Hughenden church, she had a large marble tablet erected in his memory, with the inscription, 'This memorial is placed by his grateful Sovereign and Friend, Victoria R.I.'

SIX

'A deluded excited man'

Everyone on all sides had expected that Gladstone's new premiership was going to prove a testing one for sovereign and minister alike. The Queen alone, Gladstone told Lord Rosebery, the ministerial colleague who was destined to be his eventual successor as Prime Minister, was 'enough to kill any man'.[1] Nevertheless, on 9 May, some two and a half weeks after Disraeli's death, he paid his old political adversary a warm, statesmanlike tribute in parliament. Contemplating it beforehand, he said, had made him unwell, and confined him to bed for two days with a stomach upset; writing this eulogy was one of the most difficult things he had ever had to do in his life. Nevertheless, it was a generous, magnanimous address, in which Gladstone praised Disraeli's long career, his strength of will, long-sighted consistency of purpose and 'his great parliamentary courage – a quality which I, who have been associated in the course of my life with some scores of Ministers, have, I think, never known but two whom I could pronounce his equal'.[2]. The Queen called it 'a fine speech'; her attitude towards Gladstone softened for a while, and she even asked him to sit down at their next audience.

However, the truce did not last, and before long they were back to their old inharmonious relationship. It was only a matter of time before she was exasperated by his unwillingness to submit to what he called her 'intolerable' claims to be kept fully informed about confidential Cabinet discussions. Before he appeared at major public meetings, she issued him warnings which might have been addressed to her own sons. In October 1881, noting that he was to attend a large banquet at Leeds, she said she hoped he would take care not to say anything which might bind him to 'any particular measures'. Fifteen months later, when he was planning to go and address his Midlothian constituents for the first time since the general election, she advised him in writing of 'her earnest hopes that he will be very guarded in his language . . . and that he will remember the immense

95

importance attached to *every* word falling from him'.[3] It was a strange letter for a sovereign to write to one of her most experienced prime ministers and members of parliament.

Another incident caused further problems between them. In September 1883 Gladstone went on a holiday cruise as a guest of the shipowner Sir Donald Currie, with fellow guests including the Home Secretary, Sir William Harcourt, and the Poet Laureate, Alfred Tennyson. Originally they planned to sail around the British Isles but then decided they would make an impromptu visit to Norway and Denmark. They were entertained in Copenhagen, where King Christian and Queen Louise invited them to a dinner at which others present included Tsar Alexander III of Russia and King George of Greece. Gladstone had inadvertently broken one of the golden rules of a premier, namely that he should not set foot in a foreign country without the prior permission of the sovereign.

The Queen was highly indignant and wrote to Earl Granville of 'her unfeigned astonishment at Mr Gladstone's want of *all knowledge*, apparently, of what is due to the Sovereign he serves'. Her Prime Minister, she went on, was 'one *not* gifted with prudence in speech' and 'not a person who can go about *where* he likes with impunity'. Relations between Britain and several of the other Great Powers were rather delicate, and his absence was not only inconvenient, but 'his presence at Copenhagen may be productive of much evil and certainly lead to misconstruction'.[4]

Gladstone apologised humbly for not seeking the customary permission, excusing himself on the grounds that he and his fellow voyagers had been encouraged 'to extend their views'. She grudgingly accepted his apology, while stressing that there were so many topics which could not be discussed with foreign sovereigns by the Prime Minister without prior consultation with her Foreign Secretary and the sanction of the sovereign. While she accepted his assurances that he would have avoided politics with the crowned heads he had met at Copenhagen, a man in his position did not have the freedom to move around like a private individual, especially when every step he made was bound to be reported; and any such trip would be bound to lead 'to political speculations which it is better to avoid'.[5]

Not without justification, he found her letter 'somewhat unmannerly'. In reply he regretted that he had not considered the likelihood of her displeasure, on the grounds that 'increasing weariness of mind under public cares for which he considers himself less and less fitted, may have blunted the faculty of anticipation, with which he was never very largely endowed'.[6] He told his private secretary, Sir Edward Hamilton, that the Queen was jealous of the deference paid to an old man of whom she strongly disapproved, while she still remained in seclusion most of the time.

Yet this was no more than a minor difference. The same may be said of a rather testy moment in the summer of 1884, when the Queen seemed to be taking an intense interest in every speech made by a member of her government, as well as in those by several of the backbenchers – and then writing to Gladstone to complain about them. During a six-week period he had to write her a total of sixteen letters, with a combined length of around 4,000 words, explaining, excusing and half-apologising for the speeches as he thought fit.[7] It provoked him into one of his rare moments of answering back under extreme exasperation, that Her Majesty would readily believe that he had 'neither the time nor the eyesight to make himself acquainted by careful perusal with all the speeches of his colleagues'.[8]

A far worse rupture had occurred the previous year, after his government proposed towards the end of 1883 to withdraw British troops from the Sudan, where a Muslim, Mohammed al-Mahdi, was leading a campaign to free Egypt from foreign domination. Hoping that the Mahdi would be overthrown, the Queen insisted that the Cabinet must take firm action at once. Several thousand Egyptian soldiers were killed by rebels, and General Charles Gordon, sent out to report on the situation, was besieged at Khartoum. The Queen tried to insist on rescuing him, warning the government that she 'trembled' for his safety, and that the consequences of any disaster would be catastrophic.

Of a less imperialistic frame of mind than his sovereign, Gladstone strongly believed that the Mahdi's forces were valiant freedom fighters, and he resented the jingoistic emotions that had been inspired in Britain by Gordon's mission. He and his Cabinet considered that the General was in a position to withdraw if he wanted, and it was up to him to do so at his discretion. Yet it was increasingly apparent that the public would not tolerate any further delay in trying to ease Gordon's plight, and in the summer of 1884 an expeditionary force was mobilised in Cairo. In October it began its advance up the Nile to Khartoum, arriving within sight of the town in January 1885, but it came two days too late. Khartoum had fallen, and in the ensuing massacre Gordon had been stabbed to death; his head was cut off and sent to the Mahdi, who had it hung on a tree for three days.

Outraged, the Queen sent identical telegrams *en clair* to Gladstone, War Minister Hartington and Foreign Secretary Granville: 'to think that all this might have been prevented and many precious lives saved by earlier action is too frightful.'[9] Gladstone firmly believed he was not to blame. Bitterly wounded by her reaction, he seriously considered resigning the premiership. A dissolution of parliament was due later that year, and he vowed that nothing would induce him to fight another general election.[10]

* * *

In June 1885 the government was defeated on a vote on the budget. Gladstone resigned as Prime Minister, and the Queen offered him an earldom, which he declined on the grounds that such future small services as he could render the country would be better done if he remained in the House of Commons. Perhaps he was aware that he would not be out of office for long.

Later that month, the Marquess of Salisbury was invited to form a Conservative administration. Salisbury had been Secretary of State for India during Disraeli's administration of 1874–80, then Foreign Secretary, in which capacity he accompanied Disraeli to the Congress of Berlin. On the latter's death he took over leadership of the parliamentary opposition in the House of Lords to Gladstone's Liberal government.

As a senior minister, Salisbury often expressed views that diverged from those of the Queen, and in September 1874 Sir Henry Ponsonby had noted that they were unlikely to see him at Balmoral, because 'he is too independent and speaks his mind too freely to be acceptable'.[11] However, when he visited Osborne the following January, she found him 'particularly agreeable and gentle, and [a person] who one could not believe could be so severe and sarcastic in debate'.[12]

In January 1886 Salisbury's government was defeated and he resigned office, turning down the Queen's offer of a dukedom. When his Cabinet surrendered their seals of office to the Queen at Osborne in February, she spoke to them firmly about their duty to fight the

Home Rule Bill, which to her was an irreversible measure that ran counter to her Coronation oath. To the Earl of Cranbrook, outgoing Lord President of Council, she said that they must 'agitate', adding that 'I do not like agitation, but we must agitate every place small as well as large and make people understand.' Before he took his leave of her, Salisbury assured her that 'in whatever position he was, he would do anything to help'.[13]

* * *

Gladstone's third, and brief, administration (February–July 1886) was dominated by his determination to secure the passing of the Home Rule Bill through parliament, repealing the Act of Union with Ireland and establishing a parliament in Dublin responsible for domestic affairs. It was a divisive move bitterly opposed by several members of his own party.

In her journal, the Queen noted that her outgoing Prime Minister 'feels so much for me, and for my being alone, so cut off'. Within a week, she was sending him 'very confidential' letters, including copies of correspondence from Gladstone and his ministers, and reports on the possibility of a Liberal breakaway by disaffected members. Early in May 1886 the struggle was rising towards its climax, and she was forwarding to Salisbury not only copies of all Gladstone's important letters, instructing him to return them, but also her own replies to Gladstone.

While it was an unconstitutional business which Sir Henry Ponsonby found embarrassing, Victoria considered herself justified in keeping Salisbury properly informed. In her view, as head of state, it was part of her duty to ensure the main party leaders were fully in touch with anything to do with the issue, though in this instance she was probably too much motivated by her hatred of the idea of home rule for Ireland to see that she was exceeding her constitutional limits. In effect, her action was akin to a conspiracy – if the term is not too strong – with the opposition against the party leader and head of government, and with his own colleagues.[14] She was fortunate that Gladstone, the Prime Minister so sinned against, was as fiercely loyal to the monarchy as he was. A less compliant prime minister might not have hesitated to provoke a crisis by publicly taking the sovereign to task – an action to which Lord Palmerston would perhaps have resorted some thirty years earlier.

Salisbury behaved correctly throughout, referring her gently to the Prime Minister, and never once giving her anything but the most temperate advice. Nevertheless, he and his sovereign both passionately believed that the ends of defeating home rule fully justified the unconstitutional means involved. Among Salisbury's colleagues, there was already talk that the issue might lead to civil war in Ireland, and Salisbury himself said that while he thought it unlikely, it might happen, and they 'must not desert the loyal people of Ulster'.[15]

Queen Victoria made no effort to disguise her impatience with what she saw as Gladstone's self-inflicted predicament. Shortly after Gladstone took office again, Ponsonby had the unenviable task of conveying the Queen's thoughts in writing to Lord Granville, the Colonial Secretary. 'The Queen read your letter,' he wrote, 'and on coming to the remark "considering the state of the Irish question which Gladstone has inherited" she observed – he inherited it because he wished it. He insisted on inheriting it and now complains of what he found.'[16]

Gladstone introduced the Home Rule Bill on 8 April, and after several weeks of debate it was defeated on the Second Reading on 8 June by 343 votes to 313, with 93 Liberals voting against. Queen Victoria's comment in her journal was restrained: 'Cannot help feeling relieved, and think it is best for the interests of the country.'[17] As Elizabeth Longford observed, her lack of triumphalism might have been due to a twinge of conscience. While she had been known to point out to her relatives throughout Europe that it was her constitutional duty to support the government of the day, for the previous few months she had done just the opposite.[18]

Gladstone asked for a dissolution of parliament, which the Queen granted without hesitation. Convinced that this would be the end of his career as prime minister, again she offered Gladstone an earldom, which again he declined. He resigned on 20 July, and ten days later he was summoned to the Isle of Wight for his farewell audience with the Queen. Both took care to avoid any reference to Ireland in their conversation. She thought he looked pale and nervous, while he considered that she had become 'seriously warped'. It would, he thought, be his last audience with her after fifty-five years in political life and 'a good quarter of a century's service to her in office'.[19] As such, he found it odd that she was un-willing to discuss any matters of importance with him, apart from civil list allowances for her grandchildren.

Any reticence on her part in speaking one-to-one was remedied the next day, when she put pen to paper. She had not, she wrote, liked 'to allude to the circumstances which led to his resignation' on the occasion of his visit, but she could not resist emphasising that the country had 'unequivocally decided against his plan' with regard to Irish home rule; and she trusted that 'his sense of patriotism may make him feel that the kindest and wisest thing he can do for Ireland is to abstain from encouraging agitation by public speeches'.[20]

* * *

In August Victoria welcomed Lord Salisbury back with some relief. She was convinced she had seen the last of Gladstone, who at seventy-six seemed increasingly frail. Though Salisbury was too down-to-earth to be able, or even try, to establish the uniquely theatrical relationship with her that Disraeli had done, she soon came to respect and admire him. His relaxed, slightly detached manner to the business of government and his lack of a Gladstonian obsession with causes appealed to her. So did his skilful approach to exalting, even exploiting, the Queen–Empress as an imperial symbol, a fitting subject for patriotism and unionism at the time of the jubilee celebrations in 1887 and 1897.

The feeling was mutual, though privately he found the task of serving her as onerous as several of his predecessors had done. When a colleague commiserated with him on the inevitable strain that being prime minister and foreign secretary must entail, he remarked that he could 'do very well with two Departments; in fact I have four – the Prime Ministership, the Foreign Office, the Queen and Randolph Churchill [his maverick Chancellor of the Exchequer]';[21] to another, he said ruefully that 'the burden of them increases in that order!'[22]

While Salisbury was always ready to defend the integrity of the royal family, he shared Ponsonby's reluctance to be dazzled by them. No egalitarian, he still looked on what he termed minor royals as 'minor irritations'. After a lady-in-waiting counted seventy-six members of British and European royalty in the south of France one summer, he complained to a colleague that the coast was 'tiresomely full of minute royalties – persons known only to the editor of the *Almanach de Gotha*'.[23] If the Queen was aware of such views, she never held it against him. By June 1890 she was assuring him that

'She need not say that he knows he possesses her confidence, and how anxious she is to support him in every way.'[24]

Under the circumstances, it was magnanimous of Gladstone to celebrate the Queen's golden jubilee as he did. On 30 August 1887 he gave a special tea to all the parishioners of his country seat of Hawarden, in a tent erected below the terrace in front of his house. All those the same age as the Queen, sixty-eight, and upwards, were invited, and around 250 were present. (Gladstone himself was in his seventy-eighth year at the time.) In a special address on the occasion he told them that it was 'not too much to say that the historian in future days, when he comes to write an account of this period in which we have lived, will point to the reign of Queen Victoria as the time in which the Sovereign of this country came finally and fully to understand the constitutional position and the great and noble conditions on which a free people can be governed, and not only to understand them but to accept them and to act upon them'.[25]

In June 1892 parliament was dissolved and a general election held the following month. Queen Victoria was pessimistic about the outcome, particularly the prospect of Gladstone returning to power for a fourth time. To the alarm of his followers, in the Court Circular she announced Lord Salisbury's resignation with regret, writing to Ponsonby that 'the idea of a deluded excited man of 82 trying to govern England and her vast Empire with the miserable democrats under him is quite ludicrous!'[26] Nevertheless, Gladstone emerged victorious, with the Liberals winning 273 seats and the Irish Nationalists 81, and one Labour member being returned, making a majority of 45 over 269 Conservatives and 46 Liberal Unionists. Salisbury waited to meet parliament and was defeated on 11 August on a vote of no confidence, after which his Conservative government resigned.

Two days later, Ponsonby conveyed to Gladstone the Queen's commission to form a new administration. Increasingly resistant to change, as well as to the mere idea of having to summon Gladstone yet again, the Queen wrote to Ponsonby of her 'utter disgust'. On previous occasions, changes of government had always made it 'painful to part with those one liked and esteemed', but at least 'it was to have to do with gentlemen like Lord Russell, Lord Palmerston', and a host of others who had served her in the past.[27] It was significant that the late and much-disliked Russell now compared favourably with her new *bête noire*. She briefly considered sending for Lord Rosebery, who had impressed her greatly when he served under Gladstone as Foreign Secretary – on his inclusion in Gladstone's administration in 1886, she had called it 'the only really *good* appointment'[28] – but he declined to accept office. He considered himself too young and inexperienced, and he was still grieving for his wife, whose death from typhoid at the age of thirty-nine, less than two years previously, had shattered him.

On assuming the position of prime minister for the fourth time, Gladstone asked Ponsonby to explain to the Queen that contrary to what she might believe, Home Rule was a very conservative policy, in that it would bring peace to Ireland and would turn the Irish into loyalists – and probably into Tories as well.

When Gladstone went to Osborne to kiss hands as prime minister, the Queen awaited his appearance with great trepidation. She found him much changed, walking rather bent, with a stick, 'his face shrunk, deadly pale, with a weird look in his eyes, a feeble expression about the mouth, and the voice altered'. He was unimpressed by the Queen and thought he had noticed a further deterioration in her since their last meeting. It seemed that her intellect had become sluggish and her judgement impaired. To his ministerial colleague Sir Algernon West he remarked afterwards that the interview had been as dismal as any that might have taken place between Marie Antoinette and her executioner, and 'not one sympathetic word, or any question, however detached'.[29]

She would have been encouraged to know that he would only hold office for another eighteen months. On 23 February 1894 Ponsonby paid him a visit at Downing Street and was requested by him to ask the Queen if he might write to her in confidence. At first, the Queen feared that her Prime Minister was going to ask for a dissolution, intending to go to the country with an appeal for the abolition of the House of Lords. She was thoroughly alarmed, until Gladstone wrote to her with the news that he was planning to resign office, 'on physical grounds'. On 28 February he saw her at Buckingham Palace, where she had come to 'hold a drawing-room' (a Court reception). In his diary, he noted afterwards that she 'had much difficulty in finding topics for an adequate prolongation . . . . I thought I never saw her looking better. She was at the highest point of her cheerfulness. Her manner was personally kind throughout.'[30]

He held his last cabinet on 1 March, and on the next day the Queen invited Mr and Mrs Gladstone to dine at Windsor and stay the night. After breakfast, Mrs Gladstone saw the Queen privately and told her, with tears in her eyes, that whatever his errors, her husband had always been devoted to the Queen. On receiving his formal letter of resignation, the Queen wrote to him, trusting that he would 'be able to enjoy peace and quiet, with his excellent and devoted wife, in health and happiness'. She added that she would gladly have conferred a peerage on him, but she knew he would not accept it.[31]

Although Gladstone was her least-liked Prime Minister, it has been argued by one of his biographers, Sir Philip Magnus, that his greatest failure – his relationship with the Queen – ironically proved to be his most enduring success. He cut a new pattern of constitutional monarchy which was rejected by her but 'triumphantly followed by all her successors'. His achievement was to transform the Crown politically into a rubber stamp, yet at the same time enhance to an incalculable degree the force of its moral and emotional appeal.[32]

On Gladstone's retirement the Queen sent for Lord Rosebery. By far the youngest of her Prime Ministers (only forty-five when he took office) and the only one who was born during her reign, in personality he was quite similar to her. His 'nerves' and chronic shyness at their first audience pleased the monarch. (In later life, he would say that the only two people who had thoroughly frightened him were Queen Victoria and Prince Bismarck.)[33] His imperialistic views were also closer to her own than those of Gladstone. When she had seen him privately after he accepted office as foreign secretary again under Gladstone eighteen months earlier, he found that she spoke to him 'quite maternally', especially when she told him that she thought the work would do him good, and he answered sadly that he had nobody to look after his children.[34] Soon afterwards he had made a series of speeches which aroused her wrath, and she complained bitterly to Ponsonby that one such address was 'radical to a degree to be almost communistic'. Previously, she said, he had claimed he had nothing whatever to do with home rule, only with foreign affairs, 'and *now* he is as violent as any one . . . . Sir Henry must try and get at him through some one, so that he may know how grieved and shocked The Queen is at what he said.' If the government was to go down to sudden defeat she meant to send for him first, but after his 'violent attack on Lord Salisbury' and his 'attempt to stir up Ireland', she would find it impossible.[35]

Evidently Ponsonby, or someone else, communicated the royal displeasure, for Rosebery was soon back in favour. In August 1893, at an audience with him, Victoria told him she wished he was prime minister, and when he had told her that he might be accepting the vacant viceroyalty of India, she suggested that he was indispensable as regards her government at home, as he was the only one of the ministry with whom she could talk freely.

Seven months later, her wish had come true. Ponsonby, who brought to Rosebery the Queen's letter asking him to form a government, passed on the news from her that she was 'immensely delighted'. Whether her delight was at having the Foreign Secretary as prime minister or at being assured that 'the G.O.M.' (the Grand Old Man, as she sometimes referred to Gladstone) would not hold high office again, one must wonder. At the same time she wrote to Lord Rowton, asking him to tell Salisbury that 'her wish to see him again at the head of affairs is as great as ever', but she could not act differently than she had done, as the Liberal government still had a majority in the House of Commons.[36] On 5 March Rosebery kissed hands on his appointment as prime minister. The task she had entrusted to him, he told her, 'was very difficult, and not what he would have wished to undertake, but I repeated that he was the only person in the Government I considered suited to the post, and in whom I had absolute confidence'.[37]

As prime minister, Rosebery found his relations with the Queen were not untroubled. He recognised that she was personally sympathetic to him, though hostile to his ministry. 'She does not object to Liberal measures which are not revolutionary,' she assured him, '& she does not think it possible that Lord Rosebery will destroy well tried, valued & necessary institutions for the sole purpose of flattering useless Radicals or pandering to the pride of those whose only desire is their own self gratification.'[38]

Nevertheless, his was a thorny premiership. Within a week of taking office, he was finding it impossible to please everyone – or indeed almost anyone. During a House of Lords debate on the Queen's Speech, he dismayed his followers, as well as the Nationalists, by as good as agreeing with an address by Lord Salisbury assuring him of a hearty welcome and saying that Home

Rule was now in suspense: 'England as the predominant member of the partnership of the Three Kingdoms will have to be convinced of its justice and equity.'[39] *The Times* asserted that Rosebery had at one blow shattered the fabric of Liberal policy.[40] When the radical Henry Labouchere proposed an amendment to the address which virtually abolished the power of the House of Lords, the Queen delivered a furious rebuke to Rosebery, accusing him of being negligent towards the Whips. It prompted him and his Cabinet colleague Sir William Harcourt to comment that the spirit of George III survived in his granddaughter.[41]

He needed to tread carefully, retaining his position by virtue of a slender majority in the Commons while never losing sight of the fact that he was distrusted by the Liberal Party rank and file. He once lamented being pledged to Gladstonian policies, 'shut up in a House almost unanimously opposed to his ministry'.[42] In an address at Bradford he referred to the House of Lords as a 'permanent barrier against the Liberal Party', promptly bringing forth the Queen's disapproval. 'She fully realises the extreme difficulty of his position,' she wrote to him, 'having inherited some such (as she must call them) dangerous & almost destructive measures from his Predecessor, which she deeply regrets. But she still hopes that he will act as a check & drag upon his Cabinet. What she would however wish to say, speaking *very* openly to him, is that in his Speeches out of Parliament he should take a more serious tone, & be, if she may say so, less jocular, which is hardly befitting a Prime Minister.'[43]

Yet he would not be deflected from his theme. At another address in Bradford, on 27 October, he said that the next election would be fought not on disestablishment of the Church, home rule or the liquor question, but the House of Lords, which was 'a great national danger'. It was intolerable, he went on, that the Liberal Party should have to go cap in hand to the House of Lords to ask it to enact further legislation. 'We fling down the gauntlet; it is for you to back us up.'[44] Horrified, the Queen appealed to Lord Salisbury for advice, asking whether the Conservative and Unionist Party was 'fit for a dissolution *now*?'[45] Rosebery, she wrote, had committed a grave impropriety by not consulting her, 'not to speak of not obtaining her sanction', before advocating such far-reaching changes in the British constitution. Earlier in the year, she had stressed to him that the House of Lords 'might possibly be improved, but it is *part and parcel* of the *much vaunted* and *admired* British Constitution, and *cannot* be *abolished*'.[46] Rosebery denied this, pointing out that he had made the speech to a partisan audience of over 5,000, and he could hardly be expected to argue points under such circumstances 'in the style appropriate to a drawing room or a library'. On 3 November Ponsonby was requested to inform Rosebery that the Queen would never consent to such a resolution being tabled without an appeal to the country.

Four days later, at another audience with the Queen, Rosebery deliberately turned the conversation to the matter of the House of Lords but said that if a resolution on the subject of diminishing their powers was tabled, it would only be in a very mild form. Though mollified, the Queen was still extremely irritated with him. 'He never really seemed to know his own mind,' she remarked to another senior Liberal, Sir Henry James, a couple of years later. She said that when she scolded him for taking up so strong a position against the House of Lords, he said that she need not be troubled, as his views had fallen so flat in the country. This, she considered, was not 'a right position' for her Prime Minister to adopt, 'and I was not sorry when he was turned out'.[47]

In the following month she wrote to him at some length on the issue. He was mistaken, she said, 'in thinking that *any dealing with the H. of L.*' is distasteful to her'. She fully recognised the necessity for reform and would be interested to know the broad outlines of his plan of reconstruction. It was not 'a mere question of policy' but, as he appreciated, *'a question of enormous importance'*, a *'question of the revision of the entire constitution'*, and she believed that her sanction for its public declaration should have been obtained. Fifty-seven years ago, she reminded him, 'the Constitution was delivered into her keeping and that right or wrong she has her views as to the fulfillment of that trust. She cannot but think Lord Rosebery will feel that *his* position is not the only difficult one in these democratic days.'[48]

With this, the matter was left in abeyance, but it was not the end of Rosebery's differences with the Queen. In a speech he gave in Glasgow in late November, he proclaimed Scottish disestablishment as a permanent part of the Liberal programme. While the manses may or may not be Tory agencies, he went on, the Established Church was unrepresentative of Scotland as a whole. The Queen regarded any moves to meddle with the Church, as she saw it, just as provocative as some of Rosebery's pronouncements on the House of Lords. Once again, she drew his attention to her oath on accession to the throne, and warned him that she would do everything within her power to be true to her promise.

Within a few weeks, Rosebery's health was on the verge of breaking down. The strain of high office during the previous months, acute insomnia and an attack of influenza all left him greatly weakened. In addition, he had been deeply affected by the suicide of Lord Drumlanrig, his assistant private secretary, a son of the Marquess of Queensberry (one of the architects of Oscar Wilde's downfall in 1895), and fears that any scandal might implicate him and result in questions as to his private life, even hinting at a homosexual liaison between himself and Drumlanrig. Various crises and defeats in parliament plagued the government throughout spring and early summer, and after only fifteen months as prime minister he resigned on 23 June 1895.

Five days later, he had his final audience with the Queen, at which she invested him with the Order of the Thistle. Afterwards she noted that he was 'much attached' to her personally, and in certain respects she preferred him as a person, if not his politics, to Salisbury.[49] Rosebery's overwhelming feeling was one of relief. A comment on resignation from his biography of Sir Robert Peel, which he published four years later, will suffice. He believed that there were two supreme pleasures in life, one ideal, the other real: 'The ideal is when a man receives the seals of office from his Sovereign. The real pleasure comes when he hands them back.'[50]

* * *

At the subsequent elections, a Liberal majority of 43 was overturned with a Unionist majority of 152. Lord Salisbury became Prime Minister again, and he remained in office until after Queen Victoria's death five and a half years later. 'It is easy to see that she [the Queen] is very fond of him,' his daughter-in-law, Violet, noted at one of their tea parties in the south of France, 'indeed I never saw two people get on better, their polished manners and deference to and esteem for each other were a delightful sight and one not readily to be forgotten.'[51] On holidays there they attended church together, and sometimes at home the Queen would arrive at Beaulieu for lunch with very little notice. Though Salisbury lacked the courtliness and vividly witty conversation of Melbourne or Disraeli, he shared their non-interventionist, rather laid-back attitude to governance of the kingdom which appealed to the Queen.

William Boyd Carpenter, Chaplain to the Queen in her last years and Bishop of Ripon from 1884 to 1911, realised that she held Salisbury in high esteem. She often spoke with admiration of him, the Chaplain noticed, 'as of one in whom she had great confidence'. The impression he had 'was that she gave him, if not the highest, an equal place with the highest among her ministers'. The two prime ministers of her reign whom she praised most were Salisbury and Peel. Of the latter she 'spoke with very warm and grateful affection', particularly on account of the kindness he had personally shown her, and the trouble he took in helping her to purchase Osborne as a royal residence. She and Prince Albert, she said, 'owed it to him that we got this place'.[52]

Curiously, the spell of Disraeli had faded to some extent by this time. When Boyd Carpenter asked her whether she regarded his novel *Coningsby* as a book which gave a fairly correct picture of the English at its time, she looked blankly at him, as if not knowing how to reply. Then she pursed her lips, remarking in a quizzical manner, 'I didn't care for his novels.'[53] It was as if she had come to revise her opinions with hindsight, and as if Albert's scepticism about the rising young politician of the 1840s whom he had regarded with such distaste had come to influence her judgements once more.

In their last years, Salisbury and the Queen were both increasingly deaf. Once, when he came to Balmoral – with great reluctance, and only after his secretary had contacted Arthur Bigge (assistant secretary to Sir Henry Ponsonby) to request that his room should be kept at a minimum temperature of 60 degrees Fahrenheit – the household were amused to come across sovereign and Prime Minister sitting in different rooms on opposite sides of the corridor, shouting at each other so that every word could be overheard.

The Queen and her old adversary Gladstone were destined to come face to face once more, at Cannes, in March 1897. She and her daughter Louise were both spending a few days on the Riviera that spring, and Louise took the opportunity to invite the former prime minister and his wife to tea with her. They then joined the Queen for a few minutes. At eighty-eight, he was extremely frail, and the sight of the old man moved Victoria to pity. She gave him her hand, which he noted she had never done before in her life. He

109

too was struck by the change in her and thought that her 'peculiar faculty and habit of conversation had disappeared'.[54]

Although Gladstone was now the senior surviving privy councillor, he was not invited to take part in any of the diamond jubilee celebrations. While some might have regarded this as an unwarranted slight, by this time his health was too poor to allow him to venture far without considerable physical discomfort. Moreover, the general tone of the proceedings was thought to be too imperialist in tone for a statesman who hardly held the empire in thrall to enjoy. The Colonial Secretary, Joseph Chamberlain, a Liberal and republican firebrand some twenty years earlier, had now become one of the most loyal members of Her Majesty's government, and it was partly on his initiative that the diamond jubilee became 'a festival of empire', with prime ministers from the larger colonies invited to take part, in preference to foreign monarchs from Europe, who were not invited. Gladstone would no doubt have felt ill at ease with such an arrangement.

After a short illness, he died on 19 May 1898, aged eighty-eight. 'He was very clever and full of ideas for the bettering and advancement of the country, always most loyal to me personally, and ready to do anything for the Royal Family,' the Queen wrote in her journal, 'but alas! I am sure involuntarily, he did at times a good deal of harm.'[55] Nine days later, on the day of his funeral, she telegraphed his widow a graceful tribute, saying in conclusion that she would always 'gratefully remember his devotion and zeal in all that concerned my personal welfare, and that of my family.'[56]

'I cannot say that I think he was 'a great Englishman', she wrote to the Empress Frederick. 'He was a clever man, full of talent, but he never *tried* to keep up the *honour* and *prestige* of Great Britain. He gave away the Transvaal, he abandoned Gordon, he destroyed the Irish Church and tried to separate England from Ireland and to set class against class. The harm he did cannot easily be undone.'[57]

* * *

By the summer of 1900 Salisbury's burdens of office were of increasing concern to his colleagues and sovereign alike, and he appeared unduly apathetic over the course of the Boer war. Out of a strong sense of duty to the throne and to the Queen personally, he was reluctant to relinquish the Foreign Office, though he was heard to comment that if she asked him to resign as foreign secretary, he would. For her part, the Queen said she would press him to stay, unless he and his doctors were sure the workload he was carrying must be reduced. His nephew, Arthur Balfour, said his health would not permit him to keep both offices. Faced with this stalemate, during the autumn the Queen proposed to send Aretas Akers-Douglas, a privy councillor and close friend of Salisbury's, to consult him at Hatfield on the problem. 'She shrinks from the task of telling him she thinks he ought to go,' he wrote to Balfour.[58]

In the end, Salisbury retained both offices. He might have sensed that his sovereign would also be laying down her burdens soon enough and was reluctant to commit himself to any change, especially if doing so would cause problems for her successor.

On 12 November 1900 the Queen presided over what would be the last privy council of her reign at Windsor. Salisbury's government had been returned in the elections of the previous month with another large majority, and the new ministers were to be sworn in. Almeric Fitzroy, the new clerk to the council, was astonished by the businesslike manner in which their elderly sovereign 'guided us through the mazes of a somewhat intricate transaction whereon official records were dumb, and the recollections of ministers a blank'.[59]

It was all the more remarkable as her health had already started to fail by this time. Within a few weeks her decline was evident to all. Ten weeks later, on 22 January 1901, she was dead. It fell to Salisbury, in his address of condolence and congratulation to the new monarch, King Edward VII, in the House of Lords on 25 January, to announce that he had 'to perform by far the saddest duty that has ever befallen me'. He went on to say that 'We are echoing the accents of sorrow which reach us from every part of the Empire and every part of the globe and which express the deep and heartfelt feeling – a feeling, deeper than I ever remember – of the sorrow at the singular loss which, under the dispensation of Divine Providence, we have suffered, and of admiration for the glorious reign and the splendid character of the Sovereign whom we have lost.' Hers had been an age during which the power of the Crown had diminished. Even so, he acknowledged, 'she showed a wonderful power on the one hand, of maintaining a steady and persistent influence on the action of her Ministers in the course of legislation and government, which no one could mistake'.[60]

Rosebery, the only surviving former prime minister to serve under her, also paid his own graceful tribute. At a meeting of the Royal Scottish Corporation on 30 January, he said that 'It is not hyperbole to say that in the whole history of mankind no death has touched so large a number of the inhabitants of the globe as the death of our late Sovereign.'[61]

PART THREE

Servants

SEVEN

'He is very dependable'

Of all the men who made a significant impact on the life of Queen Victoria, none was to prove more controversial than her Highland servant or ghillie, John Brown, and since their deaths none has provoked more wild speculation or even innuendo as to the extent of their relationship. Only a year before her marriage, she had been spoken of disrespectfully as 'Mrs Melbourne'. By the mid-1860s, within three or four years of her husband's death, to some she was known behind her back as 'Mrs Brown' or even 'the Empress Brown'.

John Brown was born in December 1826 into a relatively wealthy farming family at Crathie, near Balmoral, the second of eleven children. His father, also named John, had been a schoolmaster (and, it is thought, author of a *Deeside Guide*) until he married, when he took up farming. The younger John received a thorough education at the local parish school, though like the rest of the family he was a sturdy outdoor type, more at home with a gun or fishing rod in his hand than a book or newspaper. As a young man, and one of a large family, he needed to support himself as soon as he could go out and work. At first, he was an ostler's helper at a coaching inn near Ballater, then worked as a pony herder on the Balmoral estate leased by Sir Robert Gordon, owner of the property until his death in 1847. Like the other ghillies employed in a similar capacity, he kept his job after Queen Victoria and Prince Albert leased the property.

The first mention of John Brown in the Queen's journals appears in the entry for 11 September 1849. One day on their second holiday at Balmoral, she and Albert were setting out from Altnaguithsach to the hills behind Glen Muich. During their previous excursions they had been slightly unnerved by the passage of their carriage on narrow mountain roads, and Albert decided that they would be safer if an undergroom was to ride on the box and keep the vehicle steady. At twenty-two years of age, Brown, the youngest and sturdiest of the ghillies, was chosen for the task. Two years later, he was entrusted with leading the Queen's pony on all the royal couple's Highland expeditions.

Even at this stage, he was taking on further responsibilities with regard to Her Majesty's well-being. When the royal family went out for picnics, he usually brewed the Queen's pot of tea. On one such outing during his earlier years, she commented that he had given her the best cup of tea she had ever tasted. He answered that it should have been, as he put 'a grand nip o' whisky in it'.[1]

As a local newspaper later remarked, Prince Albert was 'struck by his magnificent physique, his transparent honesty, and straightforward, independent character'.[2] If Queen Victoria was impressed by the good looks of this young man, so were some of her contemporaries. Five years later a young lady-in-waiting, the Hon. Eleanor Stanley, was writing home with enthusiasm to her family about 'the most fascinating and good-looking young Highlander, Johnny Brown'.[3]

When the royal family left Balmoral in the autumn of 1861, Brown seemed strangely reluctant for the family to go south. He told them that he hoped they would have no illness during the winter and return safely the following year, and above all trusted that there would be no deaths in the family. Earlier that year Victoria had lost her mother, the Duchess of Kent. Within a few weeks, the Prince Consort would have passed away as well.

In the dark days immediately following her husband's death, the Queen saw very little of Brown except at Balmoral. He distinguished himself with his level-headed behaviour one evening in October 1863 when they were returning to the castle from a carriage ride to Loch Muick. The driver had evidently fortified himself on that cold autumn day with something from his flask more interesting than the broth and boiled potatoes of which everybody else had partaken. As Queen Victoria noted afterwards, he was 'quite confused', lost his way in the darkness and drove so badly that he took the carriage onto very rough ground. It overturned with the passengers inside, and only the quick thinking of John Brown, who leapt clear as soon as he saw what was happening, saved the situation. He rescued the ladies, cut the traces to release the horses, produced some more alcoholic refreshment to soothe jangled nerves and sent the driver (possibly sobered up after seeing the gravity of what he had done) back on foot to procure some ponies. The bruised Queen had to have her head bandaged afterwards, while the negligent driver's royal employment was terminated forthwith; John Brown was very much the man of the moment.

Towards the end of 1864 he began to assume a more significant role in Victoria's life. That winter she was at Osborne, and her personal physician, Dr William Jenner, thought it would be good for her to take up riding again. It was agreed that a new groom would never do, and Brown, with his many years of invaluable service to the Queen and the Prince Consort in the Highlands, would probably be the most suitable aide. As someone who had been so well thought of by Prince Albert, he might be able to raise her spirits and ease her chronic mood of depression.

In December 1864 he arrived, ostensibly in order to lead her pony, Flora. Within two months he had proved his worth, and in her journal she noted that he 'should remain permanently & make himself useful in other ways besides leading my pony as he is so very dependable'.[4] A memorandum dated 4 February 1865 conferred on Brown the official status of 'The Queen's Highland Servant', to take orders from nobody but Her Majesty, and to attend her indoors and out. He was to continue cleaning her boots, skirts and cloaks, unless this proved too much. Some of these menial tasks which he was expected to perform, such as looking after her dogs and cleaning her boots, were dropped by the end of the year. Already she had promised him a cottage at Balmoral in the event of his marriage. Now, if he was to marry and wanted a cottage in the south, her promise would be strictly honoured.[5] He was engaged at a salary of £120 per annum, raised to £150 at the end of 1866, to £230 plus £70 for clothes in 1869, and £310 shortly afterwards.

At first he reported to her twice a day, after breakfast and after luncheon, for 'his orders – & every thing is always right – he is so quiet, has such an excellent head & memory', she wrote to her eldest daughter, Victoria, the Crown Princess of Prussia. 'It is an excellent arrangement, & I feel I have here always in the house a good, devoted Soul . . . . whose only object & interest is my service, & God knows how much I want to be taken care of.'[6]

It was only a matter of time before these meetings took on a more personal atmosphere, as the Queen found herself taking more and more pleasure in Brown's company. He was reliable, plain-spoken and intelligent, if not exactly learned or intellectual, and ready to devote himself entirely to her. Within a year or two, he started learning German, so he could understand what her relations were saying. Any who thought they could get away with conversing in their second language and leaving him in the dark were in for a surprise. Lord Melbourne and Prince Albert had both willingly given her their undivided attention. For the first time since she had become a widow, another man was prepared to do the same.

It was 'a *real* comfort,' she wrote to King Leopold soon after his appointment, 'for he is so devoted to me – so simple, so intelligent, *so unlike* an *ordinary* servant'.[7]

Perhaps, she believed naively, he was not really an ordinary servant. If there was a way of dispelling his ordinariness, she would do so, or at least find somebody who could assist in the matter. Accordingly, she asked Dr Andrew Robertson, the Crathie physician who had originally delivered the illustrious second child of John and Margaret Brown in the family cottage at Crathienaird in 1826. Robertson knew as well as anybody else that Brown was of peasant stock, and that his forebears had been agricultural workers. Aware that this would not do for Her Majesty, he applied some artistic licence to a supposed link between his own, rather more exalted, family tree and John Brown's grandmother Janet Shaw.[8] With a little imagination he produced a four-page copperplate account for the Queen, demonstrating that her Highland servant was indeed of rather better birth than had been previously supposed.

Within two years, the Queen's friendship with Brown was laying her open to serious criticism. In June 1866 he was blamed for delaying her at Balmoral during a ministerial crisis and keeping her from returning to London. This in itself may have seemed trivial to some. But it was a different matter entirely when a Swiss newspaper, the *Gazette de Lausanne*, published a report that September. In it an anonymous correspondent wrote that the Queen had cancelled diary appointments because she was expecting a child by John Brown, to whom she had been morganatically married 'for a long time'.[9] If she was not present for the Volunteers Review and at the inauguration of the monument to Prince Albert, the report continued, it was only in order to hide her pregnancy.

The British minister at Berne, the Hon. E.A.J. Harris, immediately lodged a formal complaint against the newspaper with the Swiss Federal Council, which did nothing. He would have been wiser to let the matter rest, for his action had the predictable but unfortunate

Edward, Duke of Kent, Princess Victoria's father. He died when she was eight months old.

Princess Victoria, aged about ten, 1829.

Prince Albert of Saxe-Coburg; engraving by Dalton after a painting by Franz Xaver Winterhalter.

King Leopold of the Belgians, Queen Victoria's uncle and 'second father'.

Queen Victoria at her first Council of State, surrounded by Privy Councillors. These include Ernest, Duke of Cumberland (with hand raised, seated behind table), the Duke of Wellington (standing on his left), the Earl of Sussex (seated in front, with cap), and the Prime Minister, Lord Melbourne (at end of table, holding papers and pen); engraving after the painting by David Wilkie.

Albert, Prince Consort, and Queen Victoria, *c.* 1859.

The Albert Memorial, Kensington Gardens, London, designed by Sir Gilbert Scott and unveiled in March 1876.

Sir Robert Peel.

Lord John Russell.

Henry John Temple, Viscount Palmerston.

Benjamin Disraeli, Earl of Beaconsfield.

Punch's comment on the Queen's proclamation as Empress of India by Disraeli, May 1876.

William Ewart Gladstone.

Robert Gascoyne-Cecil, Marquess of Salisbury.

Archibald Philip Primrose, Earl of Rosebery.

Queen Victoria on her pony, with John Brown, her controversial Highland servant.

Sir Henry Ponsonby, *c.* 1880, the Queen's indefatigable Private Secretary for nearly 25 years.

Sir James Reid, the Queen's doctor and much respected confidant during her last years, December 1901. *(Copyright reserved to HM the Queen)*

Abdul Karim, the Queen's Munshi (secretary). *(Copyright reserved to HM the Queen)*

Albert Edward, Prince of Wales, his mother's heir from birth.

'A Brown Study', from *Tomahawk*, August 1867; a satirical impression of John Brown and Queen Victoria, represented by an obsequious lion.

Queen Victoria with the Prince and Princess of Wales at around the time of her golden jubilee, summer 1887.

Alfred, Duke of Edinburgh, later Duke of Saxe-Coburg Gotha.

Crown Prince Frederick William of Germany, later Emperor Frederick III.

Arthur, Duke of Connaught and Strathearn.

Leopold, Duke of Albany.

Prince Louis of Hesse and the Rhine.

John Douglas Sutherland, Marquess of Lorne, later Duke of Argyll.

Prince Christian of Schleswig-Holstein.

Queen Victoria with Princess Beatrice, Prince Henry of Battenberg, and their two elder children, Alexander and Victoria Eugenia.

effect of giving the gossip a wider audience throughout much of Europe, gossip which has continued almost unabated to the present day. However, most of the British press loyally ignored the story. Even the socialist radical weekly *Reynolds Newspaper*, which generally took a thoroughly anti-monarchist stance, refrained from mentioning it.

Henry Ponsonby, by this time an equerry, told his brother that they did not know what the libel was, and he imagined the Queen to be as ignorant as the rest of them: 'I believe it to be a statement that she has married John Brown, and the idea that it could be said she was marrying one of her servants would make her angry and wretched.'[10] Later he said that the Queen was aware of the libel and had laughed at it, saying she was sorry any notice had been taken of it. Though Queen Victoria had more of a sense of humour than she was often given credit for, it is open to question whether she would have treated such an undignified assertion as a laughing matter.

It was rumoured that Brown had a hold on the Queen because he had been endowed with unique psychic powers, and that she used him as a spiritualist medium to contact Prince Albert in the spirit world. Gossips averred that she was convinced the Prince's spirit had somehow been passed on to her Highland servant, and she believed he was her late husband's living embodiment. It was also said that John Brown was married to another woman altogether. At one time he was believed to have taken Miss Ocklee, one of the Queen's dressers and his regular dancing partner at Balmoral, as his wife, a belief which persisted until she married a man from the Steward's department in 1873. After Brown's death, a pamphlet in general circulation stated that he had married a girl from his native valley.

At home, satirical journalists were beginning to take notice. The well-established, generally good-natured but sometimes quite sharp *Punch* and the shortlived, more anarchic *Tomahawk*, which was launched in May 1867 (and folded within three years), both lampooned the Queen and her servant mercilessly. In 1866 the former published a spoof Court Circular:

Balmoral, Tuesday.
Mr John Brown walked on the slopes.
He subsequently partook of a haggis.
In the evening Mr John Brown was pleased to listen to a bagpipe.
Mr John Brown retired early.[11]

Such satire was mild when seen beside the savagery of its dis-respectful young competitor. In August 1867 *Tomahawk* published a cartoon entitled 'A Brown Study'. This portrayed a sinister-looking John Brown leaning against the throne as he smoked a clay pipe, with the Queen's Crown resting underneath a glass bell in the background. In the foreground, looking up somewhat meekly at Brown, was the British lion.

Though Victoria's relationship with Brown gave rise to much unsavoury innuendo at the time, modern historians have taken a more detached view. As Dorothy Thompson has suggested, the reaction of a modern feminist to a widowed queen in her forties taking a lover would probably be on the lines of 'So what?' The choice would nonetheless have embarrassed or distressed members of Victoria's own family. However, such a close liaison with a man who was a social inferior, yet who lacked political ambition and only made modest personal demands on the sovereign, would be far preferable to any such relationship with someone else from the upper classes or a member of a foreign royal family, around whom political suspicions would inevitably have gathered.[12] Three of Victoria's Hanoverian predecessors on the throne (Kings George I, II and IV) had mistresses during their married lives, and the latter two outlived their wives by several years, during which time the mistresses remained at Court. George II was said to have wept at his wife's deathbed, and when she told him he should marry again, he reassured her brokenly between sobs that he would still have mistresses. It stretches the imagination considerably to picture Queen Victoria even contemplating, while Prince Albert was on his deathbed, that she would take lovers after he was gone.

The Queen's fervent relationship with Brown was simply another instance of her constant quest for a father-figure. John Brown may have been seven and a half years younger than her, but she found in him as an adult, and a very handsome man in his prime, the qualities she needed. Her passionate nature probably did not require physical relief, and unless she was a hypocrite, it is difficult if not impossible to imagine her being unfaithful to the memory of her 'beloved angel'. All she wanted and needed was intense, undivided attention and affection producing a sense of safety and comfort. 'My poor old birthday, my 51st!' she wrote in her journal in 1870. 'Alone, alone, as it will ever be! But surely, my dearest one blesses me.'[13]

Herbert Tingsten believed that Elizabeth Longford's theory of Queen Victoria's lack of sensuality was not wholly convincing, and that it seems unreasonable to assume the Queen could never have allowed herself to fall into the arms of her servant without feeling she would have to marry him afterwards. It can hardly be assumed that, had the Queen felt obliged to marry a second time, a sense of propriety would have ruled out marriage with her Highland servant. On the contrary, to take this argument to its logical conclusion, had an intimate relationship developed between them, propriety would all the more have required her to marry him.[14]

The trickle of 'Queen Victoria married John Brown' stories, supported by new so-called evidence that has just miraculously been unearthed, has never abated and probably never will. At least they provide lively, if futile, speculation for those who are interested enough to indulge their somewhat over-developed imaginations.

In 1979 Dr Micheil MacDonald, curator of the Museum of Scottish Tartans, Perthshire, claimed after ten years' research that the Queen and Brown were married and had a child. This rested partly on interviews with the relations of those who lived in or near the Queen's residences, and particularly on a tape-recorded account of an eye-witness who heard the deathbed confession of a church minister who was said to have officiated at the marriage ceremony. This supposed child of the relationship lived as a recluse in Paris until the age of ninety, returning from time to time to visit Balmoral. Dr MacDonald saw the royal widow of forty-two as 'a frightened little girl who hid behind the weeds of widowhood to avoid life's realities',[15] and Brown was the only one who could guide her through this extremely difficult time.

At least two more instances have been recorded since 1979. One was by a daughter of one of the Queen's chaplains who allegedly married her to Brown (how many different clergymen have been reputed to have performed this ceremony, one wonders), and another was by the diarist James Lees-Milne, who lunched with an elderly daughter of the late royal doctor Sir James Reid who claimed that she was confident the Queen slept with Brown.[16]

Another rumour came into circulation more than a century after the Queen's death. While rummaging in the Royal Archives at Windsor, the historian Sir Steven Runciman had apparently found a marriage certificate confirming that Victoria had been through such a ceremony with John Brown. He showed it to Queen Elizabeth, the

121

Queen Mother, who grabbed it and threw it on to a blazing fire. Runciman and Queen Elizabeth had both died not long before this story appeared in the press, but such an account could surely convince none but the most gullible. Any scholar or researcher granted access to the Royal Archives is only permitted to see specific documents relevant to their particular area of interest. As a medieval historian, Runciman would not have been handed any Victorian documents, let alone had the freedom to 'rummage' through unsorted piles which might have contained such a controversial item – if indeed such an item had ever been preserved, let alone existed in the first place.[17]

As Queen of Great Britain, and answerable to nobody else in the kingdom, she could in theory marry any man she wanted to, now that she was a widow. A few years later, in 1880, her fellow-sovereign, Tsar Alexander II of Russia, secretly married his mistress, Catherine Dolgorouky, and the mother of his three youngest children, six weeks after his Empress consort died and in the face of severe disapproval, if not outright condemnation, from most of his family. Queen Victoria could therefore have disregarded the weight of family and public opinion and made Brown her husband.

Yet in practice, she would never have gone against the grain in such a way. Any theory of a secret marriage does not fit the pattern of the portrait of her which has emerged from her journals and letters over the years. Tempting and highly amusing as it might be for gossips and republicans to imagine one of the great icons of British monarchy in bed with a Highland servant, whether she was wearing his ring on her finger or not, even her worst enemies would never have accused her of such hypocrisy.

Perhaps the last word, for now, should go to Sir Frederick Ponsonby, an assistant private secretary to Queen Victoria at the time of her death and devoted (though not always uncritical) servant to King Edward VII and King George V until his own death in 1935. In his posthumous memoirs, he noted that while the numerous stories about the Queen and John Brown were untrue, he did not completely rule out 'some grain of truth' in the idea that he might have been something more than a faithful servant to her. When he mentioned the rumour to several people in the household that they were secretly married, they all laughed at the idea. The Duchess of Roxburghe, who was said to have been present at a secret marriage ceremony, told him emphatically that it was a mere fabrication inspired by those who wished to ridicule the monarchy. While there was something to be said for the 'no smoke without fire' theory, Ponsonby said, he was convinced that if there had ever been 'any quite unconscious sexual feeling' in Queen Victoria's regard for John Brown, he believed it was unconscious on both sides,.and 'their relations up to the last were simply those of employer and devoted retainer'.[18]

* * *

In May 1867 the Royal Academy of Arts Spring Exhibition included an equestrian picture by Sir Edwin Landseer, entitled 'Her Majesty at Osborne, 1866'. It showed Queen Victoria reading a despatch while sitting side-saddle on her pony, Flora, while the red despatch boxes, other documents and her gloves lay on the ground. Holding the horse's bridle was the unmistakable form of the Queen's Highland servant. The *Saturday Review* felt it was a great mistake for such a painting to be exhibited, remarking in its review of the show that while they respected the privacy of Her Majesty, Landseer was inadvertently doing more harm to her popularity than he could imagine. The *Illustrated London News* agreed that it was an unfortunate painting, and that they hoped it would not be deemed disloyal to the sovereign or to the painter's reputation to say that none of Her Majesty's subjects would see 'this lugubrious picture without regret',[19] while the *Saturday Review* wrote that if anyone was to stand beside it for a quarter of an hour and listen to visitors' comments, 'he will learn how great an imprudence has been committed'.[20] Far from sharing such views, the Queen was so impressed by the painting that she ordered Landseer to make an engraving of it. Ironically, Landseer was one of the favourites at Court who had been suspected of passing anti-Brown remarks to *Punch* and *Tomahawk*.

Worse was to follow. The Queen had agreed to attend a review in Hyde Park in July of that year, but to her fury Lord Derby, her Prime Minister, dared to suggest that she leave John Brown at home, as the sight of him might lead to incidents of an 'unpleasant nature'. Derby asked the Queen's secretary, Charles Grey, to recommend that Brown might develop 'some slight ailment' on the day and thus excuse himself. Knowing that such subterfuge would never work with anybody as honest as the Queen, he approached her saying that the Prime Minister's greatest concern was for Brown's own feelings and safety: what if he was to be exposed to public humiliation?

Providentially, the impasse was resolved by a tragic event on the other side of the world. In June Emperor Maximilian of Mexico, brother of Emperor Francis Joseph of Austria and the husband of Queen Victoria's cousin Princess Charlotte of Belgium, and whose so-called empire had been revealed as no more than an ill-conceived experiment in imperialism on the part of France, was captured by Mexican forces, given a show trial and executed by firing squad. The Hyde Park review was cancelled and the Court went into mourning, but not before the Queen had ensured that on any similar future occasion Brown's position would be unchallenged. 'The Queen will not be dictated to,' she wrote angrily to her equerry, Lord Charles Fitzroy, 'or *made* to *alter* what she has found to answer for her comfort.'[21]

One reason Brown was so disliked in certain sections of the Queen's entourage was that she *would* be dictated to – by Brown. If he did not approve of her clothing, he would ask disdainfully, 'What's this ye've got on today?' Once she complained about a sketching table which she found inconvenient. He told her sharply not to grumble, 'for I canna mak one for ye'.[22] A tourist walking near Balmoral one day was startled to see Brown fastening the Queen's cloak under her bonnet and scolding her: 'Hoots then, wumman, can ye no hold yerr head up?'

Members of the household, visitors and statesmen alike, were all open-mouthed at his rudeness not only to her, but also to them. Nobody around the Queen could be less of a well-spoken aristocrat or an obsequious courtier, and in this lay much of his appeal for her. To her, the 'higher classes' generally personified idleness, self-indulgence and frivolity, while the lower orders stood for industry and morality. Brown's brusque, plain-speaking manner was a breath of fresh air. She was always a little shy in intellectual or aristocratic company, and her ladies noticed that she tended to give an involuntary nervous laugh on meeting anyone new. Among the poor and unsophisticated Highland folk she was always at ease, and to have one of them as a devoted companion, someone in whom she could trust, was a tonic.

Brown's manner masked a character capable of great tenderness. In June 1866 Queen Victoria was particularly worried about her eldest daughter Victoria, who was beside herself with grief after losing her 21-month-old son, Sigismund, to meningitis. She told Brown that she was 'in great trouble' about the Princess, and he told her that he wished to take care of his dear good mistress until he died: 'You'll never have an honester servant.' Whatever he may have felt to the contrary during his remaining sixteen years, he honoured his promise faithfully.

His physical strength was another advantage. After several carriage accidents and two attempted assassination attempts, Victoria was nervous about driving out. To have someone of Brown's calibre on the box gave her a sense of security. When she sat working at home, he kept constant guard over her. He often prevented others from pestering her needlessly (in his view and hers, if not perhaps in the opinion of her illustrious would-be visitors), and ensured that she was properly wrapped up when they went out and that she did not tire herself.

He disliked travelling abroad, had little time for foreigners, foreign languages (despite his mastering German) or foreign food. He disliked the heat of hotter climes and so feared attempts on the Queen's life that he discouraged the stopping of her carriage for her to enjoy breathtaking views as she passed. Some foreign territories paid him little respect. The Queen never passed through Brussels on her way to the German Court after the death of King Leopold I and the accession of his son, who did not recognise Brown and thus refused to arrange for him to have his own suite of rooms close to those of the Queen.

Never for one moment was he overawed by her status as a sovereign or afraid of her as a person. Unlike her family and her ministers, he could see that his monarch was at heart a helpless female, still fervently mourning her husband, in need of being pampered, looked after, even sometimes being ordered around. He could say things to her which no courtier, statesman or relative would ever dare – and with the death of King Leopold in December 1865, there was no relation who would even contemplate doing so. As her private secretary, Sir Henry Ponsonby, noted in a letter to his wife a few weeks after Brown's death, he was 'the only person who could fight and make the Queen do what she did not wish'.[23]

Being on a pedestal was a lonely business, and sometimes the greatest queen of the nineteenth century was the most lonely of all. The only child who had never been certain of her mother's love had the time-honoured Hanoverian aversion to her son and heir, and she had been widowed at an early age. It was hardly surprising 'that she numbered her servants among her best friends'.[24] In addition, she had spent a large part of her life among servants and thought very highly of them – far more of them, in fact, than of most of her family.

In 1867 a limited edition volume of extracts from the Queen's private journal, *Leaves from a Journal of Our Life in the Highlands*, was produced for her family and courtiers. Her editor was Arthur Helps, clerk to the privy council and the uncredited editor of a volume of the Prince Consort's principal letters and speeches published in 1862. It described many of her Highland expeditions in great detail, with what some of her family and household thought was undue emphasis on the presence and role of John Brown. 'His attention, care and faithfulness cannot be exceeded,' she wrote, 'and the state of my health, which of late years has been sorely tried and weakened, renders such qualifications most valuable and indeed most needful.'[25]

When *Leaves* was issued for private circulation, Helps was foremost among those who persuaded the Queen that it should be given the benefit of general publication. However carefully the recipients of this edition were selected, he advised her, parts of the text, 'or incorrect representations of its contents, might find their way into the public journals'.[26] Some of the household thought general publication would be unwise. In particular, her lady-in-waiting Lady Augusta Stanley feared the reaction of 'the more educated classes' and that reviewers would serve the Queen ill, with 'ignorant, stupid remarks [which] are calculated to do great harm to our dear One'.[27] The view of Helps and others prevailed. In 1868 Smith, Elder & Co. issued an edition for the public which proved an instant success, with 100,000 copies sold within three months.

That same autumn, during the annual royal visit to Balmoral, John Brown was absent for a week. It was announced that he was suffering from a chill. When he reappeared, his face was battered and bruised. The staff whispered among themselves that the Prince of Wales and one or two friends had arranged for a prize-fighter from Aberdeen to pick a quarrel with Brown and give him a thrashing. This, it was alleged, was payback time for an incident earlier that year when the Prince had arrived at Windsor to see his mother, only to be told by Brown that he would not be seeing the Queen until five o'clock that afternoon, and he would have to go and amuse himself for a couple of hours. The idea that the Prince of Wales would stoop to such tactics to get his way seems absurd to say the least, but the story was widely believed on Deeside for many years afterwards.[28]

EIGHT

'Absolutely fair and lucid'

The height of the Brown controversy coincided with the appointment of a new private secretary to Queen Victoria. For some years the position had been filled by General Charles Grey, who had served as a Whig member of parliament from 1831 to 1837. On his re-election to the seat of High Wycombe in 1834, he was the victorious opponent of Disraeli. Becoming an equerry to the Queen on his departure from political life, he was appointed private secretary to the Prince Consort in 1849, and on the latter's death continued to serve Queen Victoria in the same capacity, though the title was not officially conferred on him until 1867.

After Albert's death, the Queen proclaimed she was unable to receive ministers personally for a while and gave orders that they must be received instead by her second daughter, Princess Alice, who had initially been her mother's greatest prop in the family since the onset of her father's last illness, or Grey, on whom she had become increasingly dependent for help. Despite her determination, expressed in a letter to King Leopold ten days after Albert's death, that '*no one* person, may *he* be ever so good, ever so devoted among my servants – is to lead or guide or dictate to me',[1] she needed a permanent official who was in a position to speak to her ministers with full authority. After twelve years of faithful service to her husband, it was clear to the Queen that nobody was better qualified than Grey to fill the role, and she became more reliant on him for help. In January 1863 she wrote to him that he was her 'main support', and whenever he was away 'she always feels additionally anxious'.[2]

Grey continued to act as her secretary, though ministers had looked askance at the Prince Consort's increasing influence over his wife, regarding him as king in all but name. Some of them, particularly Lord Palmerston, wrongly suspected that Grey was eager to assume a similar role. Grey knew that some thought he was becoming 'a power behind the throne' and defended himself by saying he would never venture an opinion without the Queen's approval; he merely obeyed her orders. Not for another six years did the Queen manage to persuade her ministers that it was vital that Grey's position as her chief helper with government business be recognised, by his formal appointment as her private secretary; Prime Minister Lord Derby accordingly did so in 1867.

Sometimes Grey felt he was being asked to undertake tasks beyond the call of duty. When a young lady-in-waiting appeared at court wearing too much make-up, the Queen said that 'Dear General Grey will tell her.' When the message was passed on to him, he murmured, 'Dear General Grey will do nothing of the kind.'[3]

Under the Queen's direction, Grey had helped to prepare for publication a biography, *The Early Years of the Prince Consort*, which covered Albert's life from birth to marriage. She had hoped Grey would complete the work in a second volume, but by the time it was published his health was beginning to fail. (Perhaps fortuitously for Grey, the task of completing the biography of the Prince Consort, again very much under the Queen's direction, devolved on Theodore Martin, but far from requiring one further volume, it took five. They were published between 1874 and 1880.)

Nevertheless, Grey was not uncritical of his mistress. He felt her seclusion was unwarranted and believed she was taking advantage of ill-health to evade some of her duties as a sovereign. As she reportedly declined to open parliament at the beginning of 1870 on the grounds that it was 'a very unwholesome year',[4] his complaints were not unjustified. To him, her excesses of grief were little more than self-indulgence. In a moment of impatience he once referred to her to Gladstone as 'the royal malingerer' and urged him to try to counteract the strong feeling against the Queen by ordering her in a more peremptory tone to do her royal duty. Her moans, said Grey, might satisfy her doctor, the complaisant Sir William Jenner, but they had no effect on him whatsoever.[5]

To add to Grey's problems, he had shared the general detestation of Brown ever since being sent one of his very rudely worded messages, which he refused to accept because of the tone, and both men had always borne each other a grudge afterwards as a result. Towards the end of his years of service, his own health was failing, and increasing deafness made it difficult for him to do the job properly. By 1869, the year of his sixty-fifth birthday, he was keen to retire, but only after he had suffered several small strokes did the Queen realise that a successor would need to be found.

Fortunately, the right man was not far away. Henry Ponsonby, a former Army officer who had served in the Crimean war with the Grenadier Guards and been promoted to lieutenant-colonel, had been in royal service since his appointment as equerry to Prince Albert in January 1857. While he found the Prince oddly humourless, he was impressed by his intellectual seriousness and welcomed the chance to accompany him to various lectures, exhibitions and meetings of the Fine Arts Commission. Such activities opened his eyes and his mind to the gaps in his education: he took to spending many of his days off in visiting the British Museum, or long periods as an equerry, when he might have been waiting around and doing nothing, by making profitable use of his time, going to read and study in the Royal Library at Windsor. All this turned him into a much more bookish, better-informed man than many others at Court.

In April 1861 he married one of the Queen's maids of honour, Mary Elizabeth Bulteel, Colonel Grey's niece. Later that year she was expecting their first child, and he received the unwelcome news that as a result of the heightened tension between Britain and the United States of America, he might be ordered to serve with his regiment in Canada. The tension soon subsided, but it was shortly followed by even more shocking news – the sudden illness and death of the Prince Consort. His salary ended with the Prince's death, but after a short period of uncertainty as to his prospects, he was given the news that he and the other three equerries to the Prince would be reappointed equerries to the Queen, though with a reduction in salary.

In March 1870 Ponsonby was informed by Sir Thomas Biddulph, Keeper of the Privy Purse, that the Queen planned to offer him the post of private secretary. After a short illness, Grey died on 31 March, and on 8 April Ponsonby was gazetted to the office. At the same time he was placed on half-pay of the Grenadier Guards, in accordance with arrangements which he had already made. The appointment was not generally popular. The Queen's notoriously reactionary cousin George, Duke of Cambridge, expressed regret that 'one who was known to have such extreme radical tendencies should be placed in such a position', while her son-in-law Prince Christian was opposed to it for similar reasons, especially as he regarded Mary Ponsonby as a holder of 'extreme views'.[6]

The Queen was cautious about Ponsonby's ability to fill the post. She already knew him well enough, she wrote to Princess Victoria, to be aware of his 'excellent abilities, great facility in writing, great discretion and very good temper'. General Grey's experience could never be replaced, 'but that is the dreadful misfortune as they grow old and no one feels this more acutely than I do'. Fortunately, she recalled the words of Baron Stockmar many years before, advising her to 'make more and more use' of Ponsonby.[7]

Despite her reservations, his appointment was fortuitous, and not for a moment would she have good reason to take issue with Stockmar's favourable impression of the man. By 1870 the Queen's popularity in the country was at a low ebb. Ponsonby's more progressive outlook put him naturally in sympathy with Gladstone, who had an unenviable task in trying to persuade the Queen to abandon her seclusion. Republicanism was on the rise, with journals such as the *National Reformer* warning that Her Majesty, 'by doing nothing except receive her Civil List, is teaching the country that it can get on quite well without a monarch'.[8] Enjoying a good relationship with Gladstone and the Liberal ministers, naturally self-effacing, with a dry wit and sense of humour which ensured that he never took life too seriously, Ponsonby performed an invaluable service to the monarchy by helping to keep the Crown above politics in a similar, if less overt, way as the Prince Consort had done.

Whereas the Queen had generally been more inclined towards the Whigs and Liberals, regarding her first Tory Prime Minister, Sir Robert Peel, as a Liberal in all but name, from around the age of fifty onwards she was becoming increasingly conservative and Conservative. Ponsonby and his equally progressive-minded wife helped to reduce the damage that might otherwise have been done. He had a natural dislike of ceremony and grandeur for its own sake. A spell in North America reinforced his liberal views and inbuilt admiration of a more egalitarian society, perhaps only serving to accentuate the importance he attached to what his biographer William A. Kuhn called 'the smallness of attending to the whims of princes and princesses'.[9]

While he and Mary were never republicans, they were curious to learn more about the republican movement and studied the radical papers with keen interest, and their moderate yet unashamedly slightly left-of-centre attitudes went some way towards making Queen Victoria and her Court more acceptable to left-wing opinion in Victorian England. By their very presence at Court, they proved that the Crown could tolerate and even rise above political dissent, and it might not be overstating the case to suggest that the monarchy's survival into the twentieth century owed more than a little to their presence.

Even so, Mary was not generally invited to what were described as 'Court junketings', or visits to members of the royal family in other European countries. Though the Queen and her household could claim that she did not have an automatic invitation to such occasions as she was merely the wife of the private secretary, she believed that this was being used as an excuse to keep her out of the way. She was said to be slightly embittered at being marginalised in such a manner, and thus had little compunction in seeking out and spreading dubious gossip about the family,[10] though as the loyal wife of the Queen's private secretary, there is reason to doubt whether she would ever have resorted to such questionable tactics.

Much as the Queen might disagree with Sir Henry Ponsonby or shake her head at the sight of his untidy clothes, his scruffy jackets and ill-fitting, too-long trousers, she respected his views and his patience. Gladstone must have counted himself fortunate that his dealings with a sovereign who disliked him, and was not anxious to conceal the fact, had in Ponsonby a ready friend and partisan so close to the royal presence. Ponsonby was not blind to the faults of the man who became prime minister four times, and when he was minister in attendance at Balmoral in August 1873 admitted that he sometimes thought him 'earnestly mad, and taking up a view with an intensity which scarcely allows him to suppose there can be any truth on the other side'.[11] However, Gladstone was the kind of honest, unaffected politician whom Ponsonby trusted as well as respected.

Ponsonby and Gladstone regularly compared notes and ideas on the contemporary power and influence of the Crown. After reading an article by Gladstone on the Prince Consort in 1875, Ponsonby wrote to him to say how struck he was by a paragraph 'on the altered character of the Regal office' and how they saw it as a substitute for the influence of power. He believed that the power still remained, though unused. In some ways, he went on, he thought the dormant power 'is so great that it might almost be dreaded if we had a bad and clever King and a weak Minister'. While he thought such an occurrence unlikely, he considered that it supported his argument that the latent power still existed, 'and though it is dormant indeed is the force which gives to the royal influence the strength it possesses'.[12]

Like many admirers of Gladstone, Ponsonby was a little suspicious of Disraeli, not just on political grounds, but because he found something unappealing, if not mildly distasteful, about his showmanship and flattery of the Queen. He could never be sure whether Disraeli really respected his sovereign or was just flattering her for the sake of it and exploiting her admiration for his own ends. He seemed 'always to speak in a burlesque' and was 'cleverer than Gladstone with his terrible earnestness. But how anyone can put faith in Dizzy is what I don't understand.'[13]

Ponsonby took a balanced view of the royal family. He was not above making gentle fun of them, enjoying the odd joke at their expense as long as nobody was offended in the process, or taking an objective analysis of their status. He was no sycophant, and like Brown he refused to be dazzled by the aura of monarchy. 'If they had real determination and strong convictions they would be a danger to the state,' he wrote to his wife in 1884. 'As it is they are what they should be.'[14]

From the start of his duties, he had been reassured to learn that his predecessor, General Grey, had been no shrinking violet. Grey, he was aware, was in the habit of writing to the Queen boldly about his views on anything, and 'tho' it irritated her, it sunk in and did good'. While her ministers often thought he might have gone further, he had long since learnt exactly how far he could go, and as a result his advice was never disregarded.[15]

During the early years, Ponsonby himself was sometimes obliged to discuss with the Queen the delicate subject of gossip, rumours and greatly exaggerated reports on her seclusion. Had he been more brave and more clever, he said, he 'might have read her a lecture on her duties', but knew that for him to do anything of the sort would mean that he would 'never have the subject approached again'. Whenever any contentious matter needed consideration, he took care never to open with a direct negative or contradiction. His manner of dealing with an employer unused to contradiction was masterly. If she insisted that two and two made five, 'I say that I cannot help thinking that they make 4. She replies that there may be some truth in what I say, but she knows they make 5. Thereupon I drop the discussion. It is of no consequence and I leave it there, knowing the fact.' Someone else in an identical situation, a woman to whom he referred as 'X', did not know when to let well alone, and would try to use arguments and other statements in order to prove her point. This the Queen found intolerable, as 'no one can stand when they are wrong, women especially; and the Queen can't abide it.'[16]

It is hard to imagine any of the men with whom she regularly came into contact at around this time telling her on such an occasion that it was rubbish to suggest that two and two made five. John Brown might have done so and got away with it; Gladstone would have argued to the contrary at inordinate length; Disraeli would probably have conjured up some ingeniously flattering explanation to suggest she was right after all. Ponsonby was astute enough to tread a middle path.

Later on, when his patience was wearing thin with age and the increasing burdens of office, he was tempted to be more forthright with his employer. It would sometimes be necessary for his wife to warn him that when 'the Queen makes a remark he must not say "It is absurd."'[17]

* * *

In August 1871 the Queen was seriously ill, with symptoms which left her physicians baffled. These included a swelling in her throat which prevented her from swallowing and speaking properly, and at one point Dr Jenner feared she might have only twenty-four hours to live. An abscess followed soon afterwards, with flying gout and rheumatic pains. Her lady-in-waiting Lady Churchill wanted to know why the Queen's children had not been sent for, only to be told promptly by Sir Thomas Biddulph that to do so would have killed her at once. Though his remark was widely taken as flippancy and indicated antipathy to her often-difficult progeny, for all her children to gather by her bedside might indeed have induced a presentiment in her, if it had caught her at the wrong moment, that she was indeed mortally ill. When Ponsonby saw her again on 13 September, he thought she looked 'rather pulled down, thinner and paler'.

Unlike members of the Queen's family, John Brown was allowed unrestricted access to her bedroom, lifting her from her bed to her couch, and delivering her orders to the household in his typically blunt manner. All of her sons and daughters bitterly resented him being accorded such privileges. The Prince of Wales had always been infuriated and humiliated by her taking Brown's side against his in his quarrels with the servant. It particularly rankled with him that the Queen should consider there was 'no male head' in her family after the Prince Consort's death, and that she should always bow to Brown's judgement rather than that of the eldest son who would succeed her as sovereign was a gross insult. Princess Alice, who was married to Prince Louis of Hesse, complained to Ponsonby that while Brown was totally unfit for more than menial work, he alone talked to the Queen 'on all things while we, her children, are restricted to speak on only those matters which may not excite her or which she chooses to talk about'.[18]

Her second son, Alfred, Duke of Edinburgh, arrived at Balmoral in September and made a point of shaking hands with everyone on his arrival except Brown. There had been differences between both men since the previous summer, when they had been present at a ball and the Duke had ordered the music to be stopped after the revelry was showing signs of getting out of hand, and Brown had reputedly told him that he would not take orders from the Duke or any other man. The Queen sent word that the quarrel must be patched up at once, and the Duke agreed, as long as Ponsonby was present as a witness. If he saw a man on board ship on any subject, he argued, it was always in the presence of an officer. When the Queen heard about it, she was furious with her son: 'This is not a ship, and I won't have naval discipline introduced here.'[19] In the end, a meeting was arranged at which Ponsonby persuaded Duke and servant, somewhat grudgingly, to patch things up.

In February 1872 Brown acquitted himself so well during what could have been an extremely serious incident that nothing could diminish the Queen's confidence in him. While she was returning to Buckingham Palace from a drive, a youth named Arthur O'Connor pointed an unloaded pistol at her and came within inches of her face, ostensibly with the aim of attempting to frighten her into releasing Fenian prisoners. Prince Arthur tried to jump over the carriage and apprehend him but was too slow. Brown grabbed hold of O'Connor and kept him pinned until the police could come to arrest him. The weapon in itself was not a threat, for the flintlock was broken, and instead of being properly loaded the pistol was stuffed with wads of paper and bits of old leather. But this attempt on the Queen's life, futile though it was, frightened her more than all the others.

For his efforts, Prince Arthur was presented with a gold pin, much to the Prince of Wales's fury, while Brown became the recipient of a special award, the Devoted Service Medal. It included a specially designed medal and a life annuity of £25. Irreverently referred to as 'The Greater Order of Brown', it was thus awarded for the first and, so it seems, last time.

Brown had taken to sleeping with a loaded revolver under his pillow in order to protect the Queen. Security measures at Balmoral were not taken very seriously, as whenever she stayed there only a single policeman was on duty. Her devoted Highland servant would patrol the vicinity each night himself, to keep any eye out for any possible source of trouble. Queen Victoria had little fear of potential assassins, and those around her thought she was more concerned about disloyalty at the height of the republican agitation than any physical danger from lone gunmen or self-styled anarchists.

Within a few years, Brown was said to be threatening to leave the Queen's service. Now nearing fifty years of age, he appeared to be tiring of his bachelor status, while becoming uncle to an ever-growing number of nieces and nephews. Ponsonby was aware of the rumours, and when his wife asked him if they were true, appeared reluctant to commit himself. He assumed that Brown would leave the Queen's service if he did marry, and this he thought would be unfortunate. In theory, there was nothing to stop him from taking a wife without damaging his job security, apart from the fact that there were limited opportunities to form a close relationship with any eligible spinster at Court. He could easily have done so, as the Queen's future physician James Reid was to do towards the end of her life. Admittedly, it would have risked her intense short-term displeasure, but he would still have been able to continue to serve Her Majesty, if not as single-mindedly as before. That he never did marry (or marry openly) has only served to add to the claims of those who maintain that he went through a secret ceremony with the Queen.

While he was part of the royal household, they had 'the best and worst of him'. It was a case of better the devil they knew, as a successor, if granted the same power, might not be so harmless.[20] Everyone took it for granted that Her Majesty insisted so much on single-minded devotion from those who served her that Brown's betrothal, if and when it happened, would be tantamount to his resignation.

However, he stayed with his royal employer. In 1876 she gave him a cottage, and his lease contained the customary clause of 'Forfeiture & Irritancy', against which she wrote in the margin, 'what does this mean?' If he became increasingly embittered with his lot in life and churlish towards those around her, it was hardly surprising. Dr Hal Yarrow, a Fellow of the Royal Society of Medicine and an expert on skin diseases, believed that, from his forties onwards, Brown suffered from erysipelas. A sudden change from a healthy outdoor life to 'comparatively soft living' as the Queen's personal attendant would have made him prone to more recurrent attacks, once the condition had manifested itself.[21]

His initial duties had increased, and he had become overseer of all general below-stairs work and management. He was in effect a kind of personnel officer to the servants, especially whenever they had any private problems that might affect their royal service. As if this was not enough, he acted as general courier or message-bearer to the Queen and to her equerries. When new staff were required at Balmoral, she generally asked him for his advice. He had a habit of choosing candidates whose ways resembled his. Once he was approached by a man who was keen to find his young son of twenty a position in the royal household. The proud parent told Brown that his son was a good lad who did not swear, drink or play cards. Brown shook his head apologetically, replying that this would-be employee sounded much too good to live long, 'and the Queen disna like the quick-deeing kind'.[22]

Victoria was aware of how hard Brown worked, and on occasion she asked the equerries to refrain from sending him at all hours for 'trifling messages', as he was increasingly exhausted from such activities. His boorishness and inability to suffer fools gladly, and his increasing reliance on the bottle, could easily be understood. His love for whisky was legendary, and that the Queen cheerfully turned a blind eye towards over-indulgence in alcohol among her servants (provided they did nobody else any harm, such as causing embarrassment to her or anyone else in public) did nothing to discourage him from seeking such solace. If whisky was one of his few pleasures in life, so be it. Over a century later, the Queen's great-great-granddaughter, Queen Elizabeth II, showed similar understanding in putting up with drunkenness and other lapses of etiquette from favoured members of staff. She was equally aware of the pressures they were under, and was 'keen to keep a peaceful house'.[23]

The story is often told that on at least one occasion Brown was so drunk when he appeared in the Queen's presence that he fell to the floor, and that she kept a perfectly straight face as she told everyone else that she had distinctly felt an earth tremor. Brown was increasingly accident-prone in his later years, but at least some of his problems were caused by the obvious. In August 1877, while accompanying the Queen on a tour of the warship HMS *Thunderer*, he fell through an aperture in a gun turret, sustaining severe bruising to his shins. On another occasion, at Balmoral, he was due to escort her out on a ride but was nowhere to be found. Ponsonby went and looked in his room, saw him sleeping off a binge and, without a word of explanation, mounted the carriage himself. The under-standing Queen Victoria knew without asking what had happened. Ponsonby always got on well with Brown, admiring his honesty and lack of obsequiousness. His friendship with the Highland servant doubtless compensated for what Queen Victoria might have regarded as other shortcomings in Ponsonby's character.

Though very different, both men were quite self-effacing and unpretentious in their own way. Neither relished display or grandeur for the sake of it, and neither were dazzled by awards or honours, which they regarded as something of a hollow charade. In 1872 the Queen wished to make Ponsonby a Commander of the Order of the Bath, which he declined gracefully on the grounds that it was a civilian order and he still considered himself a soldier.[24] His real reason was that he regarded the addition of letters after one's name with distaste. Getting things done was part of one's job, and he had an egalitarian contempt for honorifics.

Though the Queen respected Ponsonby's decision, the Garter King of Arms, Sir Albert Woods, took him to task on the grounds that it was ungentlemanly to refuse an honour from a lady. In 1879 Victoria proposed to make him a Knight Commander of the Bath. Realising that to decline an honour for the second time would create difficulties in his relations with her, he reluctantly accepted. For him and his wife to be Sir Henry and Lady Ponsonby was a distinction to be endured rather than relished.

That Ponsonby should find his political views making him something of a fish out of water in the atmosphere at Court is hardly surprising. Well aware that the Queen distrusted his political instincts, especially at this time when she was under Disraeli's spell, there were times when he felt irritated at being 'muzzled' by her because of it. For Tory courtiers to make fun of Gladstone in his presence at Balmoral was a needless provocation which only made his work harder, and he did not hesitate to tell them coldly that such comments were all very well when they knew he must not speak.[25]

Sometimes the Queen made moves herself which were unnecessarily partisan. When Sir Thomas Biddulph died in 1878, she asked Montague Corry, Disraeli's private secretary, whether he would be prepared to join her staff as her own private secretary, while appointing Ponsonby to the privy purse. Fortunately for all, Corry decided he did not wish to leave Disraeli's household, while Ponsonby hinted he would rather resign than exchange his present position for another. As a result, the Queen made him keeper of the privy purse as well as her private secretary, promising that he would have assistants so his duties would be less onerous than before, and so that he could spend more time with his wife. Perhaps she had realised that he was too indispensable to her and that losing him from the household would be a grave mistake. As the only Liberal in a court of Tories of varying hue, he was the only one who could maintain friendly contact with Gladstone and his secretaries, something which would stand him in good stead after Disraeli's last period in office came to an end.

Disraeli was scrupulously fair to the man who might have been regarded as something of a political adversary, albeit a very discreet one. Ponsonby, he said, used to be a Whig, but whatever his politics, he said that he could not wish his case 'better stated to the Queen than the Private Secretary does it. Perhaps I am a gainer by his Whiggishness as it makes him more scrupulously on his guard to be absolutely fair and lucid.'[26]

* * *

While accompanying the Queen on her holiday in Italy in the spring of 1879, Brown suffered his first severe attack of erysipelas, an acute skin disease which on this occasion affected his legs and spread to his face. Within a fortnight he had recovered enough to take his place on her carriage box, but he remained out of sorts for the rest of the holiday. From then on, he was never in good health.

Whatever his failings where personal charm was concerned, Brown was always very generous to others. While they were at Osborne in the winter of 1868, unemployment was particularly severe, and when the Admiralty closed the dockyard at Portsmouth, many shipwrights and mechanics were thrown out of work; some were reduced to selling all their possessions or begging in the streets. Brown wasted no time in starting a collection among the servants at Osborne, and in February 1869 he donated £22 to the Committee of the Portsmouth Dockyard Discharged Workmen's Relief Association. Ever sociable to people of all classes, sometimes he would invite visiting dignitaries and their valets to his room for an evening of whisky, tobacco and informal 'committee on the state of the nation'.[27]

When Disraeli died in April 1881 and the Highland servant was chosen to break the news to his royal mistress, she found he was 'quite overcome'. After he had got over the shock, he personally started a subscription among the other servants and Royal Household to erect a monument to her hero. On other occasions he was always the first to pass the hat, whether subscribing to a wedding present for one of the royal family or helping out a needy servant down on his luck.

* * *

In July 1881 another young man entered the employment of Queen Victoria. Though he shared nothing with John Brown except Scottish blood, he too would become indispensable to her and, by virtue of his personality, would ultimately take on a greater and far more supportive role than his conditions of service would ever have suggested.

Earlier in the year, Queen Victoria had sought a resident medical attendant to Dr William Marshall to take responsibility for her personal health and that of the royal household. He was to be a Scotsman, if possible a native of Aberdeenshire, with suitable medical qualifications, and a fluent German speaker, so he would be able to converse easily with her visiting relations from Germany. Her Commissioner at Balmoral was asked to find a suitable local candidate, and James Reid, a young doctor of thirty-one, was recommended.

The son of a country doctor, Reid had gone to university at the age of sixteen and began reading arts subjects for three years before he was old enough to begin studying medicine. He travelled widely in Europe, completing medical studies in Vienna and spending a short time as tutor to the young Count de Lodron. He therefore knew something of the atmosphere of court life, an experience which would make him exceptionally well qualified in his role in the royal household.

After audiences with the Queen at Balmoral and with Sir William Jenner in London, Reid was duly appointed and took up his duties at Windsor Castle. For the remaining nineteen years of his life, by virtue of his character and peacemaking skills, he was to be a valued confidant of the Queen and many members of her family and household. He was quick to discover that she could be a demanding taskmistress who laid down extraordinarily precise routines. 'Let Dr Reid go out from quarter to 11 to one, unless the Queen sends before to see him, and from 5 till *near* 8', ran one of her earliest written instructions. 'If he wishes on any particular occasion to go out sooner he shd. ask. These are the regular hours. But I may send before to say he is not to go out before I have seen him shd. I not feel well or want anything. This every Doctor in attendance has done and must be prepared to do.'[28]

In time he would play almost as important a role as Ponsonby, especially after the latter's death, in speaking his mind and fearlessly telling the Queen what she did not necessarily wish to hear. During her last few years, there were few people, if any, whom she would trust more than Sir James Reid, as he had become by then.

Ponsonby and Reid soon became the best of friends. Both men not only had the capacity to get on well with others, but also infinite tact, patience and a sense of humour which enabled them to cope with life under a woman who could be exceptionally demanding. Though the Queen was in remarkably robust health for a woman of her age, with stamina and energy envied by many of those around her younger than she was, she still worried endlessly about her health. She persistently complained she was a martyr to 'sick headaches' and indigestion, though she still ate too much and took no exercise, with subsequent disastrous effects on her figure. The young sovereign who had told Lord Melbourne how much she disliked walking never overcame this particular aversion. With Reid, she had daily consultations about her generally exaggerated or imagined ailments. A more self-assertive doctor might have risked her wrath by telling her she was talking nonsense much of the time, but his tenure of employment would have been correspondingly short.

Not only was Reid obliged to look after the Queen's health, but also to an extent that of her family overseas. Any letter about ailments from her children or grandchildren throughout Europe would generally be shown to him, with an appeal for advice.

Reid appeared at a crucial time in Queen Victoria's life. In July 1881 she was still mourning the loss of Disraeli, and her only real confidant was John Brown, slowly but surely becoming a shadow of his former self. As Randall Davidson noted, she had a tendency to form 'unwise' relations with servants, as she did twice during her widowhood. Like most women, he was convinced, she needed a man in her life, someone to cherish and in whom she could confide.[29] While her relations with Brown and later with 'the Munshi' (see chapter 9) were fundamentally innocent, they did not always appear that way to others, and led to no little detrimental speculation which threatened to damage her image and her reputation.

* * *

In March 1882 Queen Victoria was once again the target of a would-be assassin. Riding into Windsor on a train from London, she heard a noise which she thought was the train letting off steam, but then she saw people running in all directions and a man being led away. The man responsible for the commotion, a mediocre Scottish poet named Roderick Maclean, had fired at her once with a revolver and was preparing to shoot a second time when he was overpowered.

Brown was in the carriage, but in stark contrast to his heroic behaviour during O'Connor's attempt on her life, he was very slow to react. His leg might have been troubling him, or he might have been slightly drunk. He seemed slow to understand what had happened and could only repeat afterwards in some amazement that 'That man fired at Your Majesty's carriage.'[30] Maclean was sent for trial and found not guilty on grounds of insanity, a verdict which enraged Queen Victoria, who told Gladstone, her Prime Minister at the time, that 'the law must be altered'.

One is tempted to speculate as to whether John Brown would have been relieved of some of his more arduous duties if his physical condition had declined much further. It was perhaps fortunate for him that the end came fairly suddenly.

In March 1883 Lady Florence Dixie, who lived near Windsor Castle, claimed that she had been assaulted on her estate by two men dressed as women, possibly Fenians, and only saved from serious injury by the appearance of her St Bernard dog, Hubert. Lady Dixie's colourful reputation was not calculated to make her a favourite with the Queen. A sister of the notorious 8th Marquess of Queensberry and aunt of Lord Alfred Douglas, both of whom would play conspicuous roles in the downfall of Oscar Wilde a few years hence, she was a big game huntress, an outspoken advocate of equality between the sexes and a champion of the right of women to wear trousers. She and her husband also had a marked love of the bottle.

A thorough police investigation of the incident, including a forensic examination of Lady Dixie's clothing, found major discrepancies in her account, which was quickly ascribed to her hysterical imagination. However, any possibility of Fenian outrages or cut-throats near Windsor was enough to alarm the Queen. It was less than a year since Lord Frederick Cavendish, her Secretary of State for Ireland, and his deputy, had gone to Dublin to take up their appointments and been assassinated in broad daylight shortly after their arrival, and only fifteen years since the Duke of Edinburgh had been shot and wounded by an Irish republican sympathiser in Australia. Brown was sent to conduct a thorough search of the plantation where Lady Dixie had allegedly been attacked.

Hours of tramping around in damp undergrowth revealed nothing, but by the time Brown returned to the castle he was thoroughly chilled. The Queen was suffering from a wrenched knee and had to be carried everywhere for a time, so he had no respite. His cold rapidly worsened, erysipelas set in and, on the afternoon of 27 March, he sank into a coma from which he never regained consciousness. His brothers William and Archibald were summoned to his bedside, just in time to see him die late that evening.

At first, Victoria's family avoided breaking the news to her directly. On the following morning, Leopold, her youngest son, undertook (or was chosen) to go to her dressing-room and tell her. 'We can feel for her, & her sorrow, without being sorry for the cause,' he wrote to his brother-in-law Louis, Grand Duke of Hesse, on behalf of the family. 'At least I can't be a hypocrit [*sic*].'[31] None of his brothers showed any hypocrisy at the death of their mother's favourite, or inclination to observe any period of mourning. It did not escape the notice of the press that the Prince of Wales and the Duke of Edinburgh seemed to be attending an unusually large number of stage plays and after-dinner parties that week.

Ironically, Dr Reid's father had died the previous day after a short illness. Reid was kept informed by telegram by his family and a fellow practitioner of his father, but the Queen felt unable to release him to be with his father at such a time. However, she wrote a letter of condolence, saying that she felt 'doubly grieved and distressed at this great sorrow and trouble which have come upon him'.[32]

The grief which the Queen felt at the loss of this most devoted servant and companion was almost as intense as that which she felt after the death of her husband. She felt 'utterly crushed', she told Ponsonby, and her life had 'again sustained one of those shocks like in '61 when every link has been shaken and torn'.[33] To Jessie, the wife of Hugh, another of the Brown brothers, she declared that her grief was 'unbounded, dreadful, and I know not how to bear it, or how to believe it possible'. Many years later, when her daughter Beatrice came to rewrite her journals for publication and destroy the originals, the reference to Brown's death read: 'Am terribly upset by this loss, which removes one who was so devoted and attached to my service and who did so much for my personal comfort. It is the loss not only of a servant, but of a real friend.'[34] Similar phrases appeared in the Court Circular, which Victoria helped to draft, announcing that 'the death of this truly faithful and devoted servant has been a grievous stroke to the Queen'.[35]

From Downing Street, Gladstone wrote a letter of condolence to the Queen. Kindly though his intentions were, the letter betrayed his habitual tactlessness. He could understand, he wrote, how she would miss 'the aid and attention of an attached, respected and intelligent domestic', and he hoped she would 'be able to select a good and efficient successor, though it would be too much to hope that anyone, however capable, can at once fill the void'.[36] One can hardly imagine the bereaved sovereign appreciating references to an 'intelligent domestic', let alone the references to a successor to 'fill the void'. One could never imagine Disraeli writing such a note. Later she appointed Brown's cousin, Francie Clark, to the position, though there could never be a second John Brown.

Any doubt that the Queen loved Brown in her own way is dispelled by a letter she wrote to his brother Hugh. She had come across, and was enclosing a copy of, the entry in her journal referring to his words of comfort to her after the death of her grandson Prince Sigismund of Prussia, and his promise to take care of her until he died. 'Afterwards so often I told him no one loved him more than I did or had a better friend than me: and he answered "Nor you – than me." "No one loves you more"'.[37]

Perhaps even more significant were her comments to the Earl of Cranbrook that 'perhaps never in history was there so strong and true an attachment, so warm and loving a friendship between the sovereign and servant as existed between her and dear faithful Brown'. (Close examination of the letter suggests that the words 'between the sovereign and servant' were added as an afterthought.) She went on to pay tribute to his strength of character, 'the most fearless uprightness' and other qualities which made him, in her estimation, 'one of the most remarkable men who could be known'. Even more significantly, she added that 'the Queen feels that life for the second time is become most trying and sad to bear deprived of all she so needs', words which could be interpreted as expressing a relationship on a deeper level than had been previously thought.[38]

For the rest of her life, she ordered that two small salt cellars, a gift from Brown, should be placed on her luncheon table, and that a fresh flower should be put daily on the pillow of his bedroom in Balmoral. There was a plethora of In Memoriam memorabilia, including statuettes and plaster of Paris busts of Brown, funeral brooches and gold tie pins set with diamonds around images of his head, distributed to his relatives and to courtiers alike. Dr Alexander Profeit, who had always been one of Brown's most outspoken enemies at Balmoral, was among the recipients of a tie pin. He knew he would be a laughing-stock among the household if he wore it more than necessary, so, in order not to offend the Queen, he kept it in his coat pocket so he could wear it correctly whenever he had to go and see her.

The Times acknowledged Brown's popularity among his own countrymen. 'Deep regret is felt on Deeside, particularly in the Balmoral and Braemar districts,' it noted on his death. 'There he was widely known and widely respected. He was loved among his own people, and they regarded his good fortune as an honour reflected upon them.'[39]

A funeral service was held at Windsor on 3 April, attended by the Queen, before Brown's coffin was taken north for another ceremony and burial at Crathie cemetery two days later. Among the tributes and memorials to John Brown was a lifesize bronze statue by the Viennese-born sculptor Edgar Boehm, initially placed alongside the Queen's garden cottage at Balmoral until removed after her death, on the orders of King Edward VII, to a suitably remote hillside. Brown might not have appreciated the statue, for the ample Boehm was one of those who had incurred his wrath some years previously during a 'Great Pony Row' in Scotland, when he complained that some of the more portly members of the Queen's German entourage were riding her small Highland ponies almost to death. Thereafter he referred to the sculptor as 'Mr Bum'.

* * *

In February 1884 the Queen published a second volume based on entries from her diary: *More Leaves from a Journal of a Life in the Highlands*. It covered the first twenty years of her widowhood, and, as she wrote in the preface, it was intended to show 'how her sad and suffering heart was soothed and cheered by the excursions and incidents it recounts'.[40] Again, the sales were considerable, and it found favour with the public, though it caused embarrassment within the family and some of the household. In particular, its dedication to 'My Loyal Highlanders and especially to the memory of my devoted personal attendant and faithful friend John Brown', the frequent references to him and its effusive conclusion, in which she dwelt on her 'irreparable loss' and how he was 'daily, nay hourly, missed by me',[41] deeply rankled with most of them. The Prince of Wales begged her to confine circulation to friends and family instead of allowing general publication, but she refused to listen. The German Crown Princess, who was no less critical of Brown but preferred to keep a more discreet silence than her brother, merely remarked to her mother than it described the charm of Balmoral 'so well'.

Much worse was to come. The family were aghast to learn that the Queen planned to write a 'little memoir' of her faithful Highland servant. She approached Sir Theodore Martin, the Prince Consort's official biographer, to assist, a task from which he excused himself with the utmost tact on the grounds that his wife's delicate health would not allow him to give the task sufficient attention. Next she contacted a Miss MacGregor, who read through the manuscript and struck out what she called 'unnecessary repetitions'.

The Queen sent the result to Ponsonby, who was appalled. Knowing that any recommendation from him not to proceed further would almost certainly produce the opposite effect, he recommended that she should send it to William Boyd Carpenter, Bishop of Ripon and Dr Cameron Lees of St Giles in Edinburgh, as they both had some experience of authorship. Neither of them wanted anything to do with the project. Ponsonby wrote diplomatically to the Queen that he doubted the wisdom of Her Majesty making public such 'innermost and most sacred feelings', which might easily be misunderstood by less sensitive readers. She told him firmly that the account was intended for private circulation only and asked him to return the manuscript so she could send it to Disraeli's private secretary, Montagu Corry, Lord Rowton. Rowton's reaction was similar, but he had an even better idea. Why not send the manuscript, he suggested, to a printer who would take at least six months to set it, by which time – if indeed she had not lost interest in the project, which was quite possible – they would all have had a better chance to persuade her of the inadvisability of publication.

Less of a shrinking violet than his peers, the new Dean of Windsor, Randall Davidson, tried a blunter approach – to reason with the Queen and talk her out of it that way. Through her lady-in-waiting Lady Ely, she asked Davidson to withdraw his remarks and apologise for the pain he had caused her. He readily offered his apologies, but at the same time said he would resign his post rather than withdraw his remarks. That Sunday, the sermon at Windsor was preached by another clergyman, and Davidson heard nothing from the Queen for a fortnight. Then he was summoned to a royal audience and found the Queen as friendly as ever. No reference was made to the notorious memoir.

The Dean of Windsor was not the first man to discover that Her Majesty admired, liked and trusted best those who were prepared to incur her wrath for the sake of what they believed was right. The memoir was postponed, and later destroyed by Ponsonby. Obstinate the Queen may have been, but she knew better than to defy the advice of half a dozen well-respected men who all said much the same thing, even if they told her in varying degrees what she did not wish to hear.

The early 1880s were a difficult time on a personal level for Queen Victoria, with the loss in 1881 of Disraeli, in 1883 of John Brown and one year later of her youngest son, Leopold, Duke of Albany. During these years she came to rely more and more on the support of Sir Henry Ponsonby, whose political opinions might conflict with hers but whom nevertheless she respected and trusted. All the family valued his advice and presence, and her children often depended on him to choose the right moment to propose something to their mother on which they did not dare to approach her themselves.

Her relations with Gladstone never improved, and after Ponsonby was put in the unenviable position of having to convey one of her most marked rebukes to him, he had to advise Gladstone to reply direct to the Queen rather than to Ponsonby himself as her private secretary, as he had no desire to put his 'finger in between two iron clads colliding'.[42] His attitude to the role of the sovereign in the constitution remained that of a Whig a hundred years previously. Though he devoted much of his life to serving the Queen, he always retained a down-to-earth perspective on the splendour and institution of royalty and monarchy. The lack of showiness of the British monarchy, when compared with the opulence of some European courts, clearly appealed to him.

NINE

'A sort of pet'

In June 1887, the year she celebrated her golden jubilee, Queen
Victoria acquired the first of her Indian servants. To mark her fifty
years on the throne, Sir John Tyler, governor of the north-west
provinces in India, recruited two Indians specifically to come to
England as her servants. One, Abdul Karim, was to play an
increasingly important and highly contentious part in her life, and
was in fact destined to remain in her service until her death. Twenty-
four years old at the time of his appointment, slim and intelligent, he
entered her service at the same time as his colleague Mohammed
Bukhsh. At first she had them stand behind her chair at breakfast, as
she ate a boiled egg in a gold eggcup with a gold spoon.

Abdul Karim, she thought, looked so distinguished with his black
beard and dark eyes, and she decided that he was destined for
greater things. Something in his personality evidently made a deep
impression on her. Perhaps he had exceptional powers as a
raconteur, in his telling her stories of India and fluently answering
her questions about the religions, customs and traditions of her
Indian subjects. To the end of her days, it would always be a source
of major disappointment to her that she never managed to make the
journey to her Indian empire, and there can be little doubt that
Abdul Karim provided her with the next best thing in a suitable
personal connection to this exciting yet unknown world. Her letters
suggest that she had some fascinating discussions with him,
embracing philosophy, politics and practical matters. Above all, he
appealed to her as a true man of the people, as opposed to a
representative of the viceroy's court, who could be guaranteed to tell
her something of the essence of the sub-continent, rather than the
official line.

Though Karim was barely literate, the Queen soon raised him
from the rank of *khitmagar* (waiter) to *munshi* (secretary). Instead
of cooking her curries, he progressed to giving her lessons in

Hindustani. He was relieved of such menial tasks as waiting at table, and all photographs which had been taken of him handing dishes to the Queen were soon destroyed as being beneath his dignity.

Within a few months, the Queen was employing more Indian servants, and she made it clear that Karim must be treated as the most important among them. He was put in charge of all the other Indians in her employ, and he soon graduated to Indian Secretary, being given his own office and a staff of clerks. From looking after the Queen's letters and papers, he moved on to commenting on those concerning India and helping to compose answers. If petitions from India needed nothing more than a formal refusal, she would hand them straight to him. In 1889, Karim was given John Brown's old room at Balmoral. That same year, the Queen took him to stay overnight at Glassalt Shiel, the little lodge on Lock Muick in which she had once sworn she would never sleep again after the death of Brown.

This last great emotional attachment of the Queen's life was in some ways her most blinkered. She believed everything Karim told her. He assured her that his father, Dr Mohammed Waziruddin, was a surgeon-general in the Indian Army in Agra. His family were all well-respected people who occupied important positions in government service, he said, and he himself had been a highly paid clerk in Agra before coming to England. She found his Hindustani lessons rewarding and regarded him as a very strict but capable master, and his continuous presence was a great comfort to her.

In 1890 the Munshi returned briefly to India on leave. The Queen asked Lord Lansdowne, the Viceroy of India, to obtain a grant of land for him in Agra, as well as a place for him and his father at the forthcoming Durbar, the Indian princes' state reception given in the Queen's honour. Notwithstanding considerable jealousy on the part of other Indians, Lansdowne settled the land grant and found room for him at the Durbar, but explained he could do nothing for the Munshi's father, whose low earnings automatically excluded him from attending the ceremony. This was as good as proof that Dr Waziruddin's status was less grand than his son claimed, but the Queen continued to believe her Munshi. To Dr Reid's amazement, she endorsed Karim's request for a large quantity of drugs to be sent to his father, and when the doctor disclaimed all responsibility for a consignment which he estimated as having the potential to kill up to 15,000 adults, the Queen requested that the drugs should be ordered through a British chemist in India and the bill be sent to her.

The Munshi's father was not the only one of his relations to benefit from the Queen's generosity. Before coming to England, Karim had married, and his wife, plus various female relations, followed him to Britain, settling in the three homes which the Queen had allotted to the Munshi – Frogmore Cottage at Windsor, Arthur Cottage at Osborne and the specially built Karim Cottage at Balmoral. They and others from their extended family lived quietly, playing no role in their increasingly important and self-important relative's career. Whether there was one wife or more was open to question, as Dr Reid maintained that whenever he was asked to attend 'Mrs Abdul Karim', who (as Indian custom prescribed) always remained fully clothed and veiled, a different tongue was put out for him to examine. Life within these self-contained compounds was lived along strict Islamic lines, with animals slaughtered according to religious rites.

The existence of the Munshi's exotic ménage, a stone's-throw from the Queen's own residences, struck visitors as extremely curious. Lady-in-waiting Marie Mallet wrote of going to see the Munshi's wife, whom she found 'fat and not uncomely, a delicate shade of chocolate and gorgeously attired, rings on her fingers, rings in her nose, a pocket mirror set in turquoises on her thumb and every feasible part of her person hung with chains and bracelets and ear-rings, a rose-pink veil on her head bordered with heavy gold and splendid silk and satin swathings round her person. She speaks English in a limited manner and declared she likes the cold. But the house surrounded by a twenty-foot palisade, the white figure emerging silently from a near chamber, all seemed so un-English, so essentially Oriental.'[1]

The Munshi's name began to appear not only in the Court Circular, but also in newspapers and magazines. Any attempt on the part of the royal household to belittle him by fobbing him off with a hired carriage, by seating him among the dressers at theatrical performances or by refusing to allow him use of the billiard room immediately incurred the Queen's wrath as soon as she was informed. The other Indian servants were jealous of his privileged position, but the Queen always took his side. Whether Abdul Karim was in the wrong or not, and his high-handed attitude meant he frequently was at fault, Her Majesty would never hear a word against him. Any Indian who quarrelled with the Munshi was liable to find himself being sent back to the Asiatic sub-continent almost at once.

Once, when the Munshi was suffering from a carbuncle on his neck, the Queen became very worried. She would visit Karim's sick-room several times a day, where she would examine his neck, smooth his pillows, 'stroke his hand' and have her boxes brought in so as to allow her to spend more time in his company. Suspecting that Reid was not doing enough for this 'dear good young man', the Queen suggested that he get a second opinion. The capable Reid had no need of a second opinion, and once the abscess had been opened, the Munshi quickly recovered.

If the royal household had resented John Brown's presence, they soon decided for themselves that the Munshi was far worse. Racism and snobbery both help to explain this aversion to him, for only if an Indian was a prince would the ladies and gentlemen of Queen Victoria's court consider treating him as an equal. Even liberals like Ponsonby referred disparagingly to 'the Black Brigade'. The Queen had been obliged to give instructions that the Indians in her employ must never be referred to as 'black men', and even Lord Salisbury had to apologise for doing so.

At the Braemar games in 1890 the Queen's third son, Arthur, Duke of Connaught, was so angered at seeing the Munshi, 'a very conspicuous figure, among the gentry', that he complained of his presence to Ponsonby. The secretary had long since become an expert in the handling of these delicate situations and told him that Abdul stood where he was on the orders of the Queen. Perhaps it would be better, he suggested, to mention it directly to Her Majesty himself. 'This entirely shut him up.'[2] As Ponsonby had foreseen, Queen Victoria's favourite son thought better of it.

Any speculation on the Munshi's humble origins, no matter how well justified, infuriated the Queen. But the household's antipathy towards the Munshi was understandable. He undoubtedly misled the Queen about his origins. He would never have been employed, as it was claimed in one press report, in a secretarial capacity by the Nawab of Jawara. Moreover, his father was not a surgeon-general in the Indian Army, or indeed a doctor of any description. He had merely been a hospital assistant, with no medical diploma or qualification that would have secured him a place on a British medical register.

Refusing to believe this, the Queen instructed Sir Henry Ponsonby's son Fritz, then on the Viceroy's staff but soon to become one of Her Majesty's equerries, to investigate. Fritz Ponsonby duly visited 'Dr' Waziruddin and, on reporting to the Queen later that year, explained that Waziruddin was not a surgeon-general but merely 'an apothecary at the jail'. The Queen flatly rejected young Ponsonby's story, saying he must have seen the wrong person. Assuming the matter was now closed, Fritz Ponsonby was astonished to discover the extent of the Queen's anger. Though he was an equerry, he was not invited to dine at the Queen's table until a year had elapsed. It was no wonder that he shared the household's resentment of the man who seemed to him to have the status of 'a sort of pet, like a dog or cat which the Queen will not willingly give up.'[3]

Sometimes he who dares wins, and the Munshi's web of deceit about his family's origins and father's achievements had paid off. If he had told the truth, it has been pointed out, he might never have risen to such an exalted position in the royal household at all, especially in view of the attitudes which most English people had towards Indians in the Victorian age.

Yet this was not the end of the Munshi's lack of trustworthiness. The Queen was particularly fond of a brooch which had been given to her by her son-in-law the Grand Duke of Hesse. One day she asked for it to be pinned on her shawl by her dresser, Mrs Tuck. When she could not see it and asked where it was, the Queen was assured that the brooch had been pinned on as directed, but despite an extensive search it could not be found. A footman on duty that day suspected that the Munshi's brother-in-law, Hourmet Ali, had stolen it. The Queen angrily accused the dresser of having lost it.

A few weeks later it turned up at Wagland's, a jewellery shop in Windsor, where the proprietor confirmed that an Indian had sold it to him for 6*s*. When he returned it, the Munshi's enemies were delighted, convinced that they were about to see the last of him. However, when Mrs Tuck took the brooch and letter to the Queen and reported Hourmet Ali's involvement, she was furious with dresser and jeweller alike. 'That is what you British call justice!'[4] she shouted. (Her reference to 'you British' makes one wonder whether she had suddenly assumed honorary Indian nationality for the purpose.) After talking to the Munshi, she ordered Mrs Tuck not to mention a word of the matter to anyone else. The Munshi's brother-in-law, she said, would never dream of stealing anything; the Munshi himself had picked up the brooch at the 'policeman's box', and as it was an Indian custom to keep anything one found and say nothing about it, he was only acting in accordance with his national customs.

What the Queen's entourage resented more than his race or his class or his dishonesty was his bumptiousness and insufferable self-importance. Even John Brown at his most insolent had never thought of himself as anything more than a privileged royal servant, while the Munshi insisted on being treated as an equal of the gentlemen of the household, and the Queen never failed to support him. Every time she took her annual spring holidays on the Continent, when tension within the household was generally at its greatest, the Munshi's behaviour caused particular resentment.

During her stay in Florence in the spring of 1894, it reached epic proportions. Firstly he complained bitterly to the Queen about the distance of his railway carriage from hers in the royal train to Italy. Next he refused to allow any other, less important, Indians to set foot in it, and insisted that the bathroom and lavatory must be reserved for his exclusive use. Once they had arrived in Florence, he persuaded the Queen to issue instructions that he was to drive out in the same carriage as the other gentlemen of the household. He arranged for a display of photographs in a shop window in which his likeness appeared in the centre, surrounded by nine photographs of the Queen. At his behest, she gave orders that his name was to appear more frequently in the newspapers. In case these orders might not be observed, the Munshi prepared his own press release with a photograph of himself in which he was, he instructed, to be made 'thinner and less dark', and sent them to the *Florence Gazette*:

> The Munshi Mohammed Abdul Karim, son of Haji Dr Mohammed Waziruddin an inhabitant of Agra the Cheef City of NWP who left his office in India, and came to England in the service of the Queen Victoria Empress of India in the year 1887.
>
> He was appointed first for some time as Her Majestys Munshi and Indian Clerk. From 1892 he was appointed as her M's Indian Secretary. He is belonging to a good and highly respectful Famiely. All is Famiely has been in Govt. Service with high position. His father is still in the service of the Govn. 36 years ago. One brother of his is a city Collector. All the Indian attendants of the Queen are under him and he also wholes different duties to perform in Her Majesty's Service.[5]

During the Queen's visit to the south of France in March 1895 a newspaper in Nice printed the information that Karim had helped the Queen from her carriage. He was grossly insulted at the suggestion that he had performed any such menial function, and she readily endorsed his efforts to correct this misunderstanding. 'By telegraphic error it was made to appear that the Munshi assisted the Queen from her carriage on her arrival at Nice, which is of course not the case, as Her Majesty is always assisted by an Indian servant,' reported the *Galignani Messenger* dutifully. 'The Munshi, as a learned man and the Queen's Indian Secretary and preceptor in Hindustani, is one of the most important personages "*aupres de la Reine*" having several men under him, and being often privileged to dine with his Royal Mistress and pupil.'[6]

The Munshi's presence was resented not only by the household, but also by Queen Victoria's three surviving sons, the Prince of Wales, the Duke of Edinburgh and the Duke of Connaught. For them, John Brown's rudeness had been bad enough, but at least he was honest and they never had any reason to distrust him. The same could never be said of the Munshi, and his pomposity was intolerable. Perhaps Brown's brusque demeanour and lack of manners had not been so bad after all.

In the spring of 1894 the Queen went to Coburg for the wedding of two of her grandchildren, Grand Duke Ernest Ludwig of Hesse and Princess Victoria Melita of Saxe-Coburg Gotha. The bride's father was Prince Alfred, Duke of Edinburgh and, since the death of his uncle Ernest, now also Duke of Saxe-Coburg Gotha. Inevitably, the Munshi went as part of the Queen's entourage.

Shortly after their arrival, the Duke told Sir Henry Ponsonby that under no circumstances would he allow the Munshi into the church for the wedding ceremony. The indignant Queen insisted that he must be allowed to attend; to exclude him would be most hurtful to his feelings. As a compromise, it was arranged that he would be personally conducted into the gallery of the chapel by the son of one of the Prince's equerries, provided there were no other servants present. On being escorted in, the Munshi caught sight of a couple of grooms and was so incensed at being seated with them that he stormed out of the building before the ceremony had started. He then wrote an outraged letter to the Queen, which was handed to her after the newly wedded couple had gone.

At first, she was thoroughly upset. Then she sent for the Duke's private secretary to tell him that she was putting him in charge of everything to do with the Munshi's 'position' for the rest of her stay in

Coburg. She realised she could frighten her son's secretary into obeying her more easily than the experienced Ponsonby, who was doubtless glad to be relieved of such duties. From then on, the Munshi was invited to all functions and was driven about, in splendid isolation, in a royal carriage with a liveried footman on the box.

* * *

By the summer of 1894 Sir Henry Ponsonby seemed much older than his sixty-eight years. The Queen was sometimes less than sympathetic to this most hard-working of men, who had given such faithful service over twenty years and who, it might be said, literally wore himself out as a result. To Dr Reid, she had commented rather coldly in September 1893 that Sir Henry gave her no help in her difficulties with the government, as he lacked backbone and was too placid. 'He has no courage, but agrees with me, and then is talked over by others and agrees with them. He agrees with everybody.'[7] In his position, this most courteous and easy-going of gentlemen would have found his task even more onerous had he not played the diplomat and dared to do otherwise.

Had Sir Henry's political views been closer to hers, the Queen would have surely been more accommodating. But old age had made her increasingly dogmatic and set in her ways. Like many elderly people, she disliked change, resented new ways of doing things and was inevitably less patient than before. However, it seems a little strange that she did not properly appreciate and value the impartiality of his dealings with sovereign and ministers, or his desire for peace and his quiet determination to smooth difficulties out. With her failing eyesight she was having difficulties with reading his handwriting, but even others familiar with it observed a change in his handwriting for the worse, and a general appearance of apathy, of increasing forgetfulness, on his part. Like her, his reserves of patience were probably wearing thin with the advancing years.

One detects a note of mild exasperation in his comment of 1893 (probably to Lady Ponsonby) that Her Majesty 'is full of business and sending ticklers all round, as much as to say "I'm back, so look out!"'[8] At what would be his last interview with her late the following year, he was reputed to have said to her face, 'What a funny little old woman you are.'[9] Astonished at being spoken to in this candid way, the Queen told him that he could not be well.

Sadly, she was quite correct. By this time he had probably suffered a series of minor seizures and may have been in the early stages of senile dementia. But nobody was prepared for the paralytic stroke on 7 January 1895 which rendered him unconscious for a while. When he came to, his right arm and leg were completely paralysed, and his speech was incoherent and indistinct. He was confined to his bed, and by May it was evident to all around him that he was most unlikely to recover.

Since the start of Ponsonby's illness, Reid had become the person in the household whom the Queen and most of her family trusted more than anyone. He had to undertake the painful duty of telling Lady Ponsonby that she would need to resign her husband's offices for him. The Queen permitted them to stay at Osborne Cottage for the duration of his illness, and it had previously been agreed that Lady Ponsonby could keep the rooms they occupied at St James's for the rest of her lifetime. However, his salary of £1,700 per annum was reduced to a pension of £1,000 when he became ill.

For the next six months he lingered, a helpless shadow of his former self, until the end came on 21 November. 'My heart bleeds for you and your children,' the Queen telegraphed to Lady Ponsonby, 'and I feel deeply the loss of so faithful and devoted a friend.'[10] To their daughter Magdalen she wrote that there was one person who felt her beloved father's loss more than anyone, 'and whose *gratitude* to him is *very deep*, and that is my good Munshi Abdul Karim. Your dear father was kinder to him than anyone, always befriending him, and the loss to him is, as he says, that of "a *second* Father". He could not well go to the funeral tomorrow to his regret, but sends a wreath, and I enclose what he wrote on it as I fear in the multitude of similar wreaths this tribute of gratitude might be overlooked.'[11] However, neither wreath nor card had been the Munshi's doing. The former, Reid assured Magdalen Ponsonby, had been made at Her Majesty's special command, and she herself had dictated to the Munshi what he was to write on it.

It says something for the enormous workload undertaken by Ponsonby during the previous few years that two members of the household needed promotion to the position of private secretary in order to succeed him. One was Arthur Bigge, the other was Fleetwood Edwards. Bigge found his task very difficult in the early stages, telling Reid that the Queen often found it 'inconvenient' to see him, and he could only communicate with her through written messages. Declaring it was impossible to do such a job under these conditions, Reid intervened to persuade Her Majesty that it would be necessary for her to see Bigge regularly.[12] Yet Reid was now indispensable as the only male member of the household who could readily approach her, and his importance as a liaison between his sovereign and the outside world was invaluable.

Reid's faithful service and increasing importance in the household had been rightly recognised. In May 1895 Lord Rosebery had told him he intended to offer him a knighthood on the Queen's birthday. Reid declined, making as his excuse to Dr Jenner that 'a simple knighthood' was 'rather looked down on here', and that the fact it was being offered to him showed that he was 'not put on the same platform as the rest of the people here', though his services to the Queen were more arduous and responsible than those of most of the men in royal service who had already been similarly honoured.[13] His attitude was mildly frowned on by his colleagues, and he evidently reconsidered his views. On 20 June he was knighted at Balmoral. Two years later, the Queen conferred on him a baronetcy as part of the diamond jubilee honours.

* * *

The year 1897 was that of the Queen's diamond jubilee, but for Dr Reid it was also to be remembered, unhappily, as 'the year of the Munshi'. In January he and Randall Davidson, Bishop of Winchester, had frequent discussions on the subject of the Queen and the Munshi, and he remarked with regret that Her Majesty was 'off her head on this point'.[14] He had been asked to treat the Munshi for an unpleasant disease which, he found, was venereal in origin, and 'had an interesting talk with her' about it. It was more than likely that she regarded any comments on the possibility of his having such a complaint as a disgraceful slur on the character and morals of her disgracefully persecuted Indian servant.

That spring, the household's difficulties with the Munshi came to a head. Queen Victoria had planned that she would take her spring holiday at Cimiez, near Nice, and it was beyond question that she intended to take the Munshi with her. This would necessitate his dining with her gentlemen. After previous occasions they had had enough, and they strongly objected to the fact that they would have to take their meals with him in the somewhat cramped accommodation offered by the Hotel Excelsior Regina. The Queen's personal secretary, Harriet Phipps, was chosen by the less than gallant gentlemen of the household and asked to tell her that if the Munshi was to accompany her to Cimiez, the gentlemen would not be prepared to associate with him.

When the message was delivered, her reaction was swift. She lost her temper, rose from her chair and angrily swept everything off her writing table on to the floor. This stalemate was only brought to an end when Lord Salisbury persuaded her that the French, being a somewhat odd race, would not understand the Munshi's position. If he accompanied her, he might be exposed to insults. She gave in, but with bad grace. While he did not accompany her entourage to the Côte d'Azure, he turned up soon afterwards. His friend Rafiuddin Ahmed, who had tried and failed to become a lawyer and was now calling himself a journalist, joined him, but the household objected to his presence so strongly that the Queen was obliged to ask Ahmed to leave.

The household were determined to get rid of the Munshi. Reid warned the Queen that people in high places were saying that the only charitable explanation of her extraordinary obsession with her Indian servant was that she was no longer quite sane. He feared that a time might come when, for the sake of her good name, he might find it necessary for him as her doctor to announce that she had indeed gone mad. It was a brave thing for him to say to her face, but, unpalatable as it was, she apparently took his words seriously – for the time being.

Next Dr Reid spoke firmly to the Munshi, accusing him of dishonesty, lying about his origins and education, telling the Queen that in India no receipts were ever given for money and that therefore he did not need to give any, and having certain letters of the Queen's in his possession which he was refusing to give up. If the Munshi did not stop his double-dealing and curb his pretensions, the doctor would feel himself obliged to reveal to her the full extent of his duplicity.

If he had hoped for any results after his interview with the Queen, he was to be disappointed. She insisted that the household had all behaved disgracefully, that the Munshi was to be treated with all due respect, that her gentlemen were not to go talking about such a painful subject either among themselves or with those from outside, and, above all, that they must not unite with the household against one person.

Frederick Ponsonby said wearily that all of them had done their best, but the Queen declared that they were all racially prejudiced and jealous of the Munshi. The Queen's views were in fact well ahead of their time. Her positive discrimination in having Indian members of the household contrasted impressively with the record of Queen Elizabeth II, whose reign over a multi-racial Britain at the millennium was in no way reflected in her household, which had not one secretary, equerry or household servant of Asian or Afro-Caribbean background.[15]

But the gentlemen of Victoria's household still tried to get rid of the Munshi and telegraphed the Viceroy in India for any further information about his background and anything that might make his position untenable. Meanwhile, the Prince of Wales was on holiday in Cannes. He had become increasingly alarmed about the harm which his mother's obsession with the Munshi was doing the monarchy, especially in jubilee year. He sent for Reid to ascertain the extent of the situation and assured him that he was prepared to support the gentlemen in any reasonable moves they might need to take, and to intervene personally if necessary.

The Queen enlisted the help of her grandson-in-law Prince Louis of Battenberg. As a member of the family who owed much of his current standing in public life to her intervention, particularly with regard to his joining the English Navy as a young man despite his German birth, and as the husband of her granddaughter Princess Victoria, she was sure he would support her. She sent him to tell her gentlemen, through Sir Arthur Davidson, the groom-in-waiting, that they must 'associate more' with the Munshi. He did so with some reluctance, only to find the household up in arms and threatening to resign if she insisted on pressing the matter. Endless conferences between various senior officers of the household followed. The result was akin to a nervous breakdown on the Queen's part. She finally admitted to Dr Reid that she had been foolish in acceding to her Indian servant's constant requests.

A few days later, when Reid told the Queen he had received a letter from Sir Edward Bradford, Chief of Police for London, about the Munshi's complicity in the somewhat suspect Muslim Patriotic League affairs, she broke down, admitted 'she had played the fool about the Munshi, begged to be "let down easily" and promised to do what they wanted, though not abruptly, for fear of any scandal'.[16]

Yet it was not enough to prevent 'a very excited interview' between the sovereign and her doctor a day or two later, in which he firmly warned her that the only reasonable excuse that could be given was that Her Majesty was not sane, and that the time would come when he would find it necessary, for her memory and reputation, to say so, 'and that is a nice position to be in'.[17]

It had no lasting effect. Having evidently slept on the problem, the Queen continued to insist that the Munshi was to be treated with all due respect, and that the household should not continue talking about this 'painful subject' among themselves or with others. The court realised that it was no use: Her Majesty would not change her view that they were all racially prejudiced, and that they were all jealous of the Munshi.

That summer, the Queen wanted to confer on the Munshi the Membership of the Royal Victorian Order. He had already been honoured with the CIE, or a Companion of the Order of the Indian Empire. Once again, the household were angered by this rank favouritism, and Sir James Reid was again prevailed on to speak to the equally weary Lord Salisbury on the matter. The Prime Minister advised her that to honour the Munshi in this way would look like favouritism towards her Muhammadan subjects and cause jealousy among the Hindus. This reasoning apparently convinced her.

By now, even the Queen was beginning to realise that her devoted Indian servant was not totally blameless. If he was attracting such hostility, surely there was something in the comments being made against him. Yet to admit that he was in the wrong would have meant losing face in front of her household, and she did not wish to give the impression – no matter how true it might have been – that she was afraid of him. The more she favoured and protected him, the more he took advantage of the situation, and the more his bullying and insolence increased.

In October 1897 a large photograph was published in the *Daily Graphic*, showing the Munshi standing by the Queen while she sat at her table, signing documents. Underneath it ran the caption: 'The Queen's Life in the Highlands, Her Majesty receiving a lesson in Hindustani from the Munshi Hafiz Abdul Karim C.I.E.' Reid discussed the photograph with the Queen, who was uncomfortable about the matter and felt she had been made to look foolish. That week Reid interviewed the photographer, who told him that the Munshi himself had ordered its publication.

Another round of 'painful interviews' ensued, especially after the furious Munshi resented Reid's discussing the matter with the photographer. The Queen realised that she had made a mistake, writing Reid a fourteen-page letter which started with her admission that she was 'terribly annoyed and upset by all this stupid business which unfortunately I am to blame for, and regret extremely'.[18] The persistent aggravation was telling on Reid, who was feeling gravely put upon in having to deal with matters far beyond the call of normal duty. In severe pain as a result of a boil on his right thigh, and worried almost beyond endurance, after a sleepless night he wrote a letter of resignation. Thankfully, the Queen must have sensed how upset he was and changed her attitude towards him for the better, evidently realising that she dare not lose him; the letter was never sent.

* * *

By early 1898, the relationship between Queen and Indian servant was fraying at the edges. Both were beginning to raise their voices to each other, and her dresser noted in February that he shouted at her, after which she wrote him a long letter about it. Lord Salisbury remarked that Her Majesty could always get rid of the Munshi if she really wanted to – but such an outcome seemed most unlikely. He firmly believed that 'she really likes the emotional excitement, as being the only form of excitement she can have'.[19]

There was another, stronger, underlying reason. The Queen would not be dictated to, as she had made plain during one of the 'Brown rows'. Nobody, whether family, government or household, was going to tell her whom she should employ or even have as friends and confidants. To her, it was a person's character which was important, not their position in the social hierarchy, let alone their racial origins or the colour of their skin. She also had a keen sense of fair play and the British instinct for championing the underdog, which was perhaps more than could be said of many of those around her.

In fact, if the Munshi was not blue-blooded, this could be a positive virtue. Queen Victoria was not going to place her blind trust exclusively in aristocrats or courtiers. She would defend those in whom she placed her trust to the last breath in her body against any unfounded charges which she believed to be based on prejudice or jealousy, hence her spirited rebuff to those who dared to hint that he had probably stolen her jewellery for financial gain. While she knew that the Munshi, like John Brown, was only human and had his faults like anyone else, she must have felt a certain inward delight in forcing family and household to accept a man whom they hated or despised. Any attempts to poison her mind against him backfired with a vengeance. Only a decade or so later, others would find a similar parallel in the relationship between her granddaughter, Empress Alexandra of Russia, and the Russian peasant Grigori Rasputin.

The Munshi remained in Queen Victoria's service for the remaining three years of her life. After her last holiday in Cimiez, her problems with the household regarding his presence diminished. Like John Brown, he proved himself a faithful companion in a way that nobody from her household or family ever could be.

Additionally, she had a vested interest in not wishing to lose face. After having braved a solid coalition of opposition from her household and their evident determination to try to force him out, either by shaming him into leaving or blackening him so much to the Queen that she would give in and dismiss him – both campaigns on their part proving counter-productive – she would have lost face had she given in to them. For better or worse, she had no alternative but to retain his services until he decided to leave of his own accord, something he was unlikely to do, or until she decided she had really had enough of him, another unlikely scenario.

* * *

In time, Sir James Reid would also cause his employer some, but only temporary, distress – if for a very different reason. Unlike John Brown, he was not destined to remain a bachelor for life. At the age of forty-nine he fell in love with Susan Baring, a lady-in-waiting at court and niece of Lady Ponsonby. What began as friendship rapidly blossomed, and on 24 July 1899 he proposed to her. Normally so understanding in many personal matters, the Queen had an uncommonly proprietorial attitude where bachelors and spinsters in her employ suddenly announced that they intended to get married. Naturally, Reid ensured that she was among the first to be informed. She was 'much less ferocious about it' than he and his affianced ever expected, but she asked them to refrain from announcing the news or telling the other members of the household, at Osborne at the time, for a few days.[20]

They had to wait for a full month before they were allowed to make the news public. Moreover, they had to agree to 'the Queen's Regulations'. Certain conditions had to be observed scrupulously once they were married, regarding the times of day he was in attendance on the Queen, times of year when they could go on holiday and where the future Mrs Reid could and could not go when they were at Windsor. He was still required to come round after breakfast to see what the Queen needed and be back before luncheon. Moreover, while Mrs Reid might occasionally visit his room, 'this must not interfere with his other duties'.[21]

A less amenable employee, particularly an eminent physician aged almost fifty, might have reacted angrily to such conditions, but Reid treated the business light-heartedly. He posted 'the Queen's Regulations' to Susan, who fortunately found them as amusing as he did. They knew that an elderly lady of eighty deserved to be treated lightly in her declining years, and there was nothing to be gained by upsetting her and making a fuss about something they had expected anyway. She might be a demanding and authoritarian employer, but at heart a kindly one.

The wedding took place at St Paul's, Knightsbridge, on 28 November. The Queen did not herself attend, but the guests of honour included her daughters the Princesses Helena, Louise and Beatrice. So many members of the royal household and staff were there that the Queen, who remained behind at Windsor, asked with some anxiety, 'And who shall bring me my tea?'[22] Her wedding present to the couple was a box of silver knives, engraved with the family crest, while Susan was given a diamond brooch inscribed with the royal cypher 'V.R.I.', an Indian shawl and a signed photograph of the Queen.

* * *

As the man upon whom Queen Victoria relied more than any other during her last years, it was not surprising that Reid played a major role in the drama which surrounded her declining days and death.

By the time she went to Osborne House for Christmas 1900, those closest to her were aware that her health had been declining since the autumn, when she had not been quite herself. With hindsight, some must have wondered if – unthinkable though it must have seemed – their apparently immortal Majesty would ever return to the English mainland alive. Canon Boyd Carpenter was invited to preach at a short service for her on the last Sunday of the century, 30 December, which was held in the drawing-room, with Princess Beatrice playing the harmonium. Afterwards he had a conversation with the Queen, and was encouraged that she spoke of hoping to go to Cimiez in the spring. She was not well, he realised, but seemed less depressed than when he saw her earlier in the month.[23]

On 13 January 1901 Reid noticed that she 'was rather childish and apathetic'.[24] The next day she officially received Field Marshal Roberts, who had commanded the British armies in the Boer War. It was to be her last official duty as Queen.

Next day, Professor Hermann Pagenstecher, a German ophthalmic doctor at the London Eye Hospital, examined the Queen's eyes for cataracts and confirmed Reid's prognosis that, far more importantly than the cataract condition, she was experiencing 'cerebral degeneration', or was in imminent danger of suffering a stroke. Her disposition had altered, and little irritations such as unnecessary noise, or bells not answered quickly enough, had now ceased to irritate her. The royal schedule for the next few weeks included a spring holiday for the Queen at the Excelsior Regina Hotel at Cimiez, but Bigge discussed the matter with Reid and prudently cancelled their accommodation with the hotel management, enclosing a cheque to the sum of £800 for costs already incurred.[25]

On 16 January the Queen's maids were unable to rouse their mistress. For the first time in his life, Reid went to her bedroom to see her. In the past she had never let her physicians see her in this most private of rooms; it had been the duty of her maids to administer all her medicines and draughts. He decided she was breathing normally and appeared in no immediate distress, though it astonished him to see how small and vulnerable the woman who was titular head of almost a quarter of the world looked at home. She remained in bed the entire day, the first time Reid could remember such a thing happening. Her dressers were summoned to help her rise at around 6 p.m., and she was wheeled into the sitting-room next to her bedroom. When she called for Reid about one and a half hours later, he found her very dazed and confused.

Sir Francis Laking, Physician-in-Ordinary and Surgeon Apothecary to the Prince of Wales, was also at Osborne, sent by the

Prince to report on his mother's health. The Prince's high opinion of Laking was not shared by Reid, and only the previous month the Queen had refused to let Laking examine her. As both men went in to dinner that night, Laking said that he had spent forty-five minutes with Her Majesty and considered she did not seem 'too bad'.

Reid suspected that the Queen had summoned what remaining strength she had to put on a show for the 'outsider', and also that Laking was going to give the Prince of Wales a falsely optimistic report on his mother's health – the kind of report he wanted to receive. After fifty-nine years as heir to the throne, perhaps he found it impossible to believe that the long-dreaded time was about to come. Anxious to ensure the future King had an accurate assessment of his mother's condition, that evening Reid visited her again, found her just as confused as she had been before, and wrote a report to the Prince which he hoped would be believed, in preference to any messages from Laking.

Throughout the remaining few days – the last of the Queen's life – Reid found himself more or less in the position of a headmaster, with Osborne being his school. He had been asked by Emperor William at Berlin to keep him informed in the case of any sudden decline in his grandmother's health, and so he telegraphed to him to warn him that the Queen's health gave cause for concern. After he sent the telegram it occurred to him that the princesses, or 'the petticoats', would hold him responsible for the arrival of their nephew, about whose presence they had such mixed feelings. Reid's conscience was salved only when he found that the Emperor had been told of the Queen's condition by the Duke of Connaught and by Baron Hermann von Eckhardstein at the German Embassy, and the Emperor had left for England with Reid's telegram lying unopened on his desk.

Reid also had to be involved in drafting and issuing regular bulletins to the public on the state of the Queen's health, preparing them for the worst. It fell to him to impress on the Prince of Wales the severity of the situation and to advise him that it would be necessary to alter his plans to go to his beloved Sandringham and come instead to Osborne, that island home with few, if any, happy memories for him. In addition, Reid was still expected to carry out his medical duties, which now included sitting up with the dying Queen and giving her regular oxygen throughout the night hours, though at least he could share this duty with Sir Richard Powell, the Queen's heart and lung specialist.

In the diary where he was keeping a careful chronicle of events as they occurred, he noted with some bitterness the absence of the Queen's daughters. While neither he nor Powell called for them, it seemed to him rather uncaring that they did not appear during the night and enquire about their mother's condition. Even after nearly twenty years of royal service, he still underestimated their timidity and the awe in which these middle-aged ladies held their formidable parent.

He was never in any doubt that she appreciated the severity of her condition and was frustrated at being physically and mentally incapable of working. On 19 January he and Powell visited her in bed in the evening, but she asked the latter to leave and turned to Reid, telling him weakly that 'I still have a few things to settle.' She reassured him that she had already arranged most things, but she needed to live a little longer to do those which were still left.[26] This, he knew, was probably the last royal command – if it could be interpreted as such – which she would ever give.

For the next three days, as royal relations converged on Osborne House and eager journalists waited outside, Reid kept a careful eye on his patient and helped to write the regular bulletins which had to be issued to the press and public, carefully worded in order to prepare them for the inevitable. Towards the middle of the afternoon on 22 January 1901 he knew that the final stage had arrived, and family members, doctors and clergymen gathered around the bed of the unconscious woman, the right side of her face slightly flattened after a minor stroke. Emperor William II, her eldest grandchild and the one who, though he had often exasperated her, always held her in special affection, supported her with his right arm. It was indeed at considerable discomfort to himself, as his deformed and almost lifeless left arm was incapable of such a function.

At 4 p.m. Reid and his colleagues wrote what was to be the final bulletin during Victoria's lifetime: 'The Queen is slowly sinking.' The end came two and a half hours later.

After a family service on the following day, Reid went to the Queen's room where her body lay, to find a rather less than welcome visitor. Emil Fuchs, a Viennese painter and sculptor working in Berlin, had been invited by Emperor William to make a death mask of the Queen. Her daughters were aghast at what they considered this uncalled-for desecration of their mother's body. No instructions had been left requesting such a move, and the Emperor had not thought to consult them first. Now King, Edward VII was contacted by telephone and asked to veto the move, which he promptly did, though he allowed Sir Hubert Herkomer to paint a deathbed portrait of her. Reid instructed the dressers to ensure that Her Majesty's body was not left alone for a moment.

Two days later, in accordance with the instructions she had written in December 1897 and left to be opened by her dressers after her death, Reid had her body transferred from her deathbed to her coffin, in the bedroom in which she had died. A series of coffins, fitting one inside another, had been ordered. The Queen's Chief Dresser and Dr Reid's assistant, Mrs Tuck, read the doctor a set of instructions with which the Queen had entrusted her regarding the items she wanted to be interred in the innermost coffin, some of which were not to be seen by any member of the family. Among the items specified were rings, bracelets and lockets, the Prince Consort's dressing gown, an alabaster cast of his hand and relics of the family's childhoods. Once the wedding veil had been placed over the Queen's face and upper body, now dressed in a white silk robe and the Order of the Garter, Reid placed in her left hand a photograph of John Brown. In a sheet of tissue paper he folded a lock of Brown's hair set in a case and concealed it under a corsage of flowers which the King's Consort, now Queen Alexandra, had laid on the body after it had been placed in the shell. To these, Reid added some additional photographs and letters between the Queen and Brown.[27] Though there were subsequent last viewings of the Queen's body by family and court members, the John Brown items remained undisturbed and unseen until the outer coffin lid was screwed down.

The King led various members of his family through the room, followed by members of the household and the servants, to take their final leave of her. The last to be summoned was the Munshi, whom the King loathed. Ironically, he could thus claim a special privilege in that he became the last person to see Her Majesty before the coffin was closed and the lid screwed down. After the final farewells, the bedroom was sealed with bronze gates, to remain a shrine for half a century.

The King ordered the Munshi to destroy all the letters written to him by Queen Victoria. As if to witness the destruction, Queen Alexandra and Princess Beatrice were summoned to attend the bonfire at the Munshi's home at Windsor, Frogmore Cottage. After that, he was sent back to India, as were the rest of the Indian servants, with pensions. Not everybody shared the royal household's low opinion of him, and Lady Curzon, wife of the Viceroy of India, remarked sadly in a letter to her husband of 'the poor man' having given up all his letters and the photos signed by the Queen before he returned to the country of his origin 'like a whipped hound'.[28]

He settled at Karim Cottage, Agra, but his last years were overshadowed by declining health, and he died in April 1909, aged just forty-six. A short obituary notice in *The Times* alluded discreetly to his years in Her Majesty's service when it concluded loftily that 'he cherished the memory of his illustrious pupil with profound veneration'.[29] As magnanimous as ever, King Edward VII sent a message of condolence to Karim's relations. Nevertheless, keen to preserve the integrity of his mother's memory, he ordered the Viceroy of India to organise a second session of letter-burning, and the Munshi's widow was allowed to retain only a few innocuous items as souvenirs.

No such ignominious fate awaited Sir James Reid, who had ended the Queen's reign as physician to her and to her son the Prince of Wales. Soon after the latter's accession, he was appointed physician to the new Prince of Wales, later King George V, and enjoyed a position of royal confidence up to his death in June 1923, at the age of seventy-three. As Sir Frederick Ponsonby, King George's assistant private secretary, readily acknowledged, he had occupied 'such a unique position in Queen Victoria's reign that I think she was guided more by him than anyone else'.[30]

PART FOUR

Sons and Sons-in-law

TEN

'One feels so pinned down'

Queen Victoria and Prince Albert's first child was a daughter, Victoria, 'Vicky', the Princess Royal, born on 21 November 1840, nine months after their wedding. 'Never mind, the next one will be a Prince,' the Queen assured everyone on being told her firstborn was a princess. Early the following year, the Queen learnt that she was 'in for it again', and within less than twelve months, on 9 November 1841, a Prince of Wales arrived.

At first known simply as 'the boy', he was christened Albert Edward after his father and maternal grandfather. Within a few years he was always 'Bertie' to the family. Sixteen months later came a third child, Alice, followed on 6 August 1844 by Alfred, or 'Affie'. Two daughters came next, at two-yearly intervals, Helena and Louise, then the two youngest sons, Arthur on 1 May 1850 and Leopold on 7 April 1853, before the family was completed with the birth of Beatrice in 1857.

Despite her brood of nine, Queen Victoria resented this regular child-bearing. Temperamentally she was not an ideal parent; she was not particularly maternal by nature, found the concept of breast-feeding utterly revolting, and thought babies frightful and ugly. Two years after the birth of the last, she confessed that she hated the thought of having children and had 'no adoration for little babies (particularly not in their baths till they are past 3 or 4 months, when they really become very lovely)'.[1] It was therefore ironic that she had such a large family. While she was keen to help provide a secure and loving environment for the children, she found it difficult to reconcile the demands of being their Queen with those of being their mother. It was the dictum of those days that children were to be seen and not heard, and in this sense she was a true Victorian. The more disagreeable aspects of motherhood were to be left to wet-nurses and governesses.

When her eldest daughter had been married for two months, the Queen admitted to some forthright beliefs on the comparative

171

liberties, or lack of them, of married and unmarried women. From a physical point of view, she maintained, the former certainly had no freedom. She herself had suffered severely for the first two years of her marriage, and for several more thereafter, from 'aches – and sufferings and miseries and plagues – which you must struggle against – and enjoyments etc, to give up – constant precautions to take'. She had to put up nine times 'with those above-named enemies and real misery (besides many duties) and I own it tried me sorely; one feels so pinned down'. Their sex, she proclaimed, was 'a most unenviable one'.[2]

Albert was a more devoted parent than his wife. To him it was a great pity, he wrote to her in 1856, that she found no consolation in the company of their children. 'The root of the trouble lies in the mistaken notion that the function of a mother is to be always correcting, scolding, ordering them about and organising their activities. It is not possible to be on happy friendly terms with people you have just been scolding.'[3]

He adored and always had a special relationship with Vicky, but with Bertie there was never to be such a close bond. It was his eldest son's misfortune to be overshadowed by his clever elder sister, and also to some extent by their mother's resentment of two pregnancies in quick succession. Initially she called him 'the Boy', which suggests a certain emotional detachment. She was left exhausted at the end of her confinement, and her pride at having produced the heir the country had expected did nothing to alleviate her postnatal depression. It was with some relief that she handed him over to the wet-nurse, Mrs Roberts.

Almost from birth, the young prince was to be moulded into a paragon of virtue and the supreme example of a perfect education, as much like his father as possible. Baron Stockmar had blamed the shortcomings of George III's sons on their education, which had 'contributed more than any other circumstance to weaken the respect and influence of Royalty in this country'.[4] Rather patronisingly, he warned the Queen and Prince Albert that they were too young to direct their eldest son and heir's studies, and it was their duty to seek the advice of those more experienced. As for the latter, he doubtless had himself in mind. The exalted, yet young and sadly inexperienced, parents obediently did as the Baron told them and consulted others, including the Bishop of Oxford, Samuel Wilberforce, who suggested that the object of the exercise was to make the future King into 'the most perfect man'. It took Lord Melbourne to give the best advice of all, namely that they should be 'not over solicitous about education. It may be able to do much, but it does not do as much as is expected from it. It may mould and direct the character, but it rarely alters it.'[5]

From his first years, it seemed that Bertie would be difficult to educate. As a small child he stammered and was inclined to be apathetic and backward, and given to tantrums in the nursery. When frustrated or scolded for bad behaviour he screamed, stamped his feet and threw things around the room until he was exhausted. Fortunately for him, the governess, Lady Lyttelton, was quick to appreciate his good qualities. At two years of age he was not nearly so articulate as his sister, having a rather babyish accent, yet even so he was 'very intelligent, and generous and good-tempered, with a few passions and stampings occasionally; most exemplary in politeness and manner, bows and offers his hand beautifully'.[6] She considered he had a particularly sweet nature and charming smile, as well as a readiness to tell the truth, unlike his elder sister, and she also appreciated the fact that he would be one of those people who learnt more from people than from books. Maybe she understood that the small boy had suffered from being aware that Vicky was their father's favourite, and that his mother gave the impression she was indifferent to him.

Any child who could follow simple conversations in three languages by the age of six was certainly not stupid. On Bertie's ninth birthday, the Queen noted in her journal, there was 'much good in him', and he had 'such affectionate feeling – great truthfulness and great simplicity of character'.[7] Yet he was not the paragon of wisdom and learning that his parents had fondly hoped he would be. There was more of the hearty Hanoverian than the earnest Coburger in him, and the Queen commented ruefully that he was her caricature. He had his dear father's name, even if he was to be 'Bertie' rather than Albert *en famille*, but neither his father's delicate looks nor his industrious nature. It was ironic that the son who was burdened by his destiny as the future King, the one of whom so much was expected, should in some senses be the son probably least fitted for it. With hindsight, though, none of his brothers had the demeanour of the born diplomat, coupled with the genial outgoing personality that he did, qualities which supremely equipped him for the burdens of state during his nine years as king.

By the time he was seventeen, the Queen was increasingly worried about him. 'Bertie continues such an anxiety,' she wrote to the Princess Royal in April 1859. 'I tremble at the thought of only three years and a half being before us – when he will be of age and we can't hold him except by moral power!' Most alarming was the thought of what would become of the kingdom if anything was to happen suddenly to her, as a vision of King Albert Edward aged about twenty with a widowed father trying to hold the reins of power as Prince Regent rose before her. 'One shudders to think of it: it is too awful a contemplation.'[8]

Affie was much more like his father. Less extroverted than Bertie, he could be just as badly behaved and disobedient, but made up for it by his readiness to learn. He adored geography, the sciences and anything to do with ships and the Royal Navy. When left to his own devices, he was happy to play with toys and mechanical devices, experimenting with them and trying to build his own. Both parents sometimes found themselves wishing that this lively, yet studious and conscientious, boy would inherit the throne one day instead of his elder brother.

From infancy, Arthur was and would always remain Queen Victoria's favourite son. A strong, healthy baby, he was even-tempered, with none of the irritability or rebellious spirits of the elder children. As the third son, with no likelihood of succeeding to his mother's throne or his childless uncle's duchy, he was free from the pressures and expectations placed on the elder two. Appropriately for the son who had been named after the Duke of Wellington, he was spellbound by anything to do with the Army, whether the sight of a military uniform, the sound of a band or just watching the changing of the guard at Buckingham Palace.

'This Child is dear, *dearer* than any of the others put together, thus *after you* he is the *dearest* and *most precious* object to *me* on *Earth*,' Victoria wrote to the Prince Consort when their son was aged eight. 'It gives me a pang if any fault is found in his looks and character, and the bare thought of his growing out of my hands and being exposed to danger – makes the tears come to my eyes.'[9] Soon afterwards she told Arthur's governor, Major Howard Elphinstone, that he was 'an easily managed child' as he was so well-tempered and 'so very obedient'.[10]

Although he was the first of Queen Victoria's children whose birth was eased by chloroform, Leopold was a sickly baby with a poor appetite and digestion, and a feeble cry. When learning to walk, he fell over and bruised badly, crying out as if in severe pain. Before long the doctors diagnosed in him the grave condition of haemophilia, a hereditary bleeding disease which prevents blood from clotting properly and bringing with it the risk of severe, even fatal, haemorrhage.

The condition was not properly recognised for several years. Leopold appeared perfectly healthy for long spells at a time, and he was quite tall, well-built for his age, with the usual share of a small boy's energy. But the signs of trouble were there, if not fully appreciated. He was inclined to stand awkwardly and sometimes screamed in agony. All this irritated Queen Victoria, who thought he was being lazy, holding himself badly and having fits of temper like his eldest brother, when the trouble was probably stiffness and severe pain in his joints. By his fifth birthday, he was also incurring her displeasure because of his lack of good looks: she thought him 'the ugliest and least pleasing of the whole family'. She admitted that he was 'not an ugly little baby, only as he grew older he grew plainer'.[11]

That summer, they learnt – probably from one of the royal doctors – that Leopold was suffering from some unusual condition. Writing to King Leopold that his 'poor little namesake' was laid up with a bad knee after a fall, the Queen made reference to 'this unfortunate defect' which would prevent him from being able to enter any of the active (or armed) services; it was '*often not outgrown – & no remedy or medicine does it any good*'.[12] Leopold was left behind at Osborne with Beatrice and the ladies-in-waiting while the rest of the family went to Balmoral a few days later. As he was proving so accident-prone, the Queen wrote, 'it would be very troublesome indeed to have him here'. That a mother could write with such lack of concern about her youngest son shows a degree of coldness which is hard to comprehend. 'He walks shockingly – and is dreadfully awkward – holds himself as badly as ever and his manners are despairing, as well as his speech – which is quite dreadful.' She admitted that he learnt well and read fluently, but these achievements seemed to count for little against his other shortcomings; 'he is really very unfortunate.'[13]

By this time, Leopold already had a brother-in-law, for he was only two years old when his eldest sister became betrothed. Prince Frederick William of Prussia ('Fritz') and his parents, Prince William and Princess Augusta, had been guests at the opening of the Great

Exhibition in 1851, and he had made more than a passing impression on ten-year-old Vicky. In September 1855 he was invited – without his parents – as a guest at Balmoral. Though Vicky was not yet fifteen years old, it was clear that a friendship which had been sustained fitfully by letter over the intervening period of time was ripening into something stronger, and within a few days the Prince had asked her, and then her parents, for her hand in marriage. On 25 January 1858 the family were present at St James's Palace as they became husband and wife.

* * *

Though the Prince of Wales never attained any great scholastic feats, he was sent to study at Oxford and made an effort which his parents appreciated. Partly as a reward, and partly in order to initiate him into public life, in 1860 they decided to send him on a tour of Canada and the United States of America. His itinerary was set to include opening the St Lawrence Bridge at Montreal, lay a foundation stone for the Federal Parliament building at Ottawa and pay a courtesy call on the American President, James Buchanan.

Despite, or perhaps because of, the academic shortcomings he had shown at home, at last he had the chance to prove that he had the charm and social talent required for a future king. Though he had been instructed that he was to travel incognito in the States as 'Baron Renfrew', it was too much to hope that the cheering crowds which greeted him everywhere would acknowledge him as anything other than heir to the world's greatest empire. He had been unprepared for such adulation, but he relished every moment to the full. For him the highlight was a ball at the New York Academy of Music, to which 3,000 guests had been invited but 5,000 turned up. Just before the guest of honour was due to arrive the floor gave way, but luckily nobody was hurt, and everyone waited patiently as carpenters and workmen hurried to the rescue. His governor, General Bruce, wrote rather censoriously that during the trip the Prince had been 'somewhat persecuted by attentions not in strict accordance with good breeding', but the Prince did not object.

On his return home the Queen and Albert were eager to impress on him that the success of his tour had been due mainly to the efforts of Bruce and to the fact that he was their representative, but even so the Queen could not conceal her admiration for the son who had formerly proved something of a disappointment. 'He was immensely popular everywhere and really deserves the highest praise,' she wrote to the Princess Royal, 'which should be given him all the more as he was never spared any reproof.'[14]

Alfred was also playing a similar role in another part of the British Empire. He had joined the Royal Navy in 1858, and after passing his midshipman's examination he set sail for South Africa. Though only fifteen at the time, he coped very well with the itinerary set out for him, whether it was taking part in hunting expeditions, releasing the first load of stones for a breakwater in the Table Bay or opening a public library at Cape Town. Already the Queen could see similarities between him and his father, as she wrote to King Leopold soon after his return home: 'He is really such a dear, gifted, handsome child, that it makes one doubly anxious he should have as few failings as mortal men can have.'[15]

Unhappily, the Prince Consort would see little more of the development of these two sons in particular who would be so adept at representing the Queen abroad. It was unfortunate that the Prince of Wales's liaison with the actress Nellie Clifden, or rather the fact that news of it should leak out to the courts of Europe and only after that back to his horrified parents at Windsor, should coincide with the onset of Albert's final illness. In the first intense outburst of her grief, Queen Victoria blamed their eldest son for hastening his death. He and Crown Prince Frederick William of Prussia were chief mourners at the funeral at Windsor on 23 December. Alfred was away at sea at the time, but eleven-year-old Arthur attended the ceremony, the small boy sobbing as if his heart would break.

Queen Victoria spent the first few months of her widowhood in the more comforting surroundings of Osborne, which had been home more than their other dwellings. At first she was convinced that she too would die before long, and regarded her eldest son's marriage as a matter of urgency. If a young, orphaned king was to succeed her, he should at least be married and have a settled home life. In September 1861 a meeting between the Prince of Wales and Princess Alexandra, eldest daughter of Prince Christian of Schleswig-Holstein-Sonderburg-Glucksburg, heir to the King of Denmark, had been carefully arranged at Speyer Cathedral in Germany. There were very few, if any, other unmarried princesses in Europe who were eligible and pretty enough for Bertie, and both the young people involved knew their duty.

In September 1862 the Prince proposed. Alexandra accepted him, and they were married on 10 March 1863 in St George's Chapel, Windsor. Still resolutely in mourning, as she would remain for the rest of her days, the Queen took no part in the procession of royalties but instead walked from the Deanery, along a specially prepared route covered and hidden from the general gaze, to a gallery overlooking the Chapel. There she sat, in her mourning apparel and black widow's cap, relieved only by the ribbon, badge and star of the Order of the Garter, and a diamond brooch containing a miniature of the Prince Consort. After the ceremony, thirty-six royals sat down to lunch with the bride and groom, but the Queen was not among them. After a week-long honeymoon at Osborne, they spent a few days at Windsor and at the end of the month went to the Prince's country home at Sandringham, Norfolk. In April they moved into Marlborough House, which was to be their official London residence.

Bertie had not been the only one of Victoria's sons to have a 'fall' from the path of virtue. In 1862 she learnt that Affie had also known the pleasures of a young lady on Malta. In view of the behaviour of his fellow-midshipmen, and a lack of any more becoming leisure facilities on the island, it might have given a more reasonable, less censorious, parent cause for concern if he had not indulged in what she called his 'heartless and dishonourable behaviour'.

But the Queen was irritated and upset, not only because Affie had betrayed the moral code of his father, but also because he had been at the centre of a rather complicated political matter. The volatile Greeks had just deposed their unpopular and childless king, Otho, but instead of declaring a republic they wanted to install another European prince on the vacant throne. Prince Alfred of Great Britain was the most popular choice. Though he had made a brief visit to the country on one of his naval training voyages, he was hardly known there, but the Greeks recognised that there would be considerable political and territorial advantages if they chose a British prince as their king. Late in 1862 a plebiscite was held in which Alfred received over 95 per cent of votes cast. Little did the Greeks know at the time that under the terms of a protocol signed at London in 1830, a British prince could not be elected to the throne.

At one stage, the Greeks seemed so Anglophile that it was said they had even contemplated offering the crown to Gladstone. (In later years, the Queen must have felt that her life would have been easier if the latter had indeed been chosen.) The impasse was resolved some weeks later when Prince William of Schleswig-Holstein, Alexandra's brother, was chosen instead.

Alfred, who was promoted to the rank of captain in the Royal Navy and created Duke of Edinburgh, and Earl of Ulster and of Kent, in 1866, was destined to travel far more widely throughout the world than any of his siblings. That same year he was appointed to the command of HMS *Galatea*, with orders to take her on a world cruise which would include Gibraltar, South America, the remote colony of Tristan da Cunha, Australia, New Zealand, India and Ceylon. Ostensibly it was a continuation of Alfred's duties as the Queen's representative in the further territories of the British Empire, begun during his South African travels as a midshipman.

As far as Queen Victoria was concerned, there was another purpose – to separate Alfred from his London 'flatterers'. Society was turning him into the kind of fun-loving prince, ready to indulge in the life of pleasure, of which she did not approve. Moreover, he seemed a little too infatuated with his sister-in-law, Alexandra. Unlike her husband, she took her marriage vows seriously, and she would never have made the cardinal error of leading her brother-in-law on, but the Queen thought it prudent to minimise the risk of putting temptation in anyone's way.

The world tour proved a mixed blessing for all concerned. The Duke set sail in June 1867, with by far the greater part of his itinerary embracing Australia. A round of pomp and ceremony, civic receptions and mediocre concerts soon palled for him, and he did not hesitate to voice openly his occasional boredom with the tedious routine and excessively long speeches at the functions he was required to attend. There were ugly demonstrations between Catholic and Protestant communities, fuelled by expatriate Irish republican sympathisers and exacerbated when news reached the continent early in 1868 of the execution of three members of the Fenian Brotherhood in Manchester for shooting a policeman dead. In March the Duke was attending a picnic in Sydney to raise funds for a sailors' rest home when James O'Farrell, the son of an Irish immigrant butcher, shot him in the back. Initially there were grave fears for the Duke's life, but the bullet was deflected from his spine by his heavy leather braces, and within a few days he was pronounced out of danger. However, never before had an assassination attempt on a member of Queen Victoria's family come so near to succeeding.

The programme was immediately curtailed. It had been arranged that the Duke would sail to New Zealand next, but in view of Fenian demonstrations on South Island, the authorities could not guarantee his safety. *Galatea* therefore returned home and arrived at Portsmouth in June 1868. Having got over her shock at the news of the attempt on Alfred's life, the Queen hoped fervently that her second son would return 'an altered being'. When he visited her at Windsor she was disappointed to find him unbearably conceited, receiving ovations as if he had done something extraordinary, 'instead of God's mercy having spared his life'.[16] She was relieved to see him depart again after a few months of respite, visiting family and relations in England and Germany, before resuming a more informal cruise in 1869 (with heightened police protection) which included a return to Australia, New Zealand, India, Japan and the Falkland Islands. He came home in May 1871.

Though the Prince of Wales and the Duke of Edinburgh always remained close, sharing a similar taste for society and social life, in personality they were very different. Bertie was more outgoing, while Affie was inclined to be shy, with a reserve which was often taken for rudeness. Though her first words on the matter while still in shock at her husband's death suggested that she would never forgive her eldest son, the Queen's aversion to him proved but temporary. On his twenty-sixth birthday she was writing to the Princess Royal that he was 'so full of good and amiable qualities, that it makes one forget and overlook much that one would wish different'.[17] Less than two years later, she said she was 'sure no Heir Apparent was ever so nice and unpretending as dear Bertie is'.[18]

For all his faults, the Prince of Wales always fulfilled his childhood promise of being an affectionate and dutiful son to Victoria. Even so, she still thought him far too indiscreet to be trusted to carry out state duties, apart from strictly ceremonial engagements. She had grave misgivings about his friends in the 'Marlborough House set', with their preoccupation with gambling, racing, heavy drinking and smoking. When Prussia and Denmark were at war in 1864 the Prince asked his mother to let him see Foreign Office despatches instead of mere summaries from his mother's secretaries. Through General Grey she informed Lord Russell, then Foreign Secretary, that her government was forbidden to send him any such 'separate and independent communication with the Government', on the grounds that he was liable to let the wrong people be privy to such information; His Royal Highness was 'not at all times as discreet as He should be'. 'If you ever become King,' the Queen warned him five years later (note her use of the word 'if'), 'you will find all these friends *most* inconvenient, and you will have to break with them *all*.'[19]

Not long afterwards, she told Gladstone in a moment of despair that she doubted her son's 'fitness for high functions of State'. Ironically, this was at the time when general disquiet over her seclusion and her reluctance or downright refusal to be seen carrying out 'high functions of State' herself was at its greatest. Under the circumstances, Gladstone might have considered her strictures rather ironic.

Another constant bone of contention between the Queen and her heir was their differing attitude towards public appearances in order to keep the monarchy in the public eye. He appreciated, as she did not, that the public would like and respect their royal family more if they saw them regularly. When she told him that he ought to spend more time quietly in the country with his wife, especially when she was with child, he retorted that not only did they have certain duties to fulfil, but 'your absence from London makes it more necessary that we should do all we can for society, trade, and public matters'.[20] In the end they compromised, and she asked him to forgo the Derby for once; perhaps he would like to come to Balmoral for a night or two, and 'spend my sad birthday with me'.

Yet less than a year later he found it necessary to admonish her again for remaining in seclusion so much, willingly admitting that her appearance in public would be far better for public relations than the regular spectacle of himself and Alexandra ('Alix'). If his mother would only sometimes come from Windsor to London for luncheon, he suggested tactfully, then drove for an hour in the Park, where there was no noise, the people would be 'overjoyed'. It was all very well for him and Alix to do so, she replied, but it did not have the same effect when she did. They lived in radical times, he reminded her, 'and the more the *People see the Sovereign* the better it is for the *People* and the *Country*.'[21]

Not only were the Prince's friends and way of life criticised, but his and Alix's more liberal attitude towards parenthood also incurred maternal disapproval. By March 1869 they had two sons and two daughters, with a third daughter on the way. While they were visiting Alix's family in Denmark, the Queen asked her son why no governess had yet been appointed to discipline them. The Prince replied that they would be considering one on their return, adding that if children of that age 'are too strictly, or perhaps too severely treated, they get shy, and only fear those whom they ought to love; and we should naturally wish them to be very fond of you'.[22]

Though the Queen was generally much more indulgent to her grandchildren than she had been to her own children when small, she did not always welcome new additions to the new generation. For her, the novelty of 'happy events' wore off all too soon. When her seventh granddaughter and fourteenth grandchild, the Prince and Princess of Wales's daughter Victoria, was born in July 1868, the matriarch commented to her eldest child, Vicky, the Crown Princess of Prussia, that it 'becomes a very uninteresting thing – for it seems to me to go on like the rabbits in Windsor Park!'[23]

In late middle age, the Queen was saddened at the way her sons changed as they became adults. 'Alas!' she wrote to Sir Howard Elphinstone, 'she feels more and more *how* her children become strangers to her and no longer seem to fit in with her ways and habits (which she thinks are simple and good) when they once go out a great deal into Society.'[24]

* * *

As both Bertie and Affie had had 'falls', the Queen relied on their next brother, Arthur, to uphold the spirit of his father's purity. In her eyes, he could do no wrong, and rarely if ever did the often hard-to-please matriarch ever find fault with him. To the Prince of Wales she wrote that he 'seems to see the point of view of others, however widely their views may differ. In this he follows his dear father, and I love him most dearly for it.'[25] But there must have been times when he found her all-pervading, ever-demanding presence as suffocating as his brothers did, and once he was old enough he tried to avoid spending long periods at Balmoral and Windsor with her, knowing that in the family circle he had to take care to be on his best behaviour, and that any lapse would not be readily forgiven.

He found a limited measure of freedom at the age of sixteen when he went to begin his Army training at Woolwich. A soldier's life was well-known for exposing young men to considerable temptation, as the Prince of Wales's sojourn at the Curragh (Ireland's Sandhurst) had proved, so the Queen ordered that he should live at the Ranger's House in Greenwich Park, and not at the barracks. In 1869 he was transferred to the 1st Battalion of the Rifle Brigade, then stationed at Montreal. He was greatly impressed with the people and countryside of Canada, and exhilarated at being able to take part in an action against a band of Fenians who had entered Canada. After a year he rejoined his battalion at Woolwich.

Soon after he came of age in May 1871 he managed to displease the Queen, though there was never anything approaching a rift in the relations between mother and son. He had the temerity, or good sense, to join the rest of the family in urging her to show herself more during her long period of seclusion. Greatly pained that he should side with his elder brothers, she wrote to him severely on what she called the subject of good manners – which, in her case, meant not arguing with a mother who had the experience of having been thirty-four years on the throne. To Elphinstone, she wrote that 'he *must* be set right upon that point of her appearing . . . or she will inevitably get ill again'.[26] His tutor replied with the utmost tact, suggesting that it was but a temporary change which was probably caused as much as anything by an unconscious attempt to imitate his brother officers. It would pass off gradually and disappear with a change of companions; he would never knowingly act unkindly to others. The Queen was reassured by Elphinstone's words, while admitting that she could not deny 'that her good Arthur causes her some anxiety as she thinks he is wanting in reflection and stability of purpose. These are no doubt *some* of the many defects of youth but *still* they are dangerous in his position.'[27]

As expected, Arthur soon grew out of some, if not all, of 'the many defects of youth'. In 1873 he was attached to the staff of an infantry brigade at Aldershot, and during manoeuvres there he was promoted to the rank of brigade-major. In May 1874 he was created Duke of Connaught and Strathearn and Earl of Sussex.

* * *

Leopold had become an intelligent but often frustrated young man. Like most over-protected children he chafed at the fuss made of him and was ever ready to argue with and contradict his mother. With every major attack of internal bleeding that he suffered she was most distressed, but still she managed to find a strange consolation in his ill-health. After one attack when he was aged ten, she told Vicky that 'the illness of a good child is so far less trying and

distressing than the sinfulness of one's sons'. The transgressions of
Bertie and Affie weighed heavily on her mind, and to her 'death in
purity is so far preferable to life in sin and degradation!'[28] Protecting
him from what could be 'corrupting conversation' with other men,
even his own flesh and blood, was vital. When Leopold took up
smoking he was banned from the smoking-room at Balmoral, and
when the Duke of Edinburgh arrived back from his second cruise on
Galatea, she gave orders that Leopold could not go fishing with his
elder brother.

He had undoubtedly inherited his father's brains and thirst for
knowledge. From an early age he learnt Latin and Greek, and
enjoyed reading poetry in both languages as well as in English. He
adored the work of Shakespeare, and when he was fourteen a
special new edition of the playwright's work was dedicated to him.
More than his brothers, he had inherited a love of painting and fine
arts, and among other things he collected china, autographs and,
later, card-mounted photographs of celebrities of the day. As a
musician he showed some promise, playing the piano (including
duets with his mother or sister Beatrice), harmonium and flute.
Science, current affairs and politics fascinated him equally, and,
when kept in bed by attacks of internal bleeding, he read
newspapers from cover to cover and eagerly discussed contemporary
issues of the day with anyone who could spare the time.

These activities must have been some consolation for being
forced to lead such a protected life, but all too often Leopold
railed against the restrictions placed on him by his well-meaning
mother. Not surprisingly, in time he would rebel and astonish her
with his defiance.

* * *

All but one of the princes who were destined to become Queen
Victoria's sons-in-law were German, though Fritz was the only
sovereign heir among them, being second in line to the Prussian
crown. In 1860 Alice was engaged to Prince Louis of Hesse and the
Rhine. It was not such a grand match as that of her elder sister,
though Louis was to become Grand Duke of Hesse fifteen years
later. Their wedding, delayed by Court mourning because of the
Prince Consort's death, took place at a subdued ceremony in the
dining-room at Osborne House in July 1862. The ceremony was

dominated by Winterhalter's vast painting of the royal family in 1846 which hung on the wall behind the improvised altar, as if to symbolise the Prince Consort's blessing of their union.

Even less prestigious still, though in the end a far more contented marriage, was that of Helena in July 1866 to the penniless Prince Christian of Schleswig-Holstein, whose family had been deprived of their duchy by the machinations of Prussian politics and military might. He was fifteen years older than his wife, and when originally told that he had a chance of marrying the Queen's daughter he misunderstood the message and thought he was going to marry the Widow of Windsor herself.

Nevertheless, 'the Christians' settled down to a relatively uneventful and untroubled fifty-one years of married life in England, first at Frogmore House and then at Cumberland Lodge, both in the grounds of Windsor Castle. Despite the difference in their ages, they were the only couple among Queen Victoria's children who lived long enough to celebrate their golden wedding. He demanded little except a happy, comfortable family life, and this he found with his wife and their children. With his passion for literature, he taught them to share his love of poetry and German fairy tales, telling them stories as they gathered round his armchair before they went to bed. He also had several outdoor interests, and loved shooting, riding, gardening and flowers.

If he was ever bored with his existence, he was careful enough not to show it. The Queen gave him what she termed 'light duties', mainly as Ranger of Windsor Castle Park. This was hardly an arduous post, especially as it rarely involved much more than general supervisory duties or looking after the place in the most general terms. Once, at the appropriately named Frogmore, there was a plague of frogs with which he was required to deal. He consulted the naturalist Frank Buckland, who advised him to introduce more ducks.

The Queen insisted he should have nothing to do with shooting arrangements. It would have been as well for him if he had denied himself the pleasures of such a sport. In 1892 the Duke of Connaught – who should have known better, as a senior Army officer – accidentally shot Christian in the eye, which subsequently had to be removed under anaesthetic. Magnanimously, he forgave the Duke for his carelessness, and amassed a large collection of glass eyes to fill the socket, one of them a bloodshot specimen which, he proudly told visitors when showing them his ocular assortment, he wore whenever he had a cold.

In March 1871 Louise married John Douglas Sutherland Lorne, Marquess of Lorne, heir to the Duke of Argyll. It was a controversial match, as Lorne was a Liberal member of parliament, representing Argyllshire from 1868 to 1878 and, after an interval, Manchester South in the Unionist interest from 1895 to 1900. No such marriage between a British princess and a subject had been given official recognition since the wedding of King Henry VII's daughter to the Duke of Suffolk in 1515, though the literary-minded Lorne was a backbench politician whose membership of the House of Commons never embroiled the royal family in any political issues of the day.

In terms of Victorian royal marriages, this one proved popular with the public. There had been increasing resentment of Germany and German marriages, and so when one of the Queen's daughters married a Scotsman it made a welcome change. Radicals who were displeased by a parliamentary grant of £30,000 towards the couple were mollified by the thought that at least it would be spent 'at home'.[29] *Punch* had hailed news of the engagement as 'a real German defeat', and when the court at Berlin expressed indignation that Louise had not taken one of its princes as her husband, Lorne good-humouredly told the Queen that his ancestors the Argylls were kings when the Hohenzollerns were *parvenus*.[30]

Sir Henry Ponsonby never ceased to be surprised, or sometimes amused, by Queen Victoria's attitude to her sons and sons-in-law. Her affection for her children, he observed, 'does not appear in their manner when they are grown up', although she generally adored her grandchildren. Her sons were 'all in terror of her', while she tended to give the impression that she did not like her sons-in-law.

Sometimes she was positively irritable towards Christian, whose hardly avoidable lack of purpose and activity grated on her. One morning at Osborne, she looked out of the window, watched him pottering about aimlessly in the garden and promptly ordered an equerry to take him a message saying he must either occupy himself with something or else go for a ride somewhere. This was probably down to temporary low spirits on her part, when she felt she had to have something or someone to vent her irritation on. She was 'terribly bored with Christian', Sir Henry wrote to his wife, and could not understand why Helena liked him, as he was 'bald and fat and it's nonsense their being so affectionate with each other'.[31] By and large, though, her children's spouses rarely found her anything less than kind and affectionate as a rule, so her secretary had evidently caught her on a bad day.

On the whole, her relations were more amicable with the sons-in-law, who either saw less of her or else did not find her particularly intimidating, than with the sons who saw her regularly and were often summoned to the matriarchal presence as adults for a dressing-down, or received billets-doux informing them of some slight they had committed – or to take care they avoid committing one. Like most women, Victoria was particularly drawn to good-looking men. She was often critical of her sons as children or adolescents, particularly the Prince of Wales and Leopold, because she thought them ugly or objected to some physical characteristic such as the way they did their hair.

Her sons-in-law were all mature men, and therefore not subject to such fault-finding. Moreover, most of them were blessed with strikingly handsome looks, Christian being the exception. Though it is hard to imagine the Queen being so small-minded as to hold his ugliness against him in any way, his unphotogenic appearance may possibly have been an additional minor irritant at times when she already had some reason to take him to task. Once, when she was looking after their infant daughters, she sent a rather tactless telegram to Helena and Christian, who were wintering in France, informing them that the children were very well, 'but poor little Louise very ugly'.[32] Perhaps it is only fair to the Queen to add that Princess Marie Louise, 'poor Louise', and her sister Helena Victoria as adults were indeed probably the least attractive of her grandchildren.

ELEVEN

'We are a very strong family'

In November 1871 the Prince of Wales fell ill at Sandringham with typhoid fever, the disease which had claimed the life of his father ten years earlier. Before that, Queen Victoria had never visited her son's Norfolk country house, but as soon as she was advised of the seriousness of his condition, she quickly joined the rest of the family who had gathered there. Naturally, she took charge, frequently guarding his bedroom door, it was said, like a sentry. At other times she sat by his bed, holding his hand and willing him to pull through. For a few days, he hovered between life and death, and at one stage his mother, wife and sister Alice turned to each other with tears in their eyes, all but convinced that his case was hopeless as he raved deliriously between fearful fits of coughing. The illness reached its crisis on the eve of 14 December, the tenth anniversary of the Prince Consort's death. To the astonishment of family and doctors alike, he rallied, and from the dreaded fourteenth onwards, he began to recover.

It was probably during this time that one small but amusing episode occurred, proving that while the Queen's male relatives might be grown men, she could still quite unintentionally strike fear into their hearts. Sir Henry Ponsonby recalled with great relish the day when he and Lieutenant-Colonel Arthur Haig, equerry to the Duke of Edinburgh, were going out into the garden at Sandringham by a side door when they were almost knocked down by a stampede of royals, with the Queen's cousin George, Duke of Cambridge, two months her senior, in the front, and Prince Leopold bringing up the rear. They were running so fast that Ponsonby and Haig thought there must have been a mad bull pursuing them. Instead, they cried out, 'The Queen, the Queen,' and all of them dashed, either from fright or because it was obviously the done thing, until the diminutive figure in black bombazine walked past. Once the cowed royals had slunk off, secretary and equerry 'laughed immensely'.[1]

188

Prime Minister Gladstone suggested that the Queen should take advantage of the national mood by proclaiming 27 February 1872 Thanksgiving Day, and that the royal family should attend a service at St Paul's to mark the Prince of Wales's restoration to health. The Queen had little enthusiasm for the idea and objected particularly to the length of the planned service, but the Prime Minister would not be deflected. Eager crowds, cheering the royals as they made their way to the cathedral, bore evidence to the lack of any deep-rooted republican sympathies. As the press noted, 'an extraordinary reversion of feeling towards the Prince has taken place during the last few months, and he has suddenly come to be one of the most popular men in the country'.[2]

The Queen was particularly struck by the apparent transformation in her son. A few days before the service, while he was recuperating at Osborne, she wrote to Vicky, the Crown Princess of Prussia, describing him as very weak and drawn, but 'quite himself, only gentler and kinder than ever; and there is something different, which I can't exactly express'. Even the trees and flowers 'gave him pleasure', which they had never done before, and he was 'quite pathetic over his small wheelbarrow and little tools at the Swiss cottage'.[3] The most encouraging sign of all was that he was spending so much time with Alix, and they seemed rarely apart. Victoria must have nursed hopes that at last he was about to become a model of family domesticity like his father.

Gladstone braved the wrath of his sovereign by choosing what seemed to him an opportune moment to propose a new role for the Prince. He advised that the heir and his wife ought to reside in Ireland for four or five months of the year, where he could undertake some form of administrative business, to be mutually agreed between the sovereign, her heir and the government. This, he argued, would give the Prince the advantage of some political training which he had not yet had. Moreover, if Her Majesty was to decide that she could no longer perform 'the social and visible functions of the monarchy', perhaps she would consider inviting the Prince and Princess to stay at Buckingham Palace in her absence for two or three months annually and perform them on her behalf.

Needless to say, such proposals were instantly dismissed. Queen Victoria was never likely to entertain such a proposal from Gladstone. Ireland was the least loyal of her dominions, she informed him coldly; it would mean exile for the Prince and do his health much harm; and he was not of sufficiently independent character to stand against the pressures that would be exerted on him to lean towards one political party or the other. The emerald isle, she declared, was 'in no fit state to be experimented upon'. As for the Buckingham Palace suggestion, the 'fashionable set' had already exercised a most harmful influence on her heir and his wife, and it would never do to encourage them still further. Experience was no prerequisite, she went on, for a successful monarch, as she could never take the slightest interest in public affairs before her own accession to the throne.

She was not alone in her view. Sir Henry Ponsonby, who did not always agree wholeheartedly with the Queen, shared her doubts about the heir to the throne and his readiness to work hard enough in any position of responsibility. He admitted that the Prince was extremely genial and pleasant, but rarely for more than a few minutes at a time, and lacked his father's sense of application to hard work. 'But he does not endure. He cannot keep up the interest for any length of time and I don't think he will ever settle down to business.'[4]

By the end of 1872 he had been thrown back onto his old habits, a life devoid of serious responsibility, relieved of necessity by the social round and distractions of his City and society companions. Now back in England after his cruises on *Galatea*, his brother, the Duke of Edinburgh, was more than happy to become one of this pleasure-loving set. Queen Victoria was determined that her second son – who as a boy had shown such promising signs of taking after his father – should also be married and settle down as soon as possible.

Fortunately for all, Alfred had already met the woman who was to become his wife on one of his family visits to Germany. Grand Duchess Marie Alexandrovna of Russia, the only surviving daughter of Tsar Alexander II, had been part of a gathering at Jugenheim with Alice, Louis and several of their relatives in the summer of 1868. After a difficult courtship, and despite the problems of the Queen having a daughter-in-law who belonged to the Greek Orthodox Church, Alfred and Marie were betrothed in July 1873 and married at St Petersburg in January 1874 at a double ceremony, one in the Anglican faith, the other according to the Russian Orthodox Church. This was the only wedding of one of her children which did not take place in England, and which the Queen did not attend in person. She had to content herself with sending Arthur Stanley, Dean of Westminster, to perform the English service.

In certain aspects, the Duke of Edinburgh was very like his father, but Queen Victoria never really understood this versatile and knowledgeable, yet shy and often morose, second son. Those who did not know him well found him bad-tempered and avaricious. It did not help matters that the Duchess was a haughty woman who never let an opportunity slip of reminding her in-laws that she was a Russian Grand Duchess while they were mere Princesses, and that the jewellery her imperial father had given her as a wedding present was much finer than any of theirs. Beside the more affable, outgoing Prince of Wales and his elegant, if sadly deaf, wife, the Duke and Duchess of Edinburgh did not make an attractive couple. When Alfred returned to England after his betrothal in the summer of 1873, the Queen looked for a change in his personality for the better, but in vain. It saddened her, she wrote to Vicky in Berlin, to find no improvement in him – only 'the same ungracious, reserved manner which makes him so little liked'.[5]

Though still largely unemployed in an official capacity, the Prince of Wales was given several opportunities to exercise his considerable diplomatic skills at home and abroad. In November 1874 he and the Princess of Wales paid an official visit to Birmingham, a city which had a reputation for radicalism with a staunch republican, Joseph Chamberlain, as Lord Mayor. The tact of his royal visitors soon won Chamberlain over completely, and in years to come he would be a fervent royalist and welcome guest at Marlborough House, along with Charles Dilke, a member of parliament who had been a particularly vociferous spokesman for the republican movement of some four or five years previously.

In October 1875 the Prince of Wales set out on a seven-month state visit to India. Queen Victoria had initially been against such a long separation from his family, but at length she was persuaded to give her approval, though she supported him in not allowing the indignant Princess to accompany him and the party. Before his departure, she urged him to take care that he did not eat too much, to ensure that he attended divine services every Sunday and to be in bed by 10 p.m. every night. As he was by now in his mid-thirties and had long since paid scant regard to such rules, he probably took little notice.

On their progress, the heir and his entourage were extravagantly entertained by Indian heads of state and generously showered with jewels and trophies. Yet it was not one great round of merry-making and big-game hunting. Like his mother, the Prince had enlightened views on racial prejudice that were well in advance of their time and at odds with many of their contemporaries'. He was displeased by the arrogance of English civilian and military officers; as a result of what he had seen, he wrote to the Queen deploring the widespread brutality and contempt shown to the Indian population, and the British governors in India were accordingly instructed to put their house in order. During his homeward journey he was irritated to learn not through the Court but from the newspapers that legislation had been passed creating the Queen Empress of India, an oversight for which she and Disraeli gracefully apologised.

Soon after returning from India, the Prince accepted the presidency of the British section of an international exhibition to be opened in Paris in May 1878. It was no mere honorary position, for he did much to organise Britain's role in the display. Two days after the opening of the exhibition, he attended a banquet at which he proposed the health of President Marshal MacMahon, after the Queen's health was toasted. It was the first time he had publicly honoured the head of the republican government, and he declared that the entente cordiale between both countries was unlikely to change. The British ambassador in Paris informed Lord Salisbury, the Foreign Secretary, that the Prince of Wales's visit and genial behaviour had made England very popular in France. His talents as an ambassador for Britain had already been recognised, and they would have no little effect on his role – indeed, Britain's role – in Europe over the following thirty years.

* * *

Though the years which followed the Franco-Prussian war of 1870–1 were relatively free of armed conflict in Europe on the scale of that which had divided Queen Victoria's family during the 1860s, the threat of another major conflict was never far away. France recovered quickly from her defeat at the hands of Germany in 1871, and nobody was willing to underestimate the danger posed by the volatile situation in the Balkan countries, 'the powder-keg of Europe'. In 1877 Russia declared war on Turkey, and the Duke of Edinburgh was put in command of HMS *Sultan*, attached to the Mediterranean Fleet, which was required to be close to Constantinople in order to protect the lives and property of British subjects in the area.

Within a year, the Turks were forced to surrender and sue for peace, and the Treaty of San Stefano, signed in March 1878, justified Europe's worst fears in seeing substantial Russian territorial gains. For weeks the threat of war between Britain and Russia hung in the balance, much to the discomfort of the Duke, Tsar Alexander's son-in-law. A well-intentioned but tactless act of his underlined the precarious nature of family loyalties.

One of his officers on board *Sultan* was Prince Louis of Battenberg, whose younger brother, Alexander ('Sandro'), was *aide-de-camp* to the Russian Commander-in-Chief, Tsar Alexander II's brother, Grand Duke Nicholas. When Louis heard from the German ambassador and his wife that Sandro was in Constantinople, he wanted to go and see him, and the Duke granted him permission to go ashore. Having been apart for so long, the brothers were overjoyed to meet again, and Louis invited Sandro on board *Sultan*. Later they went on board the flagship together, and then to *Temeraire*, a modern battleship equipped with several new devices. The Commander-in-Chief, Vice-Admiral Phipps-Hornby, was embarrassed that a foreign officer should be present on board one of his ships at such an inopportune time, though he was reluctant to spoil what was really no more than a brotherly reunion. However, as he was an officer, Prince Alexander had to be accorded certain privileges, such as being invited to watch a demonstration of fleet exercises, and then asked if he would like to dine on board the flagship. The brothers later went ashore and visited Russian Army headquarters, where they were received cordially by Grand Duke Nicholas and shown round the camp where Turkish soldiers were imprisoned and captured armaments kept.

This came at the worst possible time for the British ambassador at Constantinople, who feared that peace negotiations could be jeopardised by the entertaining of a Russian officer on board a British ship who might take advantage of his connections with royalty and be made party to confidential information. In order to prevent his sovereign and the Admiralty from hearing vague and inaccurate rumours from unofficial sources, he cabled to London. The Queen was furious, for the Duke's behaviour had come perilously close to treason. She wrote to him angrily that he had been 'most injudicious and imprudent', and that he had undoubtedly damaged any prospects of naval promotion for Louis and himself. After her temper had subsided, she was persuaded that no harm had actually been done, for Sandro had not been shown any confidential equipment or been granted access to naval secrets. The Duke had been forgiven as well by early summer, but only after he threatened to demand a court of enquiry in order to clear his name.

Once peace was declared and confirmed by the Congress of Berlin, the Duke, who had spent the summer at Coburg, where he was heir to his uncle Duke Ernest, was keen to return home, especially as there was no prospect of immediate active service to detain him on Malta. The Queen was reluctant to have him back so soon, partly as she thought it too soon after the *Sultan* affair and partly as she regarded his love of society as a potentially bad influence on the Duke of Connaught. He threatened to resign his commission if he was not allowed back, or given something constructive to do.

Providentially, his brother-in-law, the Marquess of Lorne, had recently been appointed Governor-General of Canada. Disraeli, who had made the appointment, thought the Canadians would regard it as a great honour if the Queen's son-in-law and daughter were living among them. In view of his wife's royal status, Lorne suggested that it would be appropriate for them to land at Halifax from one of Her Majesty's ships. HMS *Black Prince*, to which the Duke of Edinburgh had been transferred when *Sultan* returned to Portsmouth for refitting, was chosen to make the Atlantic crossing which was to take the new Governor-General and his wife to Canada.

* * *

Leopold longed to be given some similarly constructive role in life. He rebelled at his mother's wish to protect him from any kind of harm, and by the time he became an adult he was openly rebelling against her orders. 'He is so wanting in all dutiful and respectful forms and seems to delight in showing a childish defiance of my wishes,'[6] she complained to his sister Louise when he was aged twenty-two.

At Balmoral one evening after a game of billiards with the Liberal member of parliament John Bright, Leopold told his equerry that, if not allowed to do something useful, he would stand for parliament as an 'extreme radical'. Nobody took his threat seriously, as he was known to share the family's committed Tory politics. All the Queen's sons were basically, and not surprisingly, Conservatives at heart, if not all the daughters. The Princess Royal was more inclined towards the Liberals and remained something of a Gladstonian supporter to the end of her days, while Louise was likewise of a relatively progressive turn of mind. However, in Leopold's case it was widely recognised that he was far too intelligent for his talents to be wasted on representative duties and idleness.

He approached Disraeli, who could see the young man's resemblance to his late father. Although Leopold clearly had none of the political experience or knowledge that the Prince Consort had assimilated so rapidly during the first few years of his marriage, Disraeli felt that he might be able to take on something of a similar role as the Queen's confidential assistant. The wily Prime Minister could also see that to adopt such a course of action could reduce the work imposed on him by constant attendance on the sovereign, as well as providing the Prince with suitable employment. The Queen readily agreed with him that Leopold could perhaps be groomed as an unofficial assistant private secretary. Her official secretary, Sir Henry Ponsonby, liked and respected Leopold, though he was concerned lest the Queen might be unduly influenced in issues of the day, such as the Turkish crisis, where her youngest son's Tory leanings might threaten to bring the impartiality of the crown into question. He also saw dangers in elevating such a young and inexperienced prince into a position for which he was insufficiently qualified.

In April 1877 the Queen spoke to Disraeli about obtaining a cabinet key for Leopold, which would give him access to official papers, as well as a facility to help the Queen with private correspondence and despatches, with special emphasis on foreign affairs. The Prince of Wales was understandably indignant that his brother should be allowed access to state secrets which had always been denied to him as heir to the throne, though relations between the Princes did not suffer as a result.

On the contrary, the Prince of Wales had been magnanimous enough to make a recent approach to the Queen regarding a peerage for Leopold, who was now aged twenty-four. Arthur had been granted his at a similar age, and Alfred his when he was two years younger. She refused the request, as a result of which Leopold wrote to her, bitterly complaining that Arthur's duties in particular were far less arduous than she believed, because he had spent considerable time during the previous few months 'amusing himself' or officially on leave. Any reproach of her favourite son was like a red rag to a bull, and the Queen was furious with Leopold for his ingratitude, fiercely defending Arthur, 'who is a pattern to all young men & whom you always find fault with'.[7]

* * *

In 1878 Arthur, Duke of Connaught, announced his engagement to Princess Louise of Prussia, daughter of the German Emperor William's ill-tempered brother Prince Frederick Charles. With some asperity, the Queen wrote to the Crown Princess, Vicky, that there was really no need for Arthur to get married at all, as he was 'so good'. But she was pleased that he had found such a suitable young woman, and once she had met the prospective bride, any resistance soon evaporated. She welcomed Louise even more on learning that the Princess had led an extremely unhappy life at home in Berlin, as the daughter of estranged parents. Had she seen 'Louischen' before Arthur spoke to her of his feelings for the girl, the Queen wrote to Vicky, 'I should not have grieved him by hesitating for a moment in giving my consent to their union. She is a dear, sweet girl of the most amiable and charming character, and whatever nationality she was, I feel sure dear Arthur could not have chosen more wisely.'[8]

On 13 March 1879 the ceremony took place at St George's Chapel, Windsor. Sadly, the wedding had been overshadowed by the death of Alice from diphtheria in December 1878 (see p. 198), though Court mourning was suspended for the occasion. The Queen wore the Koh-I-Noor diamond, the Indian jewel in which she took such pride, and, for the first time since Albert's death, a Court train. Her favourite son's wedding was worthy of the best that she could do. Soon after his weding he was promoted to Major-General and placed in command of the 1st Guards Brigade, serving in Egypt under Sir Garnet Wolseley.

In Canada, the life that Louise and Lorne led free from the Queen's all-pervading presence was initially quite successful. They had settled at Rideau Hall, Ottawa, overlooking the St Lawrence River. Lorne was flexible and aware of Canadian sensitivities, and it was said that he became perhaps the most Canadian of all British holders of the office. The one minor controversy in which he was involved, regarding the dismissal of Luc Letellier, Lieutenant-Governor of Quebec, a move demanded by the Conservative federal government (a dismissal which Lorne opposed, but later approved under instruction from the Colonial Office), did him no damage.

Leopold joined them briefly at one stage, and all three travelled around Canada before making a short visit to the United States. The Queen was startled to receive an effusive New York newspaper article about their royal guests headed VIC'S CHICKS. Leopold had a terrier bitch called Vic, and when he sent the paper to England for her to read, she commented how odd it was of them to mention his dog.

Much to his delight, Leopold had managed to gain something of the independence which he had so craved. In May 1878 he had provoked the Queen's wrath by refusing to join her on a visit to Balmoral, on the grounds that he was so bored there. It was a verdict with which all the family heartily agreed. When a lady-at-waiting there said that when people were temporarily unhappy they sometimes killed themselves, Ponsonby added with tongue in cheek that 'suicide might be common here'. The Queen told Leopold that if he had such an aversion to her beloved Highland home, then he would have to stay at Buckingham Palace, in his room upstairs. On no account was he to go to Ascot or Epsom, or even join Bertie and Alix at Marlborough House. With great reluctance, she granted him permission to go to Paris for three or four days, but once he was there he coolly informed his mother that he intended to remain there for a fortnight. Initially she was outraged by his defiance, particularly as she objected to his going to the French capital of all places, that 'sinful city'. But he returned unscathed and had made his point by standing up to her. She had seen that he was capable of travelling abroad without injuring himself, and at last he had won some degree of autonomy.

Like Alfred, Leopold had a passion for music, and both brothers were friends with the Queen's favourite composer, Arthur Sullivan, a prolific writer of choral works, symphonies and songs, though known above all for his music for the Savoy Operas with librettist William S. Gilbert. Alfred persuaded them to support the cause of more free tuition for young students of music, and they made regular speeches on the subject. He was an enthusiastic amateur violinist himself and regularly performed with orchestras, though some at Court (including his own brothers) were inclined to be less than complimentary about his standard of playing as a soloist at home. He was also responsible for the foundation of what would become one of the royal family's most priceless assets. Since boyhood he had been an enthusiastic collector of postage stamps, and in 1890 he attended the inaugural ceremony of the Philatelic

Society in his capacity as first Honorary President, when he opened their first exhibition.

* * *

When diphtheria struck the grand ducal family at Darmstadt in the winter of 1878, four-year-old May succumbed. Worn out by having to nurse each member of the family in turn apart from second daughter Ella, who had been sent to stay with relatives as soon as the disease struck them, Alice also caught the infection. Weakened by years of indifferent health, she did not have the strength to withstand it, as her anxious mother had feared. By a peculiar irony of fate she died on 14 December, the seventeenth anniversary of her father's death.

Leopold had always been especially devoted to Alice, her husband and children, and of all the siblings he was the one most affected by the tragedy. Although the doctors tried to dissuade him from travelling to Darmstadt to attend the funeral lest he too catch the infection, he insisted that nothing would stop him going to pay his last respects, as did the Prince of Wales. They duly joined the other mourners at the obsequies, and in January 1879 the widowed Louis followed them back to England with his children. The brothers took them to Osborne and then to Windsor, and over the next few weeks Leopold went out with the father and his children during the mornings, before playing with the children every afternoon in the Round Tower.

The marriage between Alice and Louis had had its difficulties, as she had been all too conscious of her intellectual superiority and distressed to find how little she had in common with her husband. Nevertheless, Louis was stunned by her sudden death, and he drew great consolation from the company of his brother-in-law, whose sense of loss almost matched his. When the time came for Louis to return to Darmstadt, he felt unable to face the journey without Leopold. With some reluctance, the Queen allowed Leopold to accompany him back to Hesse.

Alice's death, pressure from the other children and, perhaps most importantly of all, the friendship of Disraeli had all combined to soften the Queen's over-protective attitude towards her youngest son. His bold stand against parental authority the previous year had also demonstrated that he could have his own way without coming to any harm. From this time onwards he was allowed to undertake a greater number of public engagements and made several speeches in support of various educational and charitable institutions. At the Mansion House he was one of several speakers on behalf of the London Society for the Extension of University Teaching. Gladstone, a fellow speaker, commented afterwards on how well he had spoken: 'keeping close to the subject, it was full of mind and it was difficult for anyone acquainted with the speeches of the Prince Consort not to recognise the father in the son'.[9]

He still desperately wanted a peerage, as confirmation of his adult status and a widening of his opportunities for work. Even the papers were beginning to wonder why he continued to be excluded from the House of Lords. Yet the Queen maintained, as ever, that his first duty was to support her. Nevertheless, two years later he was granted his wish when, on the Queen's birthday, 24 May 1881, he was created Duke of Albany, Earl of Clarence and Baron Arklow.

Now aged twenty-eight, he was very keen to marry. That autumn he was introduced to the Prince and Princess of Waldeck-Pyrmont and their daughter Helen. In November he asked Helen for her hand, and she accepted. They were married at Windsor in April 1882, though a few weeks before the ceremony he twisted his knee and was still walking with a stick on the day. The Queen took it ill; to her, the very idea of him getting married while 'still a complete invalid – not able to walk yet' seemed 'terrible'. She was afraid that everyone would be shocked, and as for the bride, 'I pity her but she seems only to think of him with love and affection.'[10]

For a little less than two years, Leopold and Helen were blissfully happy at Claremont, which had formerly been the home of his namesake, King Leopold, and Charlotte. In February 1883 Helen gave birth to their daughter, Alice. The Queen considered it remarkable that her frail son should have lived long enough to marry and have children.

Yet still he thirsted for proper employment. An opportunity appeared in 1883, when the Marquess of Lorne's five-year term as Governor-General of Canada expired, much to the Marquess's regret. He had found Canada more congenial than England and wished he could spend the rest of his days there, but Louise was thirsting to return home. Leopold applied to be considered as his successor, but the Queen asked Gladstone to veto his candidacy, largely on the pretext that the Fenian movement was particularly active there. Undaunted by the precedent of his brother's lucky escape from assassination in 1868, Leopold applied next for the governorship of Victoria, Australia, but this was rejected on similar grounds.

His young and often frustrated life was in fact nearing its end. In March 1884 he went to Cannes on medical advice to avoid the harsh, bitterly cold English winter. He enjoyed himself so much that he seriously considered buying a plot of land on the coast nearby where he could build a holiday home for the family. Helen, expecting a second child in the summer, had stayed at home. Leopold was also looking forward to attending the wedding of his niece, Victoria of Hesse, to Prince Louis of Battenberg at Darmstadt the following month. While arranging his accommodation for the ceremony, he begged the bride's father, Louis, Grand Duke of Hesse, not to be put in the same building as his mother, as they had not spoken for three months.[11]

During his stay at the yacht club in Cannes, on the afternoon of 27 March, Leopold slipped on a tiled floor at the foot of a staircase and hit his right knee hard against the bottom step. He was put to bed in considerable pain, and, after a severe convulsion early the following morning, he died. The exact cause of death was never entered on the official death certificates signed in Cannes and London. The staff at the club thought that his fall was the result of a lapse in consciousness, caused by an epileptic fit. Later it was believed that in falling he had burst a small blood vessel in the brain.

Queen Victoria had rarely been close to her youngest, often difficult, son, but this second death of a child within her lifetime was 'an awful blow', as she wrote to Vicky, the German Crown Princess. But his short life had been little more than 'a succession of trials and sufferings . . . and there was such a restless longing for what he could not have'.[12] Only after he had gone did she realise that the disagreements between them had added a certain amount of zest to her existence. To Canon Boyd Carpenter she said sadly, 'Nobody contradicts me now, and the salt has gone out of my life.'[13]

* * *

Also in 1884 Queen Victoria's peace of mind was to be shattered by two unexpected romances involving the next generation of her family. Unhindered by family mourning for Leopold, royal guests converged one month later on Darmstadt for the wedding on 30 April of Victoria, eldest child of the Grand Duke and Duchess of Hesse and the Rhine (the late Princess Alice), to Prince Louis of Battenberg, who had worked in the Royal Navy with Alfred, Duke of Edinburgh.

The bride was in a state of some nervousness, not at the thought of her own marriage, but of a more controversial union. Having been a widower for five years, her father was known to be in love with Alexandrine von Kolemine, a thirty-year-old divorcee who had formerly been married to a Russian diplomat. From all accounts, it seems the Grand Duke had kept his plans to marry Kolemine a secret and was trying to take everyone by surprise while they were preoccupied with his eldest daughter's wedding, so they would not be too bothered by his (a miscalculation if ever there was one). The Grand Duke's two elder daughters, Victoria and Ella, were well aware of his feelings and of the loneliness he would undoubtedly feel once Victoria, a mature and sensible young woman who had more or less taken over the role of mother to her siblings, was gone. Victoria herself had declared that her father would never marry again, though it was looking increasingly likely that he would take Kolemine as his wife before long.

Naturally, the Grand Duke's affair and impending marriage – which Victoria suspected would take place sooner or later – were impossible to keep secret, and by the time the Queen arrived at Darmstadt for her granddaughter's wedding, it seemed that everybody was aware of his plans except the Queen herself. On 25 April she was told by Vicky, who added that it was only a temporary passion and that the Grand Duke could be persuaded not to marry the lady. The Prince of Wales had also been informed of it by his sister, and he was chosen to speak firmly to his brother-in-law, instructing him to break off the relationship, or at least postpone any thoughts of marriage.

'The Grand Duke has behaved very badly in not telling the Queen before she came to Darmstadt because it places her in a most awkward position,' Sir Henry Ponsonby wrote to Gladstone. 'If she goes away it will create a scandal, if she remains it will look as if she approved the marriage.'[14] The Prime Minister replied that it would 'cause continual and painful embarrassment' to Her Majesty, and he could not see how the conduct of the Grand Duke in not giving her notice beforehand could be justified.

The wedding of Victoria and Louis took place as arranged on 30 April. During the banquet that evening, it was whispered by some that the bride would continue to be the first lady in the duchy as she had been since her mother's death, because 'la Kolomine' would never live in the palace. The guests were probably too wrapped up in the happy festivities or complimenting the bride and groom to notice that the Grand Duke had quietly slipped away. At another room in the palace, his Prime Minister and a few witnesses were waiting for him and 'la Kolomine', and they went through a short, secret civil marriage ceremony. The bride stayed that night with friends. According to some, it was never consummated, though another, less reliable version is that a son was born and later adopted as a brother by the Grand Duke's youngest daughter, Alix, when she was Empress of Russia.[15]

Inevitably, the news leaked out, and Lady Ely was chosen to inform her. Inwardly furious but outwardly calm, she sent for the Prince of Wales, ordered him to interview Alexandrine von Kolemine and arrange that the marriage be declared null and void. Next, the Grand Duke announced that his second daughter, Ella, was betrothed to Grand Duke Serge of Russia. The German Empress Augusta was already thoroughly indignant at the various Battenberg and Hesse alliances, not least the romance between Louis of Battenberg's brother Alexander and her granddaughter Crown Princess Victoria of Prussia. This was the last straw, and she ordered the Crown Prince and Princess to leave 'this contaminated court'[16] and come back to Berlin.

The Crown Princess had been one of the first to tell the family about 'la Kolemine' and might have helped her brother the Prince of Wales in his delicate negotiations regarding the breaking off of the Grand Duke's doomed marriage. However, Bertie was left with the unwelcome task himself, namely negotiating with his brother-in-law and the lawyers who were required to deal with the annulment of the marriage. Miss Jackson, the English nurse at Court, had always strongly disapproved of the liaison and said at the family discussions that Alexandrine von Kolemine should be sent back to Russia where she belonged. 'But if she won't go?' asked Sir Henry Ponsonby. 'Ah, but she must!' the nurse retorted.[17]

The British ambassador at Berlin, Lord Ampthill, was ordered by the Queen to persuade the German government to expedite this, and the marriage was dissolved on 9 July. Far from resenting interference from his mother-in-law, the distressed Grand Duke was grateful to her for saving him from himself. Something – possibly the family, possibly something else – told him that Alexandrine was a gold-digger, and perhaps he had had a lucky escape, embarrassing though it looked at the time. Yet against his late wife's family, he was powerless to do anything. As the Prince of Wales said, 'We are a very strong family when we all agree.'[18]

There was no question of the Grand Duke being ostracised for his behaviour. Anxious to show him that he had not incurred anything more than momentary disapproval, the Queen invited him back to stay at Windsor a few weeks later, though he was still in a state of deep depression. Later in May she wrote to her newly married grand-daughter that her father was 'in such a state of distress & grief that it is terrible to see'.[19]

* * *

Queen Victoria fervently hoped, if not assumed, that her youngest daughter, Beatrice, was always going to remain by her mother's side. Yet soon after their return home from Darmstadt, Beatrice astonished the Queen by announcing that she had fallen in love with Henry, another of Louis's younger brothers, and they intended to marry. For several weeks, mother and daughter were not on speaking terms and only communicated by means of written notes passed between them at the breakfast table. Very much her mother's daughter, Beatrice also had a will of her own.

It was not so much the thought of her youngest daughter marrying that so alarmed the Queen, it was the fear that Henry would insist on continuing his military career, and that Beatrice would go to Potsdam with him. His brother Louis and sister-in-law Victoria realised that action had to be taken, and they invited him to stay with them at their home, Sennicotts, near Chichester. Between them, they persuaded Henry to give up his military career and be prepared to make his home with Beatrice and the Queen. When she was advised of this she relented and gave her consent to the marriage. As Henry was retiring from the Prussian Army, Beatrice could stay at home and continue to be her mother's unofficial private secretary and confidante; and both of them were to live with her in England.

The press was critical of the impending marriage, calling the groom a 'German pauper' who expected to be kept at government expense. The wedding took place in July 1885 at St Mildred's Church, Whippingham, and though the marriage was to prove unhappily brief, Henry rapidly became the Queen's favourite son-in-law. Although he had had to give up his military career, the Queen insisted on his wearing his white uniform, that of the Prussian Garde du Corps, and the Princess of Wales called him 'Beatrice's Lohengrin'.

Henry, known in the family as 'Liko', a diminutive of his childhood name 'Henrico', brought back an atmosphere of happiness to the Queen's domestic life such as she had not known since before the Prince Consort's death. Once more there was a man in the family, one who was not in the least overawed by her, and one with whom she could make lighthearted conversation and laugh at meals. She gave him a yacht in which he could take pleasure cruises as far away as the Mediterranean, and a bicycle which he mastered with ease. He also took the lead in helping to revive the *tableaux vivants* which Albert had so loved when assisting his small children to prepare for their mother's amusement. Queen Victoria looked forward to these performances with almost childish enthusiasm, though requested that she must always be allowed to censor if necessary. It would never do for her daughter Louise, even if playing the part of a villainess in a French comedy, to be reproved as 'a degraded woman' by an assistant under-secretary.

Henry's position was not easy at first. He was half-German and half-Russian by birth, and neither country was particularly popular in Britain. He had to play second fiddle to his wife and submit to the authority of a powerful lady. However, he was pleasant, genial and full of fun, and soon endeared himself to everyone at Court. He was an excellent sportsman, good at sailing, riding, shooting, tennis and skating.

Above all, he managed to succeed where others had failed – by persuading the Queen to relax her attitude towards smoking. While staying with his mother-in-law, the cigar-loving Christian had only been allowed to indulge in this anti-social vice in a small cubby-hole at Osborne with bare boards and hard wooden chairs, which was reached by crossing the servants' quarters and an open yard. Now, after Henry had put the pro-smoking case, more conveniently situated, well-furnished sitting rooms at Balmoral as well as Osborne could be used for the purpose. Even so, there was to be no relaxation of the Queen's rules at Windsor. Only the billiard room was available for smoking, and only after 11 p.m. Here Alfred,

Duke of Edinburgh, tended to occupy one of the best chairs whenever he visited and hold forth endlessly about himself. In consequence, Henry preferred to give up smoking for a while rather than put up with his brother-in-law's endless naval conversation.

Christmas 1885 at Osborne was the happiest that any of the family could remember for a quarter of a century. Beatrice and Henry were allotted the use of a suite in the new wing of the house. Helen of Albany and her two children – a son, Charles, having been born three months after his father's sudden death – as well as the Connaughts were there to share the festivities, with presents on the tables, party games, theatrical performances and beech logs burning brightly in the polished steel grate of the Queen's sitting-room.

In November 1886 Beatrice gave birth to a son, whom they named Alexander. Two more sons and a daughter followed during the next five years. Henry was apparently happy and contented in his life at home, even if under the watchful eye of his mother-in-law. She gave orders that the old nursery quarters on the top floor at Osborne should be turned into a special suite for the Battenberg children, and the sovereign who normally so loved peace and quiet in her own home said that nothing made her feel so happy as the sounds of these youngest grandchildren playing around noisily in the rooms directly above her suite.

TWELVE

'A great three-decker ship sinking'

As the youngest son-in-law of Queen Victoria, Prince Henry of Battenberg could indeed count his blessings. Not the least of these was that he never shared the fate of his brother Alexander, who had reigned for three troubled years as sovereign Prince of Bulgaria, a tenure brought to a violent end in August 1886 when a gang of drunken officers acting under Russian orders broke into his palace at Sofia and ordered him at gunpoint to sign a deed of abdication. He arrived in England a few weeks later, prematurely aged and broken by his experiences.

Alexander's tragedy was soon to be bound up with that of another of Queen Victoria's daughters and sons-in-law. He had become unofficially betrothed to Princess Victoria of Prussia, eldest un-married daughter of the German Crown Prince Frederick William and Princess Victoria (Vicky). The match was warmly endorsed by the Crown Princess and by Queen Victoria, as well as the British royal family. Most of the German imperial family, and Bismarck, the German Chancellor, resolutely opposed it for political reasons, while the Crown Prince himself gave his approval only with reluctance. Prince Frederick William could not but share the view of his parents that a Battenberg, no matter how good his character, was still the child of a morganatic marriage (see note 9, chapter 7) and therefore hardly a suitable son-in-law for a Hohenzollern princess. He had already viewed the announcement of Henry's betrothal to his sister-in-law Beatrice with reservations. 'Dear Fritz speaks of Liko as not being of *Geblüt* [stock], a little like about animals',[1] the Queen wrote disapprovingly to the Crown Princess.

All the same, the Queen and her daughter hoped they would eventually persuade the Crown Prince to agree to accepting a Battenberg in his family. After he was forced to abdicate, Prince Alexander found that his importance as a political figure dwindled accordingly. When the time came for the Crown Prince to succeed

206

his father Emperor William on the throne, it was assumed that he would readily give his approval to the marriage. The Emperor celebrated his ninetieth birthday in March 1887; by then he was increasingly frail and feeble, and it would surely be only a matter of months before he passed away.

While every member of the royal family in Britain was looking forward with excitement to the celebrations for Queen Victoria's jubilee that summer, her eldest daughter had an additional cause for concern. Throughout the winter Crown Prince Frederick William had been unable to shake off a severe cold and cough, and remained unusually hoarse. In the spring he was examined by the German physicians, who, fearing he might have something more serious than a persistent sore throat and cough, decided to seek another opinion from a specialist outside Germany. A major operation could prove fatal, and it would be as well for the cause of German science if a foreign doctor was left to take any crucial decisions, and therefore all the blame, should anything go wrong.

For political reasons, given Prussia's conquests in war during Bismarck's period of power, it was inadvisable to consider a specialist from Austria or France. The name of Dr Morell Mackenzie, a Scottish laryngologist who had a thriving practice in Harley Street, seemed the most obvious. He was a renowned expert on diseases of the nose and throat, spoke fluent German and already knew Professor Gerhardt, one of the Germans on the case, on a professional basis. Above all, as he was British, it would prove to be something of a triumph for the anglophobe element at court in Berlin if one of their unpopular Crown Princess's fellow countrymen could be held responsible for the death of her husband.

At the German doctors' request, the Crown Princess asked Queen Victoria to send Mackenzie to Germany as soon as possible. This the Queen did, adding a caveat that he was clever but had a reputation in England for greed and self-advertisement. He arrived in Germany on 20 May and, after a consultation with his colleagues, examined the Crown Prince's throat. A small portion of the swelling was removed and passed to Professor Rudolf Virchow at the Berlin Institute of Pathology for diagnosis. It was deemed too small, and on request Mackenzie removed a larger sample two days later. Gerhardt insisted that Mackenzie had injured the previously healthy right vocal cord and made it bleed. He and his German doctors maintained that the only possible course of action was for them to operate on the Crown Prince at once. Mackenzie declared that if they did, the Prince would surely die.

The Crown Prince and Princess had been invited to London for Queen Victoria's jubilee celebrations, for both personal and political reasons. As the Queen's eldest daughter, and as her son-in-law who expected to ascend the throne of the most powerful empire on mainland Europe before long, they had every right to be there. Dr Mackenzie suggested that they should be in England so they could combine participation in the festivities with the Crown Prince's regular attendance as a private patient at his London surgery. The German doctors accepted this course of action, largely as they were relieved that the responsibility for their illustrious patient's health would no longer be theirs.

In June the Crown Prince and Princess came to England and stayed at a hotel in Norwood, sufficiently near the centre of London for convenience, but far enough from the worst of the heat and dust. They moved to Buckingham Palace on 18 June, so the Crown Prince could rest for a couple of days before the procession to Westminster Abbey and the service of thanksgiving.

'The day has come,' the Queen wrote in her journal that evening, happy though exhausted, 'and I am alone, though surrounded by many dear children.'[2] She was alone in the sense that the Prince Consort was long since departed, but all surviving seven children and their spouses were present, as were the widowed partners of the two deceased children, the Grand Duke of Hesse and Duchess of Albany. The Duke of Edinburgh was now a Rear-Admiral and Commander-in-Chief of the Mediterranean Fleet, based at Malta, while the Duke of Connaught was a serving officer in India, but both had obtained leave without much difficulty.

The climax of the jubilee celebrations was the procession to Westminster Abbey and the thanksgiving service on 21 June. Huge crowds lined the route and were rewarded by seeing almost every member of the royal family passing by, whether riding in carriages or on horseback. The Prince of Wales was resplendent in the scarlet tunic and plumed helmet of a British field-marshal, but everyone agreed that none looked more magnificent than Crown Prince Frederick William, in his white cuirassier uniform and silver helmet surmounted with the imperial eagle. Towering above his relations on every side, it was said that he looked like 'one of the legendary heroes embodied in the creations of Wagner'. Very few of those who stood on the streets of London to cheer him with such enthusiasm were aware of his illness.

The Crown Prince and Princess stayed in Britain for the rest of the summer, spending part of their time at Osborne and the rest at Braemar, near Balmoral. As Dr Mackenzie advised them to avoid the bitter weather of Berlin over the winter, on leaving Britain they went first to Toblach in the Austrian Tyrol, then to Venice and Baveno, and finally to San Remo on the Riviera.

It was here in November that the seriousness of the Crown Prince's illness became apparent. For some weeks it had been rumoured that he was suffering from cancer of the larynx, and at last Mackenzie had to admit that this was almost certainly the case. For some time, the Crown Prince and Princess had had another cross to bear, the growing estrangement from their eldest son and heir, William. 'Willy' shared none of his parents' liberal leanings but revered the ultra-conservative politics of his grandfather and Prince Bismarck, the Chancellor whose wars had elevated Prussia from the humble status of one of several German kingdoms to the leading military and political state in the new German Empire, created in January 1871 after the victorious war against France. Endlessly fawned on and flattered by the reactionary elements at court and the military clique, William became more arrogant and dismissive of his parents' ways than ever. Though he undoubtedly felt some sympathy for his seriously ill father, he concealed it well.

In February 1888 the Crown Prince was operated on for a tracheotomy, the operation against which he, his wife and Mackenzie had held out for so long. Without it he would have suffocated and died almost immediately, but by this stage it was realised that his life could only be prolonged by a matter of weeks. Since late the previous year he had been in constant pain, unable to speak at all except in a hoarse whisper and reduced to writing everything he wished to say on a pad of paper which he always kept within reach.

On 9 March, while walking in the garden at San Remo, he was handed a telegram from Berlin. It brought him the news that his father, Emperor William, had passed away, within two weeks of what would have been his ninety-first birthday.

'My OWN dear *Empress Victoria* it does seem an impossible dream, may God bless her!' the Queen wrote to her daughter when she learnt of her son-in-law's accession. 'You know *how* little I care for rank or Titles – but I cannot *deny* that *after all* that has been done & said, I am *thankful* & *proud* that dear Fritz & you shd have come to the throne.'[3] Like many others, not least the newly elevated Empress Victoria herself, she had often feared that Fritz might not survive his father. Now that he had come into his inheritance, and was unlikely to enjoy it for long, she begged her daughter to be firm, put her foot down and remind her elder children – particularly William, now Crown Prince – that in the previous reign they had always spoken of the Emperor and Empress with great respect and 'to remember who they are now'.

The new sovereign announced that he intended to reign as Emperor Frederick III. He, the Empress and their entourage returned to Berlin that same week, but it was evident to all that the disease was too far advanced for there to be any hope of recovery. Their existence was made worse still by the tactless behaviour of William, surrounded by toadies who already had an eye on their own advancement during the next reign.

Queen Victoria came to visit the Emperor and Empress in Berlin in April. The Empress noted sadly that it was the first time she had ever had her mother to stay under her roof – and now it was for the most poignant of reasons. As she left, the Queen kissed her son-in-law goodbye, telling him with an aching heart that he must come and visit her in England when he was better. He was able to attend the wedding of his second son, Henry, to his cousin Irene, the third daughter of Alice and Louis of Hesse, on 24 May, though he leaned on a stick the whole time and every step he took caused him great agony. After this he declined rapidly, and on the morning of 15 June he passed away.

Queen Victoria was at Balmoral at the time. In the morning she had received a telegram to say Fritz could last only a few hours, and soon afterwards Beatrice brought her another, from the new sovereign, Emperor William II, saying it was all over. 'Feel very miserable and upset,' she wrote in her journal. 'None of my own sons could be a greater loss. He was so good, so wise, and so fond of me! And now? To think of it all is such pain.'[4]

She and the old Emperor had had their minor differences. Occasionally she had criticised him and Vicky, albeit mildly, for arrogance. Nearly five years earlier, she had written to her grand-daughter Princess Victoria of Hesse that the Crown Prince and Princess were '*not* pleasant in *Germany*', and were too 'high & mighty there',[5] and they had not seen eye to eye over the lineage of the Battenbergs, but she had rarely if ever been moved to exasperation by the gentle, mild son-in-law whom she and Albert had so admired since he and his parents had been guests at the Great Exhibition of 1851. She had always been ready to make allowances for her eldest grandson, William, much as she had been dismayed at his unfilial conduct during the last few years. On his accession, she telegraphed to him, asking him to 'Help and do all you can for your poor dear mother and try to follow in your best noblest and kindest of father's footsteps.'[6]

* * *

With his extra-marital affairs and unfortunate friendships, the Prince of Wales had given his mother considerable anxiety, but as he approached his fiftieth year, even worse was to come. In September 1890 he was invited to stay with the shipowner Arthur Wilson at Tranby Croft, near Doncaster, and every evening the guests played the very popular but illegal game of baccarat. During one game, Wilson's son, also called Arthur, noticed one of their fellow-guests, the baronet Sir William Gordon-Cumming, was deliberately cheating by varying the size of his stake after looking at his cards. After being formally accused in private, he was panic-stricken and asked to discuss it with the Prince of Wales, who told him it was pointless to try to deny the charge. Gordon-Cumming signed a pledge never to play cards for money again, and the other players, including the heir to the throne himself, added their signatures as witnesses. He then left the house the following day as the price of their silence on the matter. That would have been the end of it, had Gordon-Cumming not decided to continue to protest his innocence and bring a civil action against his accusers in order to clear his name.

The Prince of Wales and Sir Francis Knollys, his secretary, tried in vain to have Gordon-Cumming brought before a military court which would look privately into the charge brought against his behaviour as an officer and a gentleman, on the grounds that once he had been found guilty, it would be virtually impossible for him to take any subsequent action in a civil court, where the Prince would be required to give evidence in public. The baronet's solicitors insisted that only a civil action would do. A further attempt by the

Prince of Wales and Knollys to institute a private inquiry held by the Guards Club Committee was defeated.

Aware that her son had become involved only in order to help his friends, Queen Victoria proved fully supportive of him, her full anger being reserved for those who had asked him to sign the document which urged Gordon-Cumming to desist from playing cards. She must have long since despaired of her eldest son's way of life but realised that there was nothing to be done other than accept him as he was and stand by him for the sake of the monarchy. It was her hope that he would promise her never to play baccarat again, but he would not commit himself to do so, and he refused to go to Windsor unless she gave him her word not to raise the matter again. As a man of nearly fifty, he felt entitled to gamble if he wanted, and despite the trouble in which he found himself, he did not intend to change the habits of a lifetime.

Nevertheless the proceedings came to court in June 1891, and the Prince was called as a witness. To a casual observer, it might almost have looked as if the heir to the throne himself was on trial. The Solicitor-General, Sir Edward Clarke, representing Gordon-Cumming, remarked that it was not the first time honourable men had been known 'to sacrifice themselves to support a tottering throne or prop a falling dynasty'. Gordon-Cumming was found guilty of cheating, expelled from the Army and his clubs, and shunned by society generally. Yet the Prince of Wales was himself the subject of strong criticism, and his gambling habits were severely censured.

The Queen's greatest fear was that the Crown was becoming tarnished by the Prince's behaviour. To the Empress Frederick she wrote that she feared the monarchy might be 'almost in danger if he is lowered and despised'.[7] The fact that light had been thrown on his habits had alarmed and shocked the country, and it was no example for the heir to the throne to set to the Queen's subjects. In an attempt to restore public confidence, she invited the Prince of Wales to write a letter to the Archbishop of Canterbury, Edward White Benson, for publication, condemning the social evils of gambling. The Archbishop and Gladstone, then leader of the opposition, endorsed this scheme, but the Prince refused to take part on the grounds that it would be hypocritical of him.

If the government considered it necessary, he replied, he would not object to issuing a statement saying that he disapproved of gambling, but only if he would be allowed to explain what he meant by gambling. To him, small racing bets, or games of baccarat played by rich men for stakes which they could afford to lose, did not count, as they did the person responsible no harm. Though it was a somewhat convoluted argument, the Prince made it clear that he was not going to lecture others and warn them against habits which they could perfectly well afford, particularly if they were aware of the risks. He also knew that to take the moral high ground would be a gift to his critics.

Nobody, it seemed, relished the affair more than his sanctimonious nephew, Emperor William, who wrote to the Queen protesting against the impropriety of anyone holding the honorary rank of a colonel of Prussian Hussars becoming involved with men young enough to be his children in a mere gambling squabble.[8] Much as she resented his intervention, she could not but feel that the Emperor's indignation was justified.

Shortly after the case was over, the Prince of Wales found himself involved in another scandal. The Princess of Wales had tolerated most of his female companions and mistresses, but one she could not abide was the unscrupulous Frances, Lady Brooke, who had become involved in an affair with a married man – Lord Charles Beresford, a naval officer and friend of the Prince of Wales and Duke of Edinburgh. When the affair ended, she wrote Lord Beresford a presumptuous, almost hysterical letter, accusing him of infidelity (ironic, in view of the fact that he was returning to his own wife) and desertion. Lady Beresford opened the letter in her husband's absence, as he had authorised her to do while he was away on active service. She deposited it with her solicitor, George Lewis, and threatened to prosecute Lady Brooke for libel if she continued to make a nuisance of herself. Lewis informed Lady Brooke, who then demanded the return of the letter, on the grounds that she wrote it and it was her property. He refused, saying that it belonged to the person to whom it was addressed.

In desperation she asked the Prince of Wales to use his influence to retrieve it for her. Though he would have been wiser not to get involved, he gallantly went to see Lewis, who showed him the letter. Agreeing it was the most shocking thing he had ever read, he asked the solicitor to destroy it, only to be told that this was impossible without Lady Beresford's consent. By way of compromise, she asked for its return and sent it to her brother-in-law for safe-keeping.

213

As a punishment for not cooperating, Lady Beresford found herself ostracised by the Prince of Wales and the rest of society. She complained that the heir to the throne had taken up the cause of 'an abandoned woman' against that of 'a blameless wife'. Lord Beresford angrily taxed the Prince with needless interference, accused him of trying to wreck their marriage and promised he would exact reparation or revenge. Eighteen months later, Lady Beresford put her London house up for sale, saying she would move abroad rather than face further humiliation at home.

This coincided with the height of the Tranby Croft case. Aware how vulnerable the Prince of Wales's standing was, Lord Beresford threatened to publish all the details of their squalid argument in the press and asked his wife to inform the Prime Minister, Lord Salisbury, of their intentions. The Prime Minister persuaded them not to make the affair public, but he could not prevent circulation of three copies of a leaflet by Lady Beresford's sister, Mrs Gerald Paget, telling the full story. These were distributed in Britain and the United States of America, and details did not remain secret for long.

Just as the Prince of Wales's stock was in danger of falling lower than it ever had before, his second son, Prince George, fell seriously ill with typhoid fever. Though he was not so ill as his father had been exactly twenty years earlier, for two or three weeks the Prince and Princess were gravely concerned. At the same time as George was declared out of danger, in December 1891, their eldest son, Albert Victor, Duke of Clarence, was betrothed to Princess May of Teck. The backward, dissipated young Duke had been a major source of worry to his father and grandfather, sharing many of his father's faults, not least his love of high living, but lacking in his personality and robust health.

In January 1892, five weeks after becoming engaged, the Duke of Clarence took to his bed at Sandringham with pneumonia. His constitution had been undermined by dissipation and perhaps venereal disease, and his death, just six days after his twenty-eighth birthday, may have been a providential one for the throne and also for his bride-to-be, who was dismayed by the young man's lack of personality and had begun to doubt whether she could really 'take this on'. But the family were heartbroken, and the country was united in mourning.

Happier times for the Prince of Wales were to come. Late in 1892 the Foreign Secretary, Lord Rosebery, sent him a gold key which had been made for the Prince Consort and used by him to open Foreign Office despatch boxes. Already he had been in the habit of receiving edited reports of cabinet meetings which were sent to the Queen. In future, while he was in Britain, he would be kept as well informed about official foreign business as the Queen herself. Informal conversations with Rosebery, ambassadors and others helped him to supplement the documents he read.

At around the same time, he accepted an invitation from Gladstone to become a member of a royal commission on the aged poor. This pleased him all the more as Lord Salisbury had rejected his offer, a year previously, to serve on an enquiry into the relations between employers and the working class. The new royal commission addressed itself to the problems of persons rendered destitute by age. At last the Prince had found a subject concerning the welfare of his mother's subjects to which he could make a genuine contribution. A fellow-commissioner, James Stuart, Liberal member of parliament for Hoxton, said that the Prince of Wales asked very good questions. He thought at first that he had been prompted to raise them, until he found out that he had brought them up on his own initiative, proving that he had a considerable grasp of his subject. As expected, the commission's final report proved a controversial one in terms of party politics. The Prince signed a statement to the effect that he was obliged to observe strict political neutrality, and it was not until the next century that state pensions were provided for by Act of Parliament.

All this was some consolation for what he perceived as persistent snubbing at the hands of his mother. When Gladstone became Prime Minister for the last time, he told his family in private that he thought the only remedy to 'the royal problem' would be for Her Majesty to abdicate in favour of her son. The Queen indignantly refused to hear of it; on the contrary, she refused to delegate any further responsibilities. During the summer season of 1892 on the Isle of Wight, Knollys sadly informed Ponsonby that the Prince of Wales had told him he believed there was no point in remaining at Cowes, though he was willing to do so. He felt that he was 'not the slightest use to the Queen; that everything he says or suggests is pooh-poohed; and that his sisters and brother are much more listened to than he is'.[9] His indiscretions of the previous year had reminded her that, notwithstanding all his good qualities, at heart he was the same Bertie with a weakness for unsuitable friends and gambling, who could still not be trusted as much as she would like.

When the Prince of Wales suggested that Mrs Gladstone should be given a peerage and appointed Mistress of the Robes, he was indeed not taken seriously. Sometimes his interventions were more successful, though they might owe something to the Queen in the first place. Under Gladstone's last administration in 1892 the Queen was particularly keen for Lord Rosebery to become Foreign Minister. The Prince spoke to him, and he accordingly informed Gladstone that His Royal Highness's intervention had induced him to accept the post after all.

Even so, the Prince was still generally not trusted. Only a few years earlier, the Queen had written to her granddaughter Princess Victoria of Hesse that he 'cannot keep anything to himself – but lets everything *out*'.[10] During her last years, when the Queen began to take annual spring holidays on the Riviera, Lord Rosebery suggested that her absence abroad should require somebody to undertake the Guardianship of the Realm, and that the Prince of Wales would be just the right person. Reluctantly, the Queen agreed to consider it, but informed Sir Arthur Bigge, her assistant secretary, that she had no intention of proposing it to the Prince herself. He might find the responsibility inconvenient, but he might find it difficult to decline if the offer came directly from her; and she did not want to prevent him from going abroad. Instead, she would rather appoint a committee, including the Dukes of Connaught and Cambridge, and the Lord Chief Justice.[11] The Prince of Wales would surely have been piqued at his favourite brother yet again being given preference for a position which should have been his by right. In the end, nothing came of the idea.

* * *

By this time, the Duke of Edinburgh's duties in England were almost complete. Soon after the expiry of his Mediterranean command in 1889, he was appointed Commander-in-Chief at Devonport for three years, a post which he took up in August 1890. On the conclusion of his command in June 1893, he was promoted to the rank of Admiral of the Fleet. A month later he attended the wedding of his favourite nephew, George, only surviving son of the Prince and Princess of Wales and recently made Duke of York, to Princess

May of Teck. George had followed his uncle into the Royal Navy, a service which he had had to leave with great regret as a result of his elder brother's death and his new status as second in succession to the throne. He had also taken after the Duke of Edinburgh in his fascination for collecting stamps.

One month after that, the Prince Consort's renegade brother Ernest, Duke of Saxe-Coburg Gotha for forty-nine years, died of a chill, aged seventy-five. As second son of the Prince Consort, Alfred had been the heir of his uncle, who had had several illegitimate children but none by his lawful wife. With little enthusiasm, the Duke took up his inheritance as the new Duke of Coburg, to spend most of the rest of his life at the small German court. He was now officially retired from his beloved Royal Navy, and to be a German Duke, subservient to the bombastic Emperor William II, whom few of the family really liked and none really trusted, was a prospect which nobody envied.

His next few months were not made any easier by unfounded rumours that he had secretly renounced the succession before Duke Ernest's death in favour of his son Alfred, and then by unseemly wrangles in parliament at Westminster and in the *Reichstag* in Berlin as to whether the new Duke of Coburg was technically a British subject or not. If Britain and Germany should find themselves at war with each other, could he be indicted in England on a charge of high treason as a result of his acts and status as a German sovereign? There was also uncertainty as to whether he should still be allowed to sit or speak in the House of Lords, or retain his membership of the privy council.

Only in the spring of 1894 was his nationality status officially confirmed. He was obliged to resign his privy councillorship and any rights pertaining to the House of Lords in England. He relinquished the annuity granted to him by parliament in 1866, but retained an allowance granted on his marriage for the upkeep of Clarence House, which remained his official residence in Britain for life. By British law, he retained his British nationality, modified 'by his status as a German sovereign'.

* * *

At Windsor and Osborne, Prince Henry of Battenberg was becoming more and more frustrated by his dull existence. His official appointments as Governor of the Isle of Wight and Honorary Colonel of the Isle of Wight Rifles did not give him much scope for activity. When he joined his elder brother Louis in Corsica while Beatrice and the Queen were on holiday in Cannes, his wife had him fetched back smartly. Rumour had it that the Battenberg princes had gone to the carnival at Ajaccio for some 'low company', and the censorious Beatrice was not prepared to sit by patiently while her husband was willingly being led into temptation. Later he joined a regiment of the volunteer battalion in Hampshire, and was delighted to find himself following his true vocation once again – sharing the camaraderie of a soldier's life.

This may have been a convenient escape from the attentions of a certain lady at Court. It was believed that Princess Louise, now unofficially separated from Lord Lorne, was flirting with Henry, and Beatrice found the situation distinctly uncomfortable. Henry found a way out of it through an opportunity for which he had long thirsted. In the autumn of 1895 an expeditionary force of West African troops and British Army officers was assembled to restore order in the kingdom of Ashanti, north of the Gold Coast Protectorate [Ghana]. Princess Helena's elder son Christian Victor, who was commissioned in the King's Royal Rifles, was invited to join the force, and a few days later Henry told the Queen that he also wanted to go to Ashanti.

Remembering the Prince Imperial's death in the Zulu War in 1879, and stressing the additional dangers he would face from tropical disease, the Queen tried hard to dissuade Henry. But Beatrice proved fully supportive of her husband's intentions, insisting that as all his brothers had seen active service he could hardly be denied such a chance himself. She also saw how desperately bored he had become with a life at home of enforced inactivity, and she may have felt it wise to remove him from her flirtatious elder sister. These reasons, and Henry's determination to volunteer in a national cause to prove his devotion to his adopted country, persuaded the Queen. On 6 December 1895 he took farewell of his mother-in-law at Windsor, as he and Beatrice left for Bagshot to stay the night with the Duke and Duchess of Connaught on his way to Africa.

From the continent Henry wrote enthusiastically to Beatrice that he was 'really happy and pleased to have received permission to see all that is going on'. However, in fact almost nothing was happening. The Ashanti chiefs had decided not to fight, instead submitting gracefully to British protection. Even so, the futile expedition continued through the tropical heat, with several men dying from fever on the way. Henry was among those to contract malaria, and the doctors ordered that he should be carried back to the coast at once. On 18 January 1896 Beatrice and the Queen received a telegram to say that he had been feverish but was improving and was about to leave for Madeira. Four days later another telegram arrived. They expected it to tell them that he had arrived safely at Madeira to convalesce and that he wanted Beatrice to go and join him. Instead it contained the news of his death.

A very few losses had affected the Queen deeply since the death of the Prince Consort, notably those of John Brown in 1883 and Emperor Frederick five years later. This came as a terrible shock. Henry had entered her life at a time when she was mourning John Brown and Leopold, Duke of Albany. His sense of humour and obvious enjoyment of life had rejuvenated her, introducing a breath of fresh air into the old-fashioned Court. He had given her another four grandchildren and thus reminded her how it felt to have a young family around – as well as a family to which she could be, and was, far more indulgent than she had ever been towards her own children.

Beatrice bore her sudden bereavement with tremendous patience and fortitude. In February she left Osborne to recuperate for a while at Cimiez. She returned to a home life which had become dull and drab without Henry. After his death, there would be no more amateur theatricals at Court. Not only was the Queen losing her eyesight and her former enthusiasm for the diversion, but Beatrice, who had been such an enthusiastic participant, no longer had the heart to return to an activity which reminded her so much of those brief, happy years with her husband.

* * *

Queen Victoria's diamond jubilee celebrations in June 1897, to celebrate the sixtieth anniversary of her accession, would be the last time that many of the family would be together. This time, it was stipulated that no crowned heads would be invited to take part in the procession and service of thanksgiving at St Paul's Cathedral, although fifteen prime ministers from the colonies would be there.

However, all the Queen's surviving children and children-in-law were also present.

This time, none among the family accompanying her that day made a greater impression than the Prince of Wales. Short of stature, overweight and hardly particularly handsome in his fifty-sixth year, he nevertheless cut a dignified, striking figure in his field-marshal's uniform as he rode by his mother's side in the procession from Buckingham Palace to the cathedral. For once, they took a route not merely through the city by the shortest possible way, but also across London Bridge and through some of the capital's poorer districts.

'No one ever, I believe, has met with such an ovation,' the Queen noted in her journal afterwards. 'The crowds were quite indescribable, and their enthusiasm truly marvellous and deeply touching.'[12]

Yet the absence of those who had died since the golden jubilee ten years earlier was noticed and sorely missed. Emperor Frederick, Henry of Battenberg, Grand Duke Louis of Hesse (who had followed his wife Alice to the grave in 1892 after a bout of pneumonia) and her eldest grandson born in England, the Duke of Clarence, had all gone. At seventy-eight, Queen Victoria was paying the common penalty of a long life, in having outlived too many members of her own family.

She may have had a presentiment that the festivities would be her own swan-song. Already one of her surviving sons, Alfred, was in poor health. As Marie Mallet, one of her ladies-in-waiting, remarked somewhat bluntly, the Duke of Coburg's life was not one likely to be accepted at any insurance office. For some years, his heavy drinking had concerned the family. For at least three years, his private secretary, Stephen Condie, had been warning Dr Reid, who passed the information on to the Queen, that unless he cut back on his alcohol consumption the consequences could be serious.

The reluctant Duke of Coburg had little to look forward to. In his German duchy he found life increasingly dull, as he missed the responsibilities of service life and the camaraderie of his naval colleagues and London society friends, whom he came to England to visit whenever he could. His marriage had never been happy. His wife, Marie, who never ceased to remind her in-laws that she was a Russian Grand Duchess and considered herself superior to them, revelled in her position as 'No. 1, and reigning Duchess', as her sister-in-law, Vicky, the Dowager German Empress, had predicted. Husband and wife had long since drifted apart, though they never officially separated and for the sake of form presented the picture of a united couple to the outside world.

The Queen was saddened that this gifted son had become almost a stranger to her, and that as a person this withdrawn, surly, over-bibulous man (or 'imprudent', as she discreetly put it) was clearly less liked than his brothers. Yet she was glad to welcome him home at the time of the diamond jubilee, and again in May 1899 when he joined the rest of the family at Windsor for celebrations in the town and at the Castle to mark her eightieth birthday.

By this time, however, he was a broken man. The Duke and Duchess's silver wedding celebrations in January, at which they put on their usual display of family unity, were marred by the plight of their only son, Alfred. He had shot himself after an unhappy love affair with a commoner, Mabel Fitzgerald, whom some sources say he had married in defiance of the Royal Marriages Act; sent to convalesce at Meran in the Tyrol, he died of his injuries a week later. For years, the official cause of his death was said to be consumption or, as an official correspondent told *The Times*, 'chronic cerebral affection'.[13] The next heir to the duchy of Coburg was Charles, the fifteen-year-old son of the Duke and Duchess of Albany who had been born three months after his father's death.

Alfred took to drinking even more heavily after his son's tragic death but managed to distance himself so much from his family that none of them had any idea how ill he was. In June 1900 a group of specialists at Vienna held a consultation and discovered a carcinomatous growth at the root of his tongue, in such an advanced stage that any operation would have been useless. He had six months to live at the most, but in his case there was nothing much left to live for. On 25 July the Queen received a telegram from the physicians, telling her that the Duke of Edinburgh's condition was hopeless. Initially it was withheld from her on the instructions of Beatrice, who wished to spare her any more upsetting news. Britain was at war with the Boers in South Africa, and the Queen was already thoroughly depressed at the news of military reverses suffered by her Army.

That weekend Alfred's surgeons at Gotha made preparations to give him a tracheotomy to assist his breathing, but it was too late. On the evening of 30 July he died in his sleep.

'Oh, God! My poor darling Affie gone too!' the Queen wrote in her journal. 'One sorrow, one trial, one anxiety, following another!

It is a horrible year, nothing but sadness and horrors of one kind and another.'[14] The news came exactly a day after the assassination of King Humbert of Italy; he was not related to the family, but any news of royal assassinations at such a time was bound to depress her further. She had seen Alfred very little during the last few years, and of all her sons he had been the one least close to her in adult life. Yet she was deeply upset by his passing, and felt her family and doctors 'should never have withheld the truth' from her as long as they did.[15] She tried to console herself with recollections of his childhood, when he had seemed to hold such great promise, with his love of building mechanical toys and learning geography. To Marie Mallet she talked sadly one evening about his happy days at Osborne, his childish likes and dislikes, and the lady-in-waiting could see that to the elderly woman 'he was once more the happy boy'.[16]

Although the Duke had never been the most popular member of the family with the British public, the Lord Mayor of London paid tribute to him in a speech opening the proceedings of a conference on the War Funds Organisation at Mansion House, the day after his death, recognising 'his devotion to his profession as a sailor, his passionate love for music, and his intense affection for his native land'.[17] In Devonport, with which he had been closely identified in the years immediately preceding his succession to the German dukedom, his identification with philanthropic institutions in the district was fondly remembered.

The Prince of Wales represented the family at his brother's funeral at Coburg. On his way back from the ceremony, he visited the widowed Empress Frederick in her home at Friedrichshof, near Kronberg. For over a year, the family had been alarmed at rumours about her state of health, and he learnt that she too was mortally stricken with cancer of the spine. She was in agony much of the time, almost bedridden, and sometimes her attacks of pain were so severe that it seemed as if she, like Affie, might predecease their mother. Bertie returned home in a mood of black depression.

At Osborne, Christmas 1900 was the saddest the family had known since the Prince Consort's death. Since the autumn, Queen Victoria's normally healthy appetite had become poor, and she was now almost blind. She knew that soon it would be time for her eldest son to come into the inheritance for which he had been destined since birth. While they had been at Balmoral in the first week of November, Marie Mallet thought it curious that the Queen remarked to her how she wished to die after the Prince Consort's death, but now she wanted to live and do what she could for her country and those whom she loved. Mrs Mallet thought it 'a very remarkable utterance' for a woman of her age, and as it was not the first time she had spoken along such lines, she wondered whether the Queen 'dreads the influence of the Prince of Wales?'[18] Even if she had forgiven and forgotten his involvement with the Tranby Croft affair and other indiscretions, she suspected that others had not.

'Another year begun and I am feeling so weak and unwell that I enter upon it sadly,'[19] she wrote in her journal on 1 January 1901, or rather dictated, as she could no longer see to write herself. On 17 January she had a mild stroke, and the family were warned to prepare for the worst. The Prince of Wales arrived at Osborne from Sandringham, and the Duke of Connaught was summoned from Berlin, where he had been attending celebrations for the bicentenary of the Hohenzollern dynasty. With them came their eldest nephew, Emperor William, who, for all the disrespectful utterances behind his grandmother's back, had always revered and respected her deeply.

They joined the hushed vigil around the bed at Osborne where the Queen lay dying, slipping away like 'a great three-decker ship sinking', in the words of her son-in-law Lord Lorne. On 22 January, shortly before she became unconscious for the last time, with a supreme effort of strength which was almost beyond her, she held out her arms to the Prince of Wales, as she softly mouthed the word 'Bertie'. At about 6.30 that evening, the Dean of Windsor was reading the prayers for the dying and noticed that she was staring at the Prince of Wales and at Dr Reid, who was sitting in front of the heir. Then her eyes flickered, and seemed to be gazing at the figure of the dead Christ in a painting over the fireplace. Then, the Bishop noticed, there was a change of look and complete calm. She opened her eyes wide, 'and knew she saw beyond the Border land and had seen and met all her loved ones'. As he finished reading the prayer, she quietly drew her last breath.

Prompted by Reid, her eldest son – who in that instant had become king – leaned forward, closed her eyes, and then broke down.[20]

* * *

When Queen Victoria died, she left a strong and prosperous country behind her. Her reign had seen enormous changes, and the next few decades would usher in many more. She bequeathed her eldest son a strong, well-respected throne which had weathered the scandals of only a few years earlier, and during his nine-year reign he would inaugurate a very different, more affable, yet equally popular style of monarchy. The political landscape of Britain was changing, with the issue of Home Rule for Ireland – as tackled with scant success by Gladstone – gaining momentum, and with Labour members of parliament on the way to supplanting the Liberals as the alternative party to the Conservatives in opposition and then in government. Britain's relations with her European neighbours would also undergo radical change, with the Queen's eldest grandson in Berlin, Emperor William, proclaiming his adoration for England, only to find himself a powerless exile in Holland less than twenty years later.

Edwardian Britain was a swan-song for, or in some respects an orderly closing chapter of, the Victorian age, before the outbreak of the First World War brought the curtain down on the old order. That the country made a relatively orderly transition to the new world beyond and came to terms with its status as a reduced world power can be attributed in part to the legacy and influence of the Queen, and the men who ruled the country, represented her and worked with her during the nineteenth century.

The Houses of Hanover and Saxe-Coburg Gotha

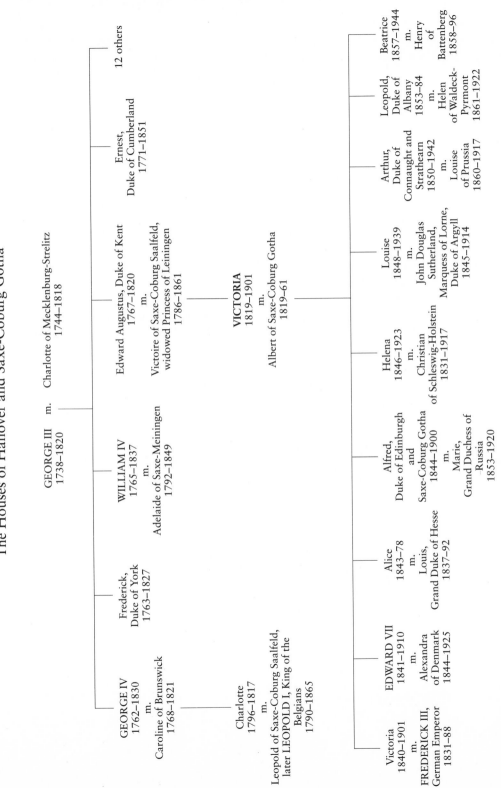

Notes

Abbreviations: QVJ: Queen Victoria's Journal (Royal Archives); NA: National Archives, London; A: Albert, Prince Consort; KL: King Leopold of the Belgians; QV: Queen Victoria (including references to her before accession); V: Princess Victoria, later German Crown Princess and Empress; RA: Royal Archives

Chapter One (pp. 3–19)

1 Crewe, *Lord Rosebery*, vol. II, p. 437
2 Fulford, *Royal Dukes*, p. 162
3 Duff, *Hessian Tapestry*, p. 127
4 Stanhope, *Notes of Conversations*, p. 128
5 Fulford, *Royal Dukes*, p. 202
6 Kuhn, *Henry and Mary Ponsonby*, p. 204
7 St Aubyn, *Queen Victoria*, p. 12
8 Duff, *Edward of Kent*, p. 294
9 Longford, *Victoria RI*, p. 24 (all subsequent Longford references are to this title unless stated otherwise)
10 *Ibid.*, p. 26; Aronson, *Victoria & Disraeli*, p. 7
11 Victoria, *Girlhood*, vol. I, p. 166, QVJ 16.9.1835
12 Woodham-Smith, *Queen Victoria*, p. 104, QVJ 6.10.1835
13 Thompson, *Queen Victoria*, p. 3
14 Victoria, *Letters 1837–1861*, vol. I, p. 72, KL to QV, 17.6.1837
15 Wilson, *The Victorians*, p. 25
16 Woodham-Smith, *Queen Victoria*, p. 128, KL to QV, 12.3.1839
17 RA Y 82/113, KL to QV, 12.4.1861
18 Woodham-Smith, *Queen Victoria*, p. 119, QV to KL, 17.5.1836

19 Victoria, *Letters 1837–1861*, vol. I, pp. 48–9, QV to KL, 23.5.1836
20 Victoria, *Letters 1837–1861*, vol. I, p. 49, QV to KL, 7.6.1836
21 Weintraub, *Victoria*, p. 100
22 Victoria, *Letters 1837–1861*, vol. I, pp. 177–8, QV to KL, 15.7.1839
23 Longford, p. 127
24 Victoria, *Girlhood*, vol. II, p. 262, 10.10.1839
25 Victoria, *Letters 1837–1861*, vol. I, p. 201, QV to A, 8.12.1839
26 Victoria, *Letters 1837–1861*, vol. I, p. 269, QV to A, 31.1.1840
27 *Ibid.*, vol. I, p. 217, QV to KL, 11.2.1840
28 Albert, *Letters 1831–1861*, p. 69, A to William zu Löwenstein, May 1840
29 RA Y54/4, Melbourne to Anson, 28.5.1840; Hibbert, *Queen Victoria*, pp. 126–7
30 RA Y/54.8, memo by Anson, 15.8.1840; Eyck, *Prince Consort*, p. 22
31 RA Y/54.3, memo by A, 15.4.1840; Eyck, *Prince Consort*, p. 24
32 Hibbert, *Queen Victoria*, p. 367
33 Fulford, *Prince Consort*, p. 276
34 Tingsten, *Victoria*, p. 81
35 Victoria, *Letters 1837–1861*, vol. III, p. 362, QV to KL, 3.2.1852

Chapter Two (pp. 20–34)

1 St Aubyn, *Queen Victoria*, p. 142
2 Victoria, *Letters 1837–1861*, vol. II, p. 7, QV to KL, 6.2.1844
3 Longford, p. 160, A to Stockmar, 16.1.1842
4 *Ibid.*
5 Eyck, *Prince Consort*, p. 30
6 Albert, *Letters 1831–1861*, p. 96, A to Stockmar, 10.5.1845
7 QVJ 12.5.1845
8 Victoria, *Letters 1837–1861*, vol. II, pp. 317–18, QV to KL, 3.5.1851
9 Eyck, *Prince Consort*, p. 164, Grey to A, 12.5.1851
10 Fulford, *Prince Consort*, p. 159
11 Victoria, *Dearest Child*, pp. 111–12, QV to V, 9.6.1858
12 *Ibid.*, p. 205, QV to V, 10.8.1859
13 *Ibid.*, p. 265, QV to V, 11.7.1860
14 Duff, *Albert and Victoria*, p. 229
15 Victoria, *Leaves 1848–1861*, p. 226, 8.10.1861
16 Longford, pp. 265–6, James Clark diary 5.2.1856
17 *Ibid.*, p. 264, A to QV, 5.11.1856
18 Tingsten, *Victoria*, pp. 89–90
19 Friedman, *Inheritance*, p. 19
20 *Ibid.*
21 Callan, 'Victoria fancied Albert'
22 Martin, *Life*, vol. V, p. 415
23 Friedman, *Inheritance*, p. 24
24 Victoria, *Dearest Mama*, p. 23, QV to V, 18.12.1861
25 Victoria, *Further Letters*, pp. 154–5, QV to Queen Augusta, 31.5.1865
26 St Aubyn, *Queen Victoria*, p. 333
27 Vitzthum, *St Petersburg*, vol. II, p. 176
28 Kuhn, *Henry and Mary Ponsonby*, p. 147
29 Duff, *Albert and Victoria*, p. 17
30 Longford, p. 305
31 Fulford, *Prince Consort*, p. 276
32 Guedalla, *Palmerston*, p. 382
33 Victoria, *Letters 1862–1885*, vol. I, pp. 218–19, KL to QV, 15.6.1864
34 *Ibid.*, vol. I, p. 287, QVJ 10.12.1865
35 Richardson, *My Dearest Uncle*, p. 217
36 Longford, p. 323

Chapter Three (pp. 37–54)

1 James, *Rosebery*, pp. 29–30
2 Longford, p. 66
3 Victoria, *Letters 1837–1861*, vol. I, p. 82, QV to KL, 3.7.1837
4 Victoria, *Girlhood*, vol. II, p. 135, 22.3.1839
5 Longford, p. 69
6 Greville, *Memoirs*, vol. IV, p. 135, 12.9.1838
7 Victoria, *Girlhood*, vol. II, p. 144, QVJ 7.4.1839
8 Woodham-Smith, *Queen Victoria*, p. 144
9 RA M7/68, Duchess of Kent to QV, 20.6.1837; Longford, p. 66
10 Greville, *Diary*, vol. II, p. 14, 21.6.1837
11 Maxwell, *Wellington*, vol. II, p. 312
12 *Ibid.*, vol. II, p. 316, Wellington to Mr Arbuthnot, 15.2.1838
13 Longford, *Wellington*, p. 347
14 Victoria, *Letters 1837–1861*, vol. I, p. 62, QV to KL, 14.3.1837
15 Greville, *Diary*, vol. II, p. 88
16 *The Times*, 13.5.1839
17 *Ibid.*, 15.5.1839
18 Thursfield, *Peel*, p. 171
19 Duff, *Albert and Victoria*, p. 99
20 Victoria, *Girlhood*, vol. II, pp. 285–6, 25.12.1839
21 RAY 54/51, memo by Anson, 12.6.1841; Rhodes James, *Albert*, p. 124
22 Victoria, *Letters 1837–1861*, vol. I, p. 305, memo by Anson, 30.8.1841
23 Cecil D., *Lord M*, p. 310
24 Victoria, *Letters 1837–1861*, vol. I, pp. 340–1, memo by Stockmar, 6.10.1841

25 Greville, *Diary*, vol. II, p. 140, 4.8.1841
26 Victoria, *Letters 1837–1861*, vol. II, p. 16, V to KL, 18.6.1844
27 Mullen and Munson, *Victoria*, p. 49
28 QVJ 9.6.1842
29 QVJ 18.2.1845
30 Mitchell, *Melbourne*, p. 249
31 *Ibid.*, p. 276
32 Victoria, *Letters 1837–1861*, vol. II, p. 203, V to KL, 21.11.1848
33 RA L16/32, V to Henry Ponsonby, 9.1.1890
34 Victoria, *Letters 1837–1861*, vol. II, p. 87, V to KL, 7.7.1846
35 Jenkins, *Gladstone*, p. 338
36 St Aubyn, *Queen Victoria*, p. 217
37 QVJ 2.7.1850
38 QVJ 12.11.1851
39 Maxwell, *Wellington*, vol. II, pp. 370–1
40 QVJ 22.4.1852
41 Victoria, *Leaves 1848–1861*, p. 137, 16.9.1852
42 Victoria, *Letters 1837–1861*, vol. II, p. 394, QV to KL, 17.9.1852

Chapter Four (pp. 55–72)

1 Airlie, *Lady Palmerston*, vol. II, p. 122
2 Victoria, *Letters 1837–1861*, vol. II, p. 264, QV to Russell, 12.8.1850
3 Connell, *Regina v. Palmerston*, p. 127, QV to Palmerston, 10.9.1850
4 Cecil A., *Queen Victoria*, p. 152, QV to KL, 22.2.1851
5 Chambers, *Palmerston*, p. 352, Lady Palmerston to Lord Palmerston, 17.9.1853
6 Ridley, *Palmerston*, p. 406
7 Longford, p. 241
8 Connell, *Regina v. Palmerston*, pp. 163–4, QVJ 5.2.1855
9 QVJ 21.8.1856
10 QVJ 20.2.1858
11 Victoria, *Dearest Child*, p. 194, QV to V, 14.6.1859
12 NA Russell MSS, Palmerston to Russell 28.12.1861
13 Victoria, *Letters 1862–1885*, vol. I, pp. 14–15, QVJ 29.1.1862
14 Ridley, *Palmerston*, p. 570, Palmerston to QV, 4.1.1864
15 Connell, *Regina v. Palmerston*, p. 360, QVJ 18.10.1865
16 QVJ 16.3.1852
17 QVJ 1.4.1852
18 Monypenny and Buckle, *Life*, vol. I, p. 1266
19 Greville, *Memoirs*, vol. VII, p. 195
20 Bradford, *Disraeli*, p. 251
21 Monypenny and Buckle, *Disraeli*, vol. II, p. 126
22 *Ibid.*, vol. II, pp. 127–8, QV to Disraeli, 24.4.1863
23 *Ibid.*, vol. II, p. 121
24 Victoria, *Letters 1862–1885*, vol. I, p. 505, Disraeli to QV, 26.2.1868
25 Magnus, *Gladstone*, p. 158
26 *Ibid.*, p. 160
27 QVJ 27.9.1868
28 Magnus, *Gladstone*, p. 194, Dean of Windsor to Gladstone, 27.11.1868
29 Morley, *Life*, p. 425
30 Guedalla, *The Queen and Mr Gladstone*, p. 8
31 Jenkins, *Gladstone*, p. 335
32 Magnus, *Gladstone*, p. 199
33 *Ibid.*, p. 200, Grey to Gladstone, 9.6.1869
34 *Ibid.*, p. 207, Gladstone to Granville, 3.12.1870
35 *Ibid.*, p. 209, QV to Hatherley, 10.8.1871
36 *Ibid.*, p. 210, Gladstone to Henry Ponsonby, 16.8.1873
37 *Ibid.*, Gladstone to Granville, 1.10.1871
38 Weintraub, *Disraeli*, p. 498
39 Magnus, *Gladstone*, p. 199, QV to Gladstone, 8.1.1869
40 *Ibid.*, p. 214, Gladstone to QV, 17.7.1872

41 *Ibid.*, pp. 214–15, QV to Gladstone, 5.8.1872

42 *Ibid.*, p. 218, QV to Henry Ponsonby, 18.11.1874

Chapter Five (pp. 73–94)

1 Monypenny and Buckle, *Life*, vol. II, p. 626

2 Aronson, *Victoria and Disraeli*, p. 126

3 Victoria, *Darling Child*, p. 130, QV to V, 24.2.1874

4 Monypenny and Buckle, *Life*, vol. II, p. 453

5 James, *Rosebery*, p. 64

6 Ponsonby A., *Henry Ponsonby*, p. 245, Henry Ponsonby to Mary Ponsonby, April 1875

7 Maxwell, *Wellington*, vol. II, p. 346

8 Cecil A. *Queen Victoria*, p. 208

9 Aronson, *Heart of a Queen*, p. 193

10 *Ibid.*, p. 197

11 Monypenny and Buckle, *Life*, vol. II, p. 788, Disraeli to QV, 24.11.1875

12 *Ibid.*, vol. II, p. 378, Princess Christian to Mrs Disraeli, 12.5.1868

13 Aronson, *Heart of a Queen*, p. 194

14 Mullen and Munson, *Victoria*, p. 102

15 Blake, *Disraeli*, p. 637

16 Marie Louise, *Six Reigns*, p. 24

17 Bradford, *Disraeli*, p. 340

18 Aronson, *Heart of a Queen*, p. 189

19 *The Times*, 8.8.1878

20 Ponsonby, M., *Mary Ponsonby*, p. 144, Mary Ponsonby to Henry Ponsonby, 5.12.1878

21 Monypenny and Buckle, *Life*, vol. II, p. 1308

22 *Ibid.*, vol. II, p. 1309

23 Aronson, *Heart of a Queen*, p. 207

24 Monypenny and Buckle, *Life*, vol. II, p. 1331, Disraeli to QV, 30.8.1879

25 *Ibid.*, vol. II, p. 1332, QV to Disraeli, 1.9.1879

26 *Ibid.*, vol. II, p. 1334, Disraeli to Lady Ely, 4.9.1879

27 *Ibid.*, vol. II, p. 1333, Disraeli to QV, 4.9.1879

28 Magnus, *Gladstone*, p. 270

29 Monypenny and Buckle, *Life*, vol. II, p. 1479, Disraeli to QV, 12.3.1881

30 *Ibid.*, vol. II, p. 1482, Disraeli to QV, 28.3.1881

31 Argyll Etkin, QV to Princess of Wales, 11.4.1881

32 Blake, *Disraeli*, p. 747

Chapter Six (pp. 95–112)

1 Crewe, *Lord Rosebery*, p. 165, Gladstone to Rosebery, 5.1.1883

2 Magnus, *Gladstone*, p. 280

3 Victoria, *Letters 1862–1885*, vol. III, p. 395, QV to Gladstone, 5.1.1883

4 *Ibid.*, vol. III, pp. 439–40, QV to Granville, 18.9.1883

5 *Ibid.*, vol. III, pp. 441–2, QV to Gladstone, 20.9.1883

6 Magnus, *Gladstone*, p. 307, Gladstone to QV, 22.9.83

7 Jenkins, *Gladstone*, p. 494

8 Guedalla, *The Queen and Mr Gladstone*, p. 617

9 Victoria, *Letters 1862–1885*, vol. III, p. 597, QV to Gladstone, Hartington and Granville, 5.2.1885

10 Longford, p. 465

11 Roberts, *Salisbury*, p. 190

12 Victoria, *Letters 1862–1885*, vol. II, p. 369, QVJ 14.1.1875

13 Roberts, *Salisbury*, p. 376

14 Tingsten, *Victoria*, p. 146

15 Roberts, *Salisbury*, p. 377

16 NA, Granville Papers, Sir Henry Ponsonby to Granville, 16.2.1886

17 Victoria, *Letters 1886–1901*, vol. II, p. 143, QVJ 8.6.1886

18 Longford, p. 491

19 Morley, *Life*, vol. II, pp. 347–8

20 Victoria, *Letters 1886–1901*, vol. I, p. 169, QV to Gladstone, 31.7.1886

21 Kennedy, *Salisbury*, p. 181

22 Tingsten, *Victoria*, p. 131

23 Roberts, *Salisbury*, p. 539
24 Victoria, *Letters 1886–1901*, vol. I, p. 617, QV to Salisbury, 27.6.1890
25 *The Times*, 31.8.1887
26 Magnus, *Gladstone*, p. 397, QV to Henry Ponsonby, 4.6.1892
27 Victoria, *Letters 1886–1901*, vol. II, p. 132, QV to Henry Ponsonby, 23.7.1892
28 James, *Rosebery*, p. 192
29 Magnus, *Gladstone*, p. 398
30 Gladstone, *Diaries*, vol. XIII, p. 390, 28.2.1890
31 Victoria, *Letters 1886–1901*, vol. II, pp. 372–3, QV to Gladstone, 3.3.1894
32 Magnus, *Gladstone*, p. 427
33 Crewe, *Lord Rosebery*, vol. I, p. 240
34 James, *Rosebery*, p. 254
35 *Ibid.*, p. 234
36 Victoria, *Letters 1886–1901*, vol. II, p. 369, QV to Rosebery, 2.3.1894
37 *Ibid.*, vol. II, p. 376, QVJ 5.3.1894
38 Crewe, *Lord Rosebery*, p. 443, QV to Rosebery, 4.3.1894
39 *Ibid.*, p. 445
40 *The Times*, 19.3.1894
41 James, *Rosebery*, p. 339
42 Victoria, *Letters 1886–1901*, vol. II, p. 399, Rosebery to QV, 14.5.1894
43 *Ibid.*, vol. II, pp. 403–4, 8.6.1894; Crewe, 457, QV to Rosebery
44 *The Times*, 28.10.1894
45 James, *Rosebery*, p. 361
46 Crewe, *Lord Rosebery*, vol. II, p. 451, QV to Rosebery, March 1894
47 Askwith, *Lord James*, p. 250
48 Crewe, *Lord Rosebery*, p. 464
49 Victoria, *Beloved and Darling Child*, p. 180, QV to V, 1.7.1895
50 James, *Rosebery*, p. 384
51 Roberts, *Salisbury*, p. 793
52 Boyd Carpenter, *Some Pages*, p. 236
53 *Ibid.*, p. 235
54 Magnus, *Gladstone*, p. 432
55 Victoria, *Letters 1886–1901*, vol. III, p. 246, QVJ 19.5.1898

56 Magnus, *Gladstone*, p. 438, QV to Mrs Gladstone, 28.5.1898
57 Victoria, *Beloved and Darling Child*, p. 215, QV to V, 31.5.1898
58 Steele, *Lord Salisbury*, pp. 354–5, Akers-Douglas to Balfour, 19.10.1900
59 Mullen and Munson, *Victoria*, p. 144
60 *The Times*, 26.1.01
61 *Ibid.*, 31.1.01

Chapter Seven (pp. 115–26)

1 Lamont-Brown, *John Brown*, p. 37
2 *Aberdeen Herald & Weekly Free Press*, 31.3.1883; Cullen, p. 43
3 Cullen, *Empress Brown*, p. 50
4 QVJ 3.2.1865
5 Longford, p. 325
6 *Ibid.*, p. 326, QV to V, 5.4.1865
7 Victoria, *Letters 1862–1885*, vol. I, p. 255, QV to KL, 24.11.1865
8 Lamont-Brown, *Royal Poxes*, p. 176
9 A morganatic marriage is one between two persons of unequal rank, generally a sovereign or senior member of a royal or imperial house and a commoner, in which any children born would have no claim on the higher-ranking parent's titles, rights or property.
10 Cullen, *Empress Brown*, p. 95
11 *Punch*, 7.7.1866
12 Thompson, *Queen Victoria*, p. 62
13 QVJ 24.5.1870
14 Tingsten, *Victoria*, p. 112
15 Gibb, 'Victoria and John Brown'
16 *Royalty Digest*, January 2005
17 Lamont-Brown, 'Queen Victoria's "secret marriage"'
18 Ponsonby F., *Recollections*, p. 95
19 Cullen, *Empress Brown*, pp. 102–3
20 *Saturday Review*, April 1867
21 Longford, p. 329
22 *Ibid.*, p. 331
23 Ponsonby A., *Henry Ponsonby*, p. 128
24 Wilson, *Victorians*, p. 504
25 Victoria, *Leaves 1848–1861*, p. 128, footnote to entry of 16.9.1850

26 *Ibid.*, pp. viii–ix
27 Stanley, *Later Letters*, p. 73, 26.1.1868
28 Tisdall, *John Brown*, pp. 141–2

Chapter Eight (pp. 127–47)

1 Victoria, *Letters 1837–1861*, vol. III, p. 476, QV to KL, 24.12.1861
2 Hibbert, *Queen Victoria*, p. 307, QV to Grey, 25.1.1863
3 Ponsonby A., *Henry Ponsonby*, p. 36
4 Jenkins, *Gladstone*, p. 344
5 Longford, pp. 379–80
6 Ponsonby A., *Henry Ponsonby*, p. 35
7 Victoria, *Your Dear Letter*, p. 273, QV to V, 2.4.1870
8 Cullen, *Empress Brown*, p. 131
9 Kuhn, *Henry and Mary Ponsonby*, p. 92
10 Lamont-Brown, 'Queen Victoria's "secret marriage"'
11 Magnus, *Gladstone*, p. 217
12 Ponsonby A., *Henry Ponsonby*, pp. 253–4, Henry Ponsonby to Gladstone, 13.7.1875
13 *Ibid.*, p. 244, Henry Ponsonby to Mary Ponsonby, October 1873
14 RA Add. A/36, Henry Ponsonby to Mary Ponsonby, 26.4.1884
15 Ponsonby A., *Henry Ponsonby*, p. 134
16 *Ibid.*, pp. 134–5
17 Mullen and Munson, *Victoria*, p. 110
18 Aronson, *Heart of a Queen*, p. 162
19 Longford, p. 386, Ponsonby Letters, 13.9.1871
20 Cullen, *Empress Brown*, pp. 170–1
21 *Ibid.*, p. 179
22 Lamont-Brown, *John Brown*, p. 62
23 Burrell, *A Royal Duty*, p. 43
24 Kuhn, *Henry and Mary Ponsonby*, p. 167
25 *Ibid.*, p. 171
26 Reid, *Ask Sir James*, p. 41
27 Cullen, *Empress Brown*, p. 192
28 Reid, *Ask Sir James*, p. 46, QV to Reid, probably August 1881
29 *Ibid.*, p. 33
30 Cullen, *Empress Brown*, p. 199

31 Lamont-Brown, *John Brown*, p. 139, Leopold to Louis, Grand Duke of Hesse, 28.3.1883
32 Reid, *Ask Sir James*, p. 53, QV to Reid, probably 28.3.1883
33 Ponsonby A., *Henry Ponsonby*, p. 129
34 QVJ 28.3.1883, Cullen, *Empress Brown*, p. 211, Lamont-Brown, *John Brown*, p. 139
35 Court Circular, 28.3.1884
36 Tisdall, *John Brown*, pp. 223–4, Gladstone to QV, 28.3.1884
37 Cullen, *Empress Brown*, p. 225
38 Fenton, 'Twice bereaved'
39 *The Times*, 29.3.1883
40 Victoria, *More Leaves 1862–1882*, pp. v–vi
41 *Ibid.*, p. 406
42 RA Add A/36, Henry Ponsonby to Mary Ponsonby, 22.7.1884

Chapter Nine (pp. 148–68)

1 Mallet, *Life with Queen Victoria*, pp. 95–6, 5.11.1896
2 Ponsonby A., *Henry Ponsonby*, p. 131, Henry Ponsonby to Mary Ponsonby, nd
3 Anand, *Indian Sahib*, p. 54, Frederick Ponsonby to Lord Elgin, 16.1.1895
4 Reid, *Ask Sir James*, p. 132
5 Aronson, *Heart of a Queen*, p. 237
6 *Ibid.*
7 Reid, *Ask Sir James*, p. 162
8 Ponsonby A., *Henry Ponsonby*, p. 135, Henry Ponsonby to Mary Ponsonby (?), *c.* 1893
9 Kuhn, *Henry and Mary Ponsonby*, p. 237
10 Reid, *Ask Sir James*, p. 164
11 *Ibid.*, p. 142
12 *Ibid.*, p. 163
13 *Ibid.*, p. 114
14 *Ibid.*, p. 142
15 Wilson, *Victorians*, p. 507
16 Reid, *Ask Sir James*, p. 144
17 *Ibid.*

18 Reid, *Ask Sir James*, p. 151
19 *Ibid.*, p. 154
20 *Ibid.*, p. 181
21 *Ibid.*, p. 184
22 *Ibid.*, p. 190
23 Boyd Carpenter, *Some Pages*, p. 295
24 Reid, *Ask Sir James*, p. 200
25 Packard, *Farewell in Splendour*, p. 30
26 Reid, *Ask Sir James*, p. 205
27 Lamont-Brown, *John Brown*, p. 162
28 Anand, *Indian Sahib*, p. 102, Lady
    Curzon to Lord Curzon, 9.8.1901
29 *The Times*, 24.4.1909
30 Reid, *Ask Sir James*, p. 255

Chapter Ten (pp. 171–87)

1 Victoria, *Dearest Child*, p. 167, QV to
   V, 16.3.1859
2 *Ibid.*, pp. 77–8, QV to V, 24.3.1858
3 James, *Albert*, p. 244, A to QV,
   1.10.1856
4 Magnus, *King Edward*, p. 5
5 Victoria, *Letters 1837–1861*, vol. I,
   p. 458, Melbourne to QV, 13.2.1843
6 Lyttelton, *Correspondence*, p. 340
7 QVJ 9.11.1850
8 Victoria, *Dearest Child*, pp. 173–4,
   QV to V, 9.4.1859
9 McClintock, *The Queen*, pp. 25–6,
   QV to A, 7.10.1858
10 *Ibid.*, p. 43, Elphinstone diary
    19.1.1860
11 Victoria, *Dearest Child*, p. 164, QV to
    V, 2.3.1859
12 RA Y104/26; QV to KL, 26.8.1859
13 Victoria, *Dearest Child*, p. 208, QV to
    V, 2.9.1859
14 Corti, *The English Empress*, p. 63, QV
    to V, 31.10.1860
15 Victoria, *Letters 1837–1861*, vol. III,
    p. 413, QV to KL, 13.11.1860
16 Victoria, *Your Dear Letter*, p. 200, QV
    to V, 8.7.1868
17 *Ibid.*, p. 158, QV to V, 9.11.1867
18 Magnus, *King Edward*, p. 88, QV to
    V, 3.7.1869
19 RA Add. MSS A.3/121, QV to Prince
    of Wales, 18.1.1869
20 RA Add. MSS A.3/1108, Prince of
    Wales to QV 1.3.1868
21 RA Add. MSS A.3/128, Prince of
    Wales to QV, 26.2.1869
22 RA Add. MSS A.3/131, Prince of
    Wales to QV, 28.2.1869
23 Victoria, *Your Dear Letter*, pp. 200–1,
    QV to V, 10.7.1868
24 McClintock, *The Queen*, p. 143, QV
    to Howard Elphinstone, *c.* 1872
25 Aston, *Duke of Connaught*, p. 115
26 McClintock, *The Queen*, p. 142, QV
    to Howard Elphinstone, 4.1.1872
27 *Ibid.*, p. 144, QV to Howard
    Elphinstone, nd
28 Victoria, *Dearest Mama*, pp. 234–5,
    QV to V, 24.6.1863
29 Diamond, *Victorian Sensation*,
    p. 23
30 Duff, *Hessian Tapestry*, p. 117
31 Epton, *Victoria and Her Daughters*,
    p. 151
32 Marie Louise, *Six Reigns*, p. 19

Chapter Eleven (pp. 188–205)

1 Ponsonby A., *Henry Ponsonby*, p. 98,
   Henry Ponsonby to Mary Ponsonby,
   nd
2 *Manchester Guardian*, 28.2.1872
3 RA Add. MSS U/32, QV to V,
   14.2.1872
4 Ponsonby A., *Henry Ponsonby*,
   pp. 100–1, Henry Ponsonby to Mary
   Ponsonby, nd
5 Victoria, *Darling Child*, p. 105, QV to
   V, 2.8.1873
6 Longford, *Darling Loosy*, p. 194, QV
   to Louise, 11.6.1875
7 Zeepvat, *Prince Leopold*, p. 129, QV
   to Leopold, nd, *c.* May 1877
8 Aston, *Duke of Connaught*, p. 98
9 Alice, *For My Grandchildren*, p. 21
10 Victoria, *Beloved Mama*, p. 117, QV
    to V, 11.4.1882

11 Zeepvat, *Prince Leopold*, p. 186, Leopold to Louis, Grand Duke of Hesse, 15.3.1884

12 Victoria, *Beloved Mama*, p. 162, QV to V, 29.3.1884

13 Boyd Carpenter, *Some Pages*, p. 281

14 Ponsonby A., *Henry Ponsonby*, p. 301, Henry Ponsonby to Gladstone, nd

15 Epton, *Victoria and Her Daughters*, p. 170

16 Hough, *Louis and Victoria*, p. 121

17 Longford, *Victoria RI*, p. 477

18 *Ibid.*

19 Victoria, *Advice to a Grand-daughter*, p. 66, QV to Victoria of Hesse, 20.5.1884

Chapter Twelve (pp. 206–24)

1 Corti, *The English Empress*, p. 225, QV to V, 7.1.1885

2 Victoria, *Letters 1886–1901*, vol. I, p. 320, QVJ 20.6.1887

3 Victoria, *Beloved and Darling Child*, p. 64, QV to V, 10.3.1888

4 Victoria, *Letters 1886–1901*, vol. I, p. 417, QVJ 15.6.1888

5 Victoria, *Advice to a Grand-daughter*, p. 56, QV to Victoria of Hesse, 21.9.83

6 Victoria, *Letters 1886–1901*, vol. I, p. 417, QV to William II, 15.6.1888

7 Magnus, *King Edward*, p. 228, QV to V, 12.6.1891

8 *Ibid.*, p. 228

9 *Ibid.*, p. 236, Knollys to Henry Ponsonby, 15.8.1892

10 Victoria, *Advice to a Grand-daughter*, p. 56, QV to Victoria of Hesse, 21.9.1883

11 Weintraub, *Importance of Being Edward*, p. 348

12 Victoria, *Letters, 1886–1901*, vol. III, p. 174, QVJ 22.6.1897

13 *The Times*, 7.2.1899

14 Victoria, *Letters 1886–1901*, vol. III, pp. 579–80, QVJ 31.7.1900

15 *Ibid.*, vol. III, p. 580, QVJ 31.7.1900

16 Mallet, *Life with Queen Victoria*, p. 201, 31.7.1900

17 *The Times*, 1.8.1900

18 Mallet, *Life with Queen Victoria*, p. 213, 2.11.1900

19 Victoria, *Letters 1886–1901*, vol. III, p. 637, QVJ 1.1.1901

20 Rennell, *Last Days of Glory*, pp. 137–8

Bibliography

Letters

Royal Archives, Windsor
The National Archives, London
Argyll Etkin, London

Books
The place of publication is London unless otherwise stated.

Airlie, Mabel, Countess of, *Lady Palmerston and her Times*, 2 vols, Hodder & Stoughton, 1922

Albert, Prince, *Letters of the Prince Consort, 1831–1861*, ed. Kurt Jagow, John Murray, 1938

Alice, Princess, Countess of Athlone, *For My Grandchildren: Some Reminiscences of HRH Princess Alice, Countess of Athlone*, Evans Bros, 1966

Anand, Sushila, *Indian Sahib: Queen Victoria's Dear Abdul*, Duckworth, 1996

Aronson, Theo, *The Heart of a Queen: Queen Victoria's Romantic Attachments*, John Murray, 1991

—— *Victoria & Disraeli: The Making of a Romantic Partnership*, Cassell, 1977

Askwith, George Ranken, *Lord James of Hereford*, Benn, 1930

Aston, Sir George, *H.R.H. The Duke of Connaught and Strathearn: A Life and Intimate Study*, Harrap, 1929

Bennett, Daphne, *King without a Crown: Albert, Prince Consort of England 1819–1861*, Heinemann, 1977

—— *Queen Victoria's Children*, Victor Gollancz, 1980

Blake, Robert, *Disraeli*, Eyre & Spottiswoode, 1966

Boyd Carpenter, W., *Some Pages of My Life*, Williams & Norgate, 1911

Bradford, Sarah, *Disraeli*, Weidenfeld & Nicolson, 1982

Brown, Ivor, *Balmoral: The History of a Home*, Collins, 1955

Burrell, Paul, *A Royal Duty*, Michael Joseph, 2003

Cecil, Algernon, *Queen Victoria and her Prime Ministers*, Eyre & Spottiswoode, 1953

Cecil, David, *Lord M*, Constable, 1954

Chambers, James, *Palmerston, 'The People's Darling'*, John Murray, 2004

Connell, Brian, *Regina v. Palmerston: The Correspondence between Queen Victoria and her Foreign and Prime Minister, 1837–1865*, Evans Bros, 1962

Corti, Egon Caesar Conte, *The English Empress*, Cassell, 1957

Crewe, Marquess of, *Lord Rosebery*, 2 vols, John Murray, 1931

Bibliography

Cullen, Tom, *The Empress Brown: The Story of a Royal Friendship*, Bodley Head, 1969

Diamond, Michael, *Victorian Sensation: Or, the Spectacular, the Shocking and the Scandalous in Nineteenth-Century Britain*, Anthem, 2003

Disraeli, Benjamin, *The Letters of Disraeli to Lady Bradford and Lady Chesterfield*, 2 vols, ed. Marquis of Zetland, Ernest Benn, 1929

Duff, David, *Albert and Victoria*, Tandem, 1973

—— *Edward of Kent: The Life Story of Queen Victoria's Father*, Frederick Muller, 1973

—— *Hessian Tapestry*, David & Charles, 1979

Epton, Nina, *Victoria and her Daughters*, Weidenfeld & Nicolson, 1971

Eyck, Frank, *The Prince Consort: A Political Biography*, Chatto & Windus, 1959

Friedman, Dennis, *Inheritance: A Psychological History of the Royal Family*, Sidgwick & Jackson, 1993

Fulford, Roger, *The Prince Consort*, Macmillan, 1949

—— *Royal Dukes: The Father and Uncles of Queen Victoria*, Collins, 1973

Gash, Norman, *Peel*, Longman, 1976

Gladstone, W.E., *The Gladstone Diaries*, 14 vols, ed. M.R.D. Foot (vols I–II), ed. M.R.D Foot and H.C.G. Matthew (vols III–IV); ed. H.C.G. Matthew (vols V–XIV), Oxford, Clarendon Press, 1968–94

Greville, Charles, *The Greville Diary*, 2 vols, ed. Philip Whitwell Wilson, Heinemann, 1927

—— *The Greville Memoirs, 1817–60*, ed. Henry Reeve, 8 vols, Longman, Green, 1873–87

Guedalla, Philip, *Palmerston*, Benn, 1926

—— *The Queen and Mr Gladstone*, 2 vols, Hodder & Stoughton, 1933

Hibbert, Christopher, *Queen Victoria: A Personal History*, HarperCollins, 2000

Hough, Richard, *Louis and Victoria: The First Mountbattens*, Hutchinson, 1974

James, Robert Rhodes, *Albert, Prince Consort: A Biography*, Hamish Hamilton, 1983

—— *Rosebery: A Biography of Archibald Philip, Fifth Earl of Rosebery*, Weidenfeld & Nicolson, 1963

Jenkins, Roy, *Gladstone*, Macmillan, 1995

Kennedy, A.L., *Salisbury 1830–1903: Portrait of a Statesman*, John Murray, 1953

Kuhn, William H., *Henry and Mary Ponsonby: Life at the Court of Queen Victoria*, Duckworth, 2002

Lamont-Brown, Raymond, *John Brown, Queen Victoria's Highland Servant*, Stroud, Sutton, 2000

—— *Royal Poxes and Potions: The Lives of Court Physicians, Surgeons and Apothecaries*, Stroud, Sutton, 2001

Longford, Elizabeth, *Victoria RI*, Weidenfeld & Nicolson, 1964

—— *Wellington: Pillar of State*, Weidenfeld & Nicolson, 1972

—— (ed.) *Darling Loosy: Letters to Princess Louise 1856–1939*, Weidenfeld & Nicolson, 1991

Lyttelton, Lady, *Correspondence of Sarah, Lady Lyttelton, 1787–1870* (ed.), The Hon. Mrs Hugh Wyndham, John Murray, 1912

McClintock, Mary Howard, *The Queen Thanks Sir Howard: The Life of Major-General Sir Howard Elphinstone, VC, KCB, CMG*, John Murray, 1945

Magnus, Philip, *Gladstone: A Biography*, John Murray, 1954

—— *King Edward the Seventh*, John Murray, 1964

Bibliography

Mallet, Victor, ed., *Life with Queen Victoria: Marie Mallet's Letters from Court, 1887–1901*, John Murray, 1968

Marie Louise, Princess, *My Memories of Six Reigns*, Evans Bros, 1956

Martin, Theodore, *Life of HRH The Prince Consort*, 5 vols, Smith & Elder, 1874–80

Matthew, H.C.G., *Gladstone, 1809–1874*, Oxford, Clarendon Press, 1986

Maxwell, Sir Herbert, *The Life of Wellington*, 2 vols, Sampson Low, Marston, 1900

Mitchell, L.G., *Lord Melbourne, 1779–1848*, Oxford, Oxford University Press, 1997

Monypenny, W.F., and Buckle, G.E., *The Life of Benjamin Disraeli, Earl of Beaconsfield*, 2 vols, John Murray, 1929

Morley, John, *Life of Gladstone*, 3 vols, Macmillan, 1903

Mullen, Richard, and Munson, James, *Victoria: Portrait of a Queen*, BBC, 1987

Packard, Jerrold M., *Farewell in Splendour: The Death of Queen Victoria and her Age*, Stroud, Sutton, 2000

—— *Victoria's Daughters*, Stroud, Sutton, 1999

Plowden, Alison, *The Young Victoria*, Weidenfeld & Nicolson, 1981

Ponsonby, Arthur, *Henry Ponsonby, Queen Victoria's Private Secretary: His Life from his Letters*, Macmillan, 1942

Ponsonby, Sir Frederick, *Recollections of Three Reigns*, Eyre & Spottiswoode, 1951

Ponsonby, Magdalen, ed., *Mary Ponsonby: A Memoir, some Letters and a Journal*, John Murray, 1927

Pope-Hennessy, James, *Queen Mary, 1867–1953*, Allen & Unwin, 1959

Priestley, J.B., *Victoria's Heyday*, Heinemann, 1972

Reid, Michaela, *Ask Sir James: Sir James Reid, Personal Physician to Queen Victoria and Physician-in-Ordinary to Three Monarchs*, Hodder & Stoughton, 1987

Rennell, Tony, *Last Days of Glory: The Death of Queen Victoria*, Viking, 2000

Rhodes James, Robert, *Rosebery: A Biography of Archibald Philip, 5th Earl of Rosebery*, Weidenfeld & Nicolson, 1963

Richardson, Joanna, *My Dearest Uncle: Leopold I of the Belgians*, Jonathan Cape, 1961

Ridley, Jasper, *Palmerston*, Constable, 1970

Roberts, Andrew, *Salisbury: Victorian Titan*, Weidenfeld & Nicolson, 1999

St Aubyn, Giles, *Edward VII, Prince and King*, Collins, 1979

—— *Queen Victoria: A Portrait*, Sinclair-Stevenson, 1991

Stanhope, Philip Henry, 5th Earl, *Notes of Conversations with the Duke of Wellington, 1831–51*, World's Classics, Oxford University Press, 1938

Stanley, Lady Augusta, *Later Letters of Lady Augusta Stanley 1864–1876*, ed. The Dean of Windsor & Hector Bolitho, Jonathan Cape, 1929

Steele, David, *Lord Salisbury: A Political Biography*, UCL Press, 1999

Thompson, Dorothy, *Queen Victoria: Gender and Power*, Virago, 2001

Thursfield, J.R., *Peel*, Macmillan, 1891

Tingsten, Herbert, *Victoria and the Victorians*, Allen & Unwin, 1972

Tisdall, E.E.P., *Queen Victoria's John Brown*, Stanley Paul, 1938

Van der Kiste, John, *Queen Victoria's Children*, Gloucester/Stroud, Sutton, 1986, new edn, 2003

Van der Kiste, John, and Jordaan, Bee, *Dearest Affie: Alfred, Duke of Edinburgh, Queen Victoria's second son, 1844–1900*, Stroud, Sutton, 1984, 1995

Victoria, Queen, *Leaves from the Journal of Our Life in the Highlands from 1848 to 1861*, ed. Arthur Helps, Smith, Elder, 1868

—— *More Leaves from the Journal of a Life in the Highlands from 1862 to 1882*, Smith, Elder, 1884

—— *The Girlhood of Queen Victoria: A Selection from Her Majesty's Diaries between the Years 1832 and 1840*, ed. Viscount Esher, 2 vols, John Murray, 1912

—— *The Letters of Queen Victoria: A Selection from Her Majesty's Correspondence between the Years 1837 and 1861*, ed. A.C. Benson and Viscount Esher, 3 vols, John Murray, 1907

—— *The Letters of Queen Victoria, 2nd Series: A Selection from Her Majesty's Correspondence and Journal between the Years 1862 and 1885*, ed. George Earle Buckle, 3 vols, John Murray, 1926–8

—— *The Letters of Queen Victoria, 3rd Series: A Selection from Her Majesty's Correspondence and Journal between the Years 1886 and 1901*, ed. George Earle Buckle, 3 vols, John Murray, 1930–2

—— *Further Letters of Queen Victoria: From the Archives of the House of Brandenburg-Prussia*, ed. Hector Bolitho, Thornton Butterworth, 1938

—— *Dearest Child: Letters between Queen Victoria and the Princess Royal, 1858–1861*, ed. Roger Fulford, Evans Bros, 1964

—— *Dearest Mama: Private Correspondence of Queen Victoria and the Crown Princess of Prussia, 1861–1864*, ed. Roger Fulford, Evans Bros, 1968

—— *Your Dear Letter: Private Correspondence of Queen Victoria and the Crown Princess of Russia, 1865–1871*, ed. Roger Fulford, Evans Bros, 1971

—— *Darling Child: Private Correspondence of Queen Victoria and the Crown Princess of Prussia, 1871–1878*, ed. Roger Fulford, Evans Bros, 1976

—— *Beloved Mama: Private Correspondence of Queen Victoria and the German Crown Princess, 1878–1885*, ed. Roger Fulford, Evans Bros, 1981

—— *Beloved and Darling Child: Last Letters between Queen Victoria and her Eldest Daughter, 1886–1901*, ed. Agatha Ramm, Sutton, 1990

—— *Advice to a Grand-daughter: Letters from Queen Victoria to Princess Victoria of Hesse*, ed. Richard Hough, Heinemann, 1975

Vitzthum von Eckstaedt, C.F., *St Petersburg and London, 1852–64*, 2 vols, Longman, Green, 1887

Weintraub, Stanley, *Disraeli: A Biography*, Hamish Hamilton, 1993

—— *The Importance of Being Edward: King in Waiting, 1841–1901*, John Murray, 2000

—— *Victoria: Biography of a Queen*, Unwin Hyman, 1987

Wilson, A.N., *The Victorians*, Hutchinson, 2002

Woodham-Smith, Cecil, *Queen Victoria, Her Life and Times: Volume One, 1819–1861*, Hamish Hamilton, 1972

Zeepvat, Charlotte, *Prince Leopold: The Untold Story of Queen Victoria's Youngest Son*, Stroud, Sutton, 1998

Journals and newspapers – articles

Callan, Paul, 'Victoria fancied Albert (and quite a bit of the other) with a passion'. In *Daily Express*, 30.12.2000

Fenton, Ben, 'Twice bereaved, Victoria's secret suffering' [after the death of John Brown]. In *Daily Telegraph*, 15.12.2004

Bibliography

Gibb, Frances, 'Victoria and John Brown "married and had a child"'. In *Daily Telegraph*, 21.5.1979

Lamont-Brown, Raymond, 'Queen Victoria's "secret marriage"' [the Queen and John Brown]. In *Contemporary Review*, December 2003

Stevas, Norman St John, 'The "Great Asian Mystery" who captured Queen and Country' [Disraeli]. In *Sunday Express Magazine*, 12.4.1981

Journals – general references

Contemporary Review
Daily Express
Daily Telegraph
Manchester Guardian
Punch
Royalty Digest
Saturday Review
Sunday Express Magazine
The Times

Index